Talking Films

Talking Films
The Best of *The Guardian* Film Lectures

Edited by Andrew Britton

FOURTH ESTATE · *London*

First published in Great Britain in 1991 by
Fourth Estate Limited
289 Westbourne Grove
London W11 2QA

Copyright © 1991 by Guardian News Service Limited
and Andrew Britton

The right of Andrew Britton to be identified as the editor of this
work has been asserted by him in accordance with the
Copyright, Designs and Patents Act 1988.

A catalogue record for this book is available from the
British Library

ISBN 1-872180-17-5

All rights reserved. No part of this publication may be
reproduced, transmitted, or stored in a retrieval system, in any
form or by any means, without permission in writing from
Fourth Estate Limited.

Designed by Lucienne Roberts, Sans + Baum
Typeset by York House Typographic Ltd., London
Printed in Great Britain by Hartnolls Ltd., Bodmin, Cornwall

Contents

1 Jack Lemmon — 1

2 David Puttnam — 29

3 Delphine Seyrig — 57

4 Satyajit Ray — 81

5 Raymond Williams — 103

6 Robert Mitchum — 133

7 Margarethe von Trotta — 163

8 Gene Kelly — 185

9 Dirk Bogarde — 203

10 Yves Montand — 225

11 Michael Cimino — 245

1 Jack Lemmon

Jack Lemmon was born in Boston, Massachusetts in 1925. He studied at Harvard while serving simultaneously as a communications officer in the US Naval Reserve, and after graduating in 1947 he moved to New York, where he worked first as a piano player in a saloon, next as an actor in radio soap opera and then as a television actor, notching up (by his own estimate) over 400 TV shows in a period of five years. He made his film debut in *It Should Happen To You* (1954, George Cukor), and signed an exceptionally liberal seven-year contract with Columbia which allowed him to appear on Broadway and to make one film a year with other studios. In 1955 he won his first Oscar, as Best Supporting Actor, for his performance in *Mister Roberts*, for which John Ford had specifically requested him. Despite this auspicious beginning, his film career did not really take off until 1959 when he made the first of his seven films with Billy Wilder, *Some Like It Hot*, in which he gives one of the most hilarious performances in the cinema. The collaboration with Wilder continued in *The Apartment* (1960), *Irma la Douce* (1963), *The Fortune Cookie* (1966), *Avanti!* (1972), *The Front Page* (1974) and *Buddy Buddy* (1981), and an equally memorable partnership with Walter Matthau in three of these films also produced *The Odd Couple* (1968, Gene Saks) and a movie which Lemmon directed but in which he did not appear, *Kotch* (1971). His versatility as an actor is astonishing, and if he is without doubt a great *farceur* he has also repeatedly demonstrated his mastery of the demands of melodrama and tragedy. His other films include *Days of Wine and Roses* (1962, Blake Edwards), *The Great Race* (1965, Edwards), *Save the Tiger* (1973, John Avildsen), *The China Syndrome* (1979, James Bridges), *Tribute* (1980, Bob Clark), *Missing* (1982, Costa-Gavras), *Mass Appeal* (1985, Glenn Jordan) and *That's Life!* (1986, Edwards). Jack Lemmon has received six Oscar nominations as Best Actor, and won the award for *Save the Tiger*. He has twice been named Best Actor at the Cannes Film Festival, for *The China Syndrome* and *Missing*, and he won the Best Actor award at the Berlin Film Festival for *Tribute*. He has repeatedly returned to the theatre, appearing in a production of *Juno and the Paycock* in Los Angeles in 1975 and in *Tribute* on Broadway in 1978, and he gave his *Guardian* lecture while he was in London playing James Tyrone in Jonathan Miller's production of *Long Day's Journey into Night*.

The following lecture took place on 7 September 1986. Jack Lemmon was interviewed by Jonathan Miller.

Jack Lemmon

Jonathan Miller One of the enviable privileges of being a director in the theatre is that every now and then you realize your wildest dreams and actually manage to work with a myth. About eighteen months ago I was walking across the lobby of a hotel in New York on the way to my room when a young producer called Roger Peters jumped out from behind a palm tree, told me that he had the rights to Eugene O'Neill's *Long Day's Journey into Night* and asked me whom I would cast in the part of James Tyrone if I were going to direct it. Without any hesitation I said that I could only imagine doing this play, which seems to be bedevilled by a reputation for slowness and pomposity, if I could have someone like Mr Lemmon – indeed, someone *so* like Mr Lemmon that it would have to be Jack Lemmon himself. I was then so intrigued by this idea that had leapt into my mind that I said I would actually consider reneging on my decision to leave the theatre if such a dream could be realized. I didn't think about it again, but three days later this young producer had the chutzpah to call Jack and say that there was a prospect of doing *Long Day's Journey*. Jack then called me, and we met in London and began to discuss the project. In the course of the next eighteen months we went into rehearsal and then went on tour and then opened in New York and finally came to London, and during that time I have come to love this man, whom I first saw and adored and admired as a young cinema-goer. [*To Jack Lemmon*] Now, since you're dressed in your Harvard suit I thought I might start simply by asking if you ever thought, when you were up there at Harvard, that a career in the theatre might be a professional possibility?

Jack Lemmon I thought about it much earlier; I'm guessing, but I'd say I was about 8 or 9. I went to school one morning and the teacher said that Billy Tyler, who lived across the street from me and who was supposed to do this part in a play we were putting on at lunch-time, couldn't do it because he'd got a bad cold, so I was going to play his part. It was about fourteen lines, so I said, 'How can I learn those lines? We've got class,' and he said, 'Well, try to learn a few of the lines. I'll be in the wings sitting on a chair, and you just come out in the costume and you face front and you say the lines, and as soon as you can't remember any more, just walk over and lean down and I'll whisper the lines to you.' Well, Billy Tyler was a big boy, about a foot taller than me, and the costume was a big, black Western hat and a cape that came down to Billy's ankles. With me it was Marie Antoinette! The train stretched way back, and the hat came down over my ears. So it came to my cue and they pushed me out and I faced front, and they started to laugh because it was so funny-looking, I guess. I muttered the first couple of lines, and then I stopped and just sauntered over and leaned into the wings, and you could hear the voice telling me the line, and I got another laugh. So I walked back centre-stage and I said the line, which was half a sentence, and stopped, and everyone laughed again. I remember it vividly, so it must have really been very important, and I think one of two things could have happened. I could have been completely mortified and never have set foot on a stage again if I could help it. Instead, for some reason, a little bulb went on in the back of my mind about the third laugh, and I said, 'I think I like this!' So even when I could remember a couple of lines I started deliberately drying up and going back to the wings, and each time I did it the laugh got bigger and bigger. From then on I just kept trying to do plays whenever I could. I don't think it had a damn thing to do with 'talent will out'. That may be, but I doubt it. I do think it had a lot to do with acceptance. It was purely and simply that I was doing something which my peers liked, and therefore I kept on doing it. Through my teens I became popular with the kids because they loved me to tell stories. I had to make up all kinds of stuff and swear it was true. I had to have a five-minute story each day to tell between classes. I think it was a very definite need to be accepted.

JM It's a very different sort of talent from the talent of the stand-up comic, who wants not only to get acceptance, but also to overcome the resistance of an audience. You felt that you were trying almost to ingratiate yourself with them, rather than overcome them?

JL Yes, there is a big difference. An actor in comedy is not funny on his own, and he has no desire to get up and *be* funny and tell jokes, or do impersonations. He needs the material; he is an *actor*. Very often, comics – including some of the very best ones – have a tremendous, almost frightening (I think) drive to control; it goes beyond being accepted. The terminology has always fascinated me. In America, at least, it's all very brutal. A comic will come off-stage and say, 'I killed them! God, I slayed 'em! Christ, I had 'em in the aisles!' It's all very manic at times, and you *cannot* get them off. About a year ago I was sitting with a young comic, who is also a very fine actor, in a little outdoor café having coffee, and he started ad libbing some stuff, and suddenly he got an idea for something funny and he couldn't stand it because there weren't many people there on the patio, so he went out to the street and when the cabs and the cars stopped for the red light, he performed. He *had* to do it, he's *on* constantly.

JM How soon was it that you began to find that the real pleasure was in playing a part rather than, as it were, being Jack being funny?

JL I think it started with imitations. I would start to imitate actors – W. C. Fields, Chaplin, Mae West (she was terrific! I really had her down!) – and while, of course, it was always *me*. I then became interested in being somebody else. What really fascinates me about some actors is that they are really only complete and happy when they *are* somebody else. I don't think it applies to me, but it does to many actors I know, and usually they are extremely good. A light comes into their eyes when that curtain goes up, and they are wonderful to the tips of their toes because they are somebody else, but then the curtain drops and – boom! They're back into their own psyche, their own neuroses, their own problems.

JM And do you yourself find a peculiar sort of fulfilment in this almost self-annihilating immersion in someone else?

JL I don't trust anybody who tries to analyse himself, but I think that my satisfaction is a totally different thing. It's the desire and the need to be as good as I can be. I never will be, but you keep striving and hoping as a professional actor who's trying to convince everybody that he is someone else. Many young actors who misuse the so-called Method think that the ideal, the *pure* performance would be if you could really totally forget yourself, even for a moment, and become that other person. That is absolutely crazy, because the moment you lose control, or lose the knowledge of what you are doing in your craft, then you can forget the performance. For instance, if you were doing *Hamlet* you could mutter 'To be or not to be' somewhere upstage, and while the entire audience would be saying, 'Wadhesay? Wadhesay?', you could be thinking, 'My God, I did it! It was pure! It was a wonderful performance!' It was a lousy performance! It was a *non*-performance! You *have* to be in control.

JM I must say that one of the things I found so refreshing and exciting when we began to work together on *Long Day's Journey* was that we were able to start rehearsing without elaborate theoretical discussions about the personality that you were trying to be. Have you ever encountered directors who have tried to lay the Method on you?

JL Oh God, yes! Perhaps I should say to begin with that I think I *am* a Method actor, for the simple reason that all that Stanislavsky really did was to put down about ten steps which are very basic and very simple, and which all actors follow in some way or another. Anybody who prepares in his mind and gets into character before he goes on stage is a Method actor. However, my basic feeling about acting is totally *anti*-Method in that I do not frankly give a damn about how a character really would behave in a scene. I could not care less! What I care a lot about is how he *could* behave – legitimately, that is. There may be twenty ways (the better the writing, the more ways there will be), and eighteen of those twenty are going to be more exciting than the two which might be credible, or probable, or the way he 'really' would behave. Whether you're on a stage or in front of a camera, an actor really exists for only one reason, and that is to try to get the highest possible level of dramatic conflict in carrying out the author's intentions. If that means you should sit and not move, then you find the damn reason why, but you don't start climbing the wall!

JM I got the impression in working with you that you don't have a clear idea of the author's intention at the outset, but that you try to discover it by finding the best possible way of doing the lines.

JL Very often, yes, and I think that the older you get and the more experience you have, the more you rely on sheer instinct and less on the intellectual process. Of course, acting *is* an intellectual process, and it's comparable to psychoanalysis in the sense that it's the study of the behaviour of one person and of what, in your opinion, makes that person tick. The acting is the very last step, where you finally show the audience what you have discovered about him and how he behaves under a certain set of circumstances. So it *is* basically intellectual, but I find that as I get older, I use less of it. I do not do as much homework prior to rehearsal as I would have done fifteen or twenty years ago, when I tended to beat a part to death with a stick. Whether it was a film or a play, I'd go through 18,000 different ideas and at times get very confused and very muddled, whereas now I rely more on instinct and on what the other people and the director are bringing, and let it happen *now*, at the moment.

JM I've often noticed during rehearsal (and indeed, even now, after performances have begun) that you will come away from a scene surprised by what you had discovered in the process of playing those particular lines, or in encountering this or that actor's playing of *their* lines. It's *so* instinctive, in fact, that often the things which you found most exciting about your own performance came from sources which you knew nothing about.

JL Yes. I'll tell you, one of the great things about the theatre is that you do get the chance to act *with* somebody as opposed to acting *at* them, and believe me, an awful lot of screen actors, even very good ones, do not know about that distinction. They do not act *with* you. They are looking at the result, and they are giving a *result* performance. It may be terribly effective, but it is not influenced enough by what the other actor is doing. Again and again I've found new things in *Long Day's Journey* because of something the other actors did and which I reacted to because, thank God, I was listening in the correct way; not just listening to the words, but to *them* underneath the words. That affected how I replied to them or what I did, and obviously that can only happen with actors who are also acting *with* you. That's why I don't really worry too much about preparation anymore, and let it happen as it happens.

JM I've seen the extraordinary exhilaration with which you and the other actors come off the stage after a scene has occurred in a certain way and a completely unprecedented novelty has taken place. Nevertheless, there are times when those novelties are, to use you own term, 'pieces of shit'! How much do you need an objective eye to say, 'Jack, that was POS!' as opposed to coming off the stage and knowing it yourself?

JL I think you know more as time goes on, but you resist wanting to admit it you know. It's the same thing as trying to get an author to cut his lines. It is just castration! You think it's just so wonderful that it can't be cut (so to speak!), and you have to learn to accept it when someone you respect looks at you and says, 'No, too much! It's a piece of shit!'

JM By what criterion do you judge when someone says of a bit of business that it's no good, even though *you* felt exhilarated by it?

JL An awful lot of that has to do with the respect that I have before I go in. I work less as time goes on, and I realize that I'm lucky: I can afford it. It's not just the part or the script; I'm interested in who the hell is going to direct it, and I want it to be somebody whom I really do respect. I can only assume and hope that the respect is mutual and that I don't necessarily have to say, 'Yes, sir!', but I can say, 'Well, wait a minute, what about this?' and we'll discuss it. But if the director then says no he will not get an argument from me, even if I am absolutely convinced that he is dead wrong. There is not a single moment that I've known in a film or a play which is so bloody important that you have to have it your way, or that one way is *it*, or the whole damn thing is down the toilet. It's not worth it. The atmosphere itself is not worth it, and your own conceit can't be that tremendous. Nobody is right all the time – and of course, that means the director too – but overall it *is* the director's production, whether it's film or theatre, and especially in film. I would only object if I really literally couldn't do something without making it look phoney. That has only happened very rarely, but then you have a serious problem that hopefully the director will understand too. That happened with us, I remember. Now and then you'd give me something and I would do it for a day or two days, and then I'd come and say, 'Jonathan, I can't do that. It's throwing everything else in the scene.' And you would be the first to know if I was right, and either you'd say, 'Yes, you can!', or you'd adapt it somehow, or you'd say, 'Forget it!'

JM Yes, directors can be perpetrators of pieces of shit as well, and it's quite a good idea to have the same sort of feelings of reticence about that! I know that one of the myths about great acting is that it's marked by the extent to which the actor can do something which is utterly unlike himself, and there are, of course, performers like Olivier and, to a certain extent, Guiness, who take pride in hiding themselves under make-up and all sorts of mannerisms which, in fact, obliterate them. But I've often felt that these are almost exotic peculiarities of the profession, whereas the most interesting performance is the one which is really not that far removed from something inside yourself. Do you feel that?

JL Yes, I do, though there's a great joy for most actors in playing the other parts which are so far removed from you that you lose your inhibitions completely and just have a field day. I remember a film years ago, *The Great Race*, where I played two or three different parts: an effete Ruritanian prince, and a villain, and so on. My God, I had fun! It really goes back to the kids going up to the attic and putting on Mummy and Daddy's old wedding clothes, or their grandfather's clothes, and playing games. We all love it. We're somebody else, you know, and the further away that person is, the more fun it is. But I do agree that the most interesting roles are characters that are, in many ways, closer to you. I have always been attracted mostly to contemporary parts, certainly in film, and I think the reason is that I could understand their difficulties and attitudes and problems and neuroses more readily than I might understand something from way back. James Tyrone in *Long Day's Journey* is one of the few parts in a long time that has not been a contemporary role.

JM And yet for most people, I suppose, you are more closely associated with a part which involves the greatest possible distance from your own personality, where you actually play another sex.

JL Yes.

JM This raises the question of the pleasure of masquerade and make-up and total transformation which you were just talking about. When you were first asked to play a woman in *Some Like It Hot*, how did you feel it would be necessary to approach that?

JL I thought, 'OK, this is risky!' – not *personally* risky, but a risky project – and my first thought was, 'Who's doing it? Who's writing it and who's directing it?' It was Billy Wilder. That's why

I did it, and I did it without the script. I was told the story and more or less the character in very general terms, but because it was Wilder, I said OK. If it had been somebody of a lesser stature, or somebody whose work I had not respected that much, I would have been very, very suspicious that it would be distasteful and a total failure, because it is a very delicate line to walk. As broad a farce as it is, it has to be handled very delicately to be successful. As for playing the musician masquerading as a woman, I had only one thought and that was, 'All right, it's one of those parts where you do not worry. You go right to the moon! Don't even consider whether they're going to think you're a little queer, or anything else. Forget it! Absolutely go all the way and don't ever hold back.' That's the only way to approach a part like that. If you hesitate, it'll show in the performance.

JM I suppose that, in a sense, there was a self-protective device built into that part in that there was no attempt to deceive the audience into thinking that you were anything other than a man playing a woman.

JL And especially in my part! Billy hired the world's foremost female impersonator (I've forgotten his name), and he refused to fly, so he had to take a liner over from France. He was hired for two weeks, at great expense, to teach Tony and I how to behave like women, and he quit the third day. He said, 'Curtis is flawless, but Lemmon is totally hopeless. If you recast I will stay and I will live with you; otherwise, I leave.' So he left! He told me that if a man wants to walk like a woman he can get away with it if he crosses one foot in front of the other with each step, and I said, 'Well, that's one damn thing that I'm not going to do, because I don't *want* to be good!' My feeling was that Daphne *wouldn't* be. Daphne is not beautiful, and Daphne is a putz, a klutz. So he got mad and he left! What all this comes down to, I think, is that *the* most important single thing about acting, without any question, is the ability to reach the one plateau where you are willing to be negative, to show yourself as somebody that's totally distasteful, or whatever it may be, but *without fear*. Rosalind Russell was addressing a bunch of girls in a drama class once, and she said, 'You must reach the point where you are willing, theoretically, to stand up in front of an audience stark naked and turn around *very* slowly.' It's important that a woman said that, because it's even tougher for a woman to think of, and that turning around very slowly would be the ultimate horrible thing for a girl. But I know what she meant, and she's right.

JM When was the moment you felt you were able to turn around stark *dressed*, as it were, as one of those two girls? You once described to me some experiment that you and Tony played with the make-up . . .

JL Yes, that was a key point, as a matter of fact, and it was before we shot. This may sound like I'm getting the Method, but normally an actor works from the inside out; you try to get the character, and then the last thing you do is put on the mannerisms, just like your costume. Those are the external things, the outer shell. But now and then you can create a shell and crawl into it. Olivier works this way fairly often, and he's talked about it. Now, with Daphne, to a great extent, I did that. I wanted a certain appearance and finally, about the third day, after looking at myself with the wig and the various make-ups, I decided that the eyebrows were important and that the lips were *very* important. I wanted the bee-sting because there were certain things that you could do with your mouth when the lipstick was on. I worked totally the wrong way on purpose in order to get certain vacuous looks when he's playing the bass; it's like there's nothing up there but air! Then I realized that all this was part of a general conception about Daphne as a character, because he never acted, he only *reacted*. He never caused anything to happen in that film out of *his* idea, and he never, ever, stopped to think: Tony would get an idea, and Daphne would say, 'Right!' When they were packing near the end of the film because the gangsters were on to them and they were trying to escape, Daphne said, 'My God, if they come in and they shoot us and I wake up in the morgue dressed like this, I'm going to *die* of embarrassment!' That was an important line, because it gave me a clue to the character. I mean, that kind of idiotic statement could only come from a man who does not stop to think! So I just let everything happen, and I said, 'I don't give a damn what I do! I'm just going to literally, honestly react.'

JM It's very interesting that a character can sometimes be arrived at by building outward from something external like the bee-stung lips. I remember being very surprised by the step forward that the rehearsals took in *Long Day's Journey* when you suddenly stepped into those slightly over-large suits. Immediately something happened to you, not because you'd gone into something inside yourself, but merely because the pants were too large for you.

JL Definitely. It's crazy what little external things can do for an actor, and images are also very important. One of the key things in rehearsal was one day when you said, 'You're beginning to get him,' and I said, 'Get what?' and you said, 'The wounded old lion.' Goddamn! – that stuck in my mind, and I can't explain why, but it helped me. *Wounded* was very important: not just a lion, but the wounded old lion. I think that in most productions of *Long Day's Journey*, Tyrone has been played as the old skinflint tyrant who's in control, but he's not in this one. He thinks he is at times, but even when he knows he isn't, he won't admit it. The bluff is there and the bluster is there, but the strength isn't, really. All of those crazy little crutches help a great deal. The best example I can think of is when I was doing *Missing*. I had no time to prepare for the character as I was just finishing another film, and I had to fly all the way from Honolulu to Mexico City and shoot the next day. They had shot everything that I wasn't in, and they were just sitting there waiting for me. But somehow one image popped into my head about a week or two before I left, while I was still working on the other film. I knew that I wanted to have a contained, controlled man who would not use his face or his hands that much, as I instinctively do. There was a straitjacket on him; everything was bottled up. I remember calling Costa-Gavras in Mexico City and saying, 'Costa, I know they've already got the suits and the wardrobe and everything, but somehow I just see this man wearing a hat every moment that he can,' and Costa thought and then he said, 'Yes, I agree.' That little hat contained everything for me. It was a crutch, but it helped me. It kicked me off into the character before I really had the time to investigate and find out what I was going to do. I damn near wore it in scenes where I was sitting in bed! I felt naked without it, but the minute I got it on I had him! I was all right, I was at home, everything was cool. That's how childish actors can get! Actors are crazy!

JM No, I don't think they're crazy, and I think they're unkind to themselves by thinking of these things as crutches. The very word implies that there is some disability involved, and I actually don't think it's like that.

JL No, you're right, it isn't. I'm not putting it down, and I think other actors would understand it completely, but it's possible that some people would fail to see how a hat, or a pair of gloves, or an umbrella could mean that much, and yet they can. It sounds silly, but it's not: it's a very important tool to an actor. All that matters is if it works. Really, anything that works.

JM Look, I think it would be much nicer now for everyone here if we were to open this up for general discussion and for questions.

Audience There is a sublime anecdote in your autobiography about the death of Edmund Gwenn, where George Seaton held him by the hand and said to him, 'It must be very hard to die,' and Gwenn replied with almost his dying breath, 'Yes, dear boy, but not as hard as playing comedy.' You are a legendary comic actor, but you've also played tragedy. Is there a difference between playing comedy and tragedy, and is comedy harder?

JL That's a good question. I approach them the same, James Tyrone the same as Daphne. Honest to God! In both cases I am trying to divine the truth of the character as best I can. What makes comedy immeasurably more difficult to achieve successfully on every level – writing, directing and acting – is timing, especially in films, where you do not have an audience to guide you. The wonderful thing about comedy in the theatre is that you *know* if it works. When you're doing a film, you don't. You're guessing, you're in the lap of the gods, and you must rely on a sense of delivery and a sense of timing over and above the character. That is not required in a drama. You are also in the laps of the editor and the director. I wish I had a nickel for every time there has been a cut which was just frames off and which wrecked a laugh because the director didn't catch it, or the editor didn't understand it or feel it. There *is* an ability to feel timing in comedy and to know that a line is funny if you read it a certain way, assuming that it's legitimate within the behaviour of the character. That you cannot learn: it's something that you're born with, like the colour of your hair. You can only sharpen it by working with good people, and by getting more experience in playing comedy. What it comes down to, I think, is that if you're going to do comedy successfully, you have to have a real *sense* of humour, which is quite different from what most people mean when they use that phrase. For example, if you tell a joke, some people will just look at you at the punch-line even if you tell the joke well. They don't get it, and they never will get it. Generally, we say that those people lack a sense of humour, but what they really lack is an *appreciation* of humour. A *sense* of humour is knowing what will be funny when it's done. That is the key to it. Neil Simon or Billy Wilder can write a scene and you'll read it, and it may not seem all that funny on the printed page, but when you play it correctly – God, it's funny! Usually, the greatest comedy writing is not a matter of funny lines. I call funny lines two-line nifties, and that's cheaper writing. They're jokes, whereas real humour comes out of the behaviour of a character within a situation. There's a very good example in a film I did called *The Out-of-Towners*, which is about this couple going to New York, where everything in the world happens to them. The shit keeps hitting the fan, and I'm screaming and ranting and raving all the time, and Sandy Dennis gets to say very little, but every now and then when some disaster strikes she says, very quietly, 'Oh, my God!' It is a brilliantly funny line, and *that* is a sense of comedy. Somebody else might say, 'What the hell is funny about that?' They wouldn't understand it. It requires that extra something, and that's what makes comedy so much more difficult than drama.

Aud The movie you directed, *Kotch*, is really a marvellous film. Why haven't you ever directed again?

JL For a number of reasons, the main one being that I am primarily an actor – good, bad or indifferent – and that is my real desire and need. I loved directing, and I do get offers, but I just haven't found a script where I've felt I was the right person to direct it, and where suddenly I've looked at it and said, 'I see it! I *must* do that film!' It just hasn't happened. I hope I will direct again, and I think directing is very good for an actor because it reinforces something he should really think of all the time, which is not what he *could* do in the scene, but what he *should* do. He has to look at the whole, the overall. Directing is *totally* concerned with that, and the more an actor thinks that way the better.

Aud I'm very curious about how you felt about working with Marilyn Monroe in *Some Like It Hot*, especially as both Billy Wilder and Tony Curtis have gone on record with some very uncomplimentary remarks about her.

JL Marilyn was fascinating. She did drive Billy crazy and she drove Tony crazy, but the reason she didn't drive me crazy was that I was a little smarter. Billy had no choice. He was making the film, and when you are the director and the writer and the producer, and you have to sit and wait for, at times, two hours until she is fully made-up, and then you discover that she won't come out of the dressing-room, that's going to drive anybody insane. Tony had most of his major scenes with her in the second half of the film, when it became a real problem, whereas I was off dancing with Joe E. Brown with a rose between my teeth. 'You having trouble, Tony? Gee, that's a shame!' I also realized very early on that the way Marilyn worked was not deliberately selfish, and that it was not a matter of prima donna temperament. It was the only way she knew how to work. Sometimes it would take thirty takes, maybe more, for something terribly simple. She would just stop in the middle of take after take. Nobody ever knew why, but *she* did. It would seem to be going fine, and she wouldn't be able to explain it. She would just stop, say sorry, and start shaking her hands in order to relax, or whatever. We had about 450,000 feet of Marilyn shaking her hands, just to relax! She had a built-in alarm clock, and if it went off, that meant 'Stop!' And then suddenly, everything would gel. There's a fairly long scene early on in the film where I'm in my upper bunk in the train, still dressed as Daphne, and Marilyn pops her head in and gets into bed with me. It's a wonderful scene, and it does go on: there are three or four pages of it. Well, we went all the way through on take one! No cuts, no nothing! It was 8.05 in the morning, and I thought Billy was going to have a conniption fit. He couldn't believe it, he was no good for the rest of the day. He says, 'What happened? What's the matter with this girl?' And it was perfect, but it was rare. She was also very ill and we didn't know it. She had a miscarriage during the film and nobody even knew she was pregnant. Anyhow, I realized that if I let it get to me, it would hurt my performance and my enjoyment, so I just didn't let it get to me. But Marilyn was fascinating. Nobody will ever know what was going on mentally with her, but that's the way she worked. When it felt right for her, as selfish as that was, it was the only way. As I said, it was not temperament or star this, that, or the other. It was the only way she knew how to work, and God knows, she did have a unique and wonderful charisma about her, some incredible thing (whatever it was) which drew you to her. There were scenes where I'd look at her and I'd swear there was a glass wall between us and there was no contact at all, but then I'd go to the rushes, and she may not have been acting with me, but she was sure going into that lens! She and the lens had something going on that I was unaware of. She had something special, there's no question of that. That character that she created was all her; no director ever gave her that. She slowly made that herself out of her early films, and she also had a hell of a gift for comedy and a wonderful sense of timing. She was just inordinately difficult, which I am convinced she could not help.

Aud What do you look for in a director, and who are your favourite directors besides Dr Miller and Billy Wilder?

JL They *are* two of my very favourites, and they're totally different. There's a lot of them I love. The main thing I look for, as I was saying earlier, is a sense of trust. The director is the captain of the ship, the general of the army, and you need to be able to trust him, you know. For example, when Costa-Gavras and I first discussed *Missing* he came to my house, and outside the window of the room where we were talking there's an eighty-foot cliff where the property just drops away. After speaking to him about the film and the character for thirty or forty minutes, I remember thinking, 'If that son of a bitch asked me to go out to the edge of that cliff and keep walking, I'd do it!' and that's when I agreed to do the film. You really have to have that much trust, and the director has to have the ability to instil that trust in you through his taste, his intelligence, his experience and his talent. Another thing that's extremely important is not to direct! That's a rare quality which all directors should possess as much as Dr Miller here. Don't direct too much, don't start giving too damn much to the actors. It's like trying to take a golf lesson, and in five minutes the guy gives you seventeen different things to do. Put this hand over here and put that hand down there . . . and you never hit the golf ball! You've got to find your own swing, and have the feeling that you can contribute, and that you can try anything and make an ass out of yourself, and nobody's going to say, 'What the hell is that?' Most of the time acting is basically an interpretive craft, but it can be creative if the director permits it, as the good ones always will.

Aud I've often wondered whether film comedy actors ever ad lib during a take. For example, there's a scene in *The Apartment* where you're getting drunk at a bar and you say, 'I'll have another one of those little mothers.' It sounds spontaneous, and I wondered if that was in the script, or if it was improvised?

JL It was in the script, and when Billy Wilder and Izzy Diamond have written a script, it is the Bible! You don't change one word – not an 'if', an 'and', or a 'but', believe me! I've done seven pictures with Billy, and finally he would let me change a line every now and then. For instance, in *Some Like It Hot* there's a scene at the beginning of the film after we've witnessed the Valentine's Day Massacre, and we're trying to hide and we go to see an agent and he says, 'There's some kind of an all-girl orchestra playing over in Jersey, it's a one-night gig. D'you want to do that?' My line was, 'Now you are talking!' and it took me half an hour, but I convinced Billy just to let me repeat it, that's all. 'Now you're talking! *NOW* YOU ARE TALKING!' He finally let me do that, but usually you don't change a bloody thing, and you'd better hope it's one of his better ones because you don't alter a syllable with Billy. With most people you can to some extent, but then with Billy, and with Neil Simon also, I have found that there is no *need* to change, or to add, or subtract. I think that one of the keys to the good Wilder scripts is not *what* Wilder has written, but what he has *not* written. It is cut right down to the nub, so you can't take out that 'and', or 'if', or 'but', and you can't add anything either. If the line is, 'I'll come in the door,' it doesn't work as well if you say, '*Well*, I'll come in the door.' He once said that he felt that 80 per cent of the film was done when he had completed the script, and the rest was the chore of putting it on film. He has always considered himself to be basically a writer, actually, and like many writers who become directors, he only directs so that he can do his material in the way he saw it, without some other interpretation being overlaid.

Aud In both *Missing* and *The China Syndrome* you play conservative middle-American types who are members of the so-called 'silent majority'. Did you get any feedback from people who really are like that?

JL Yes, but not as much as I thought I'd get, or that the films would get. Obviously, if a work of art has a point of view, it is not going to appeal to everybody, and when you have a point of view as politically loaded as in those two films, you're going to offend a lot of people. That is not why I did the films, but it definitely pleased me that they had those points of view, and as a matter of fact I think that lasting works of art always have a point of view, though, of course, they also have to stand on their own as a viable dramatic entity. Whether you agree or disagree I don't think is important. What's very important is that it should make you think, whereas you might not have thought if you hadn't seen it. That's the function of art, really, to make you think, and unfortunately very few people understand that. It's such as shame that in our culture we think of art as a luxury: going to the theatre or the movies is 'entertainment'. Camus once said that if we understood the enigmas of life, there would be no need for the arts, and everyone tends to forget that. Art can make you see as well as entertain, and those films *did*, I think.

Aud How do you feel about critics? Do you pay any attention to them?

JL I would like to be able to say (as some actors can) that I really don't care that much about the critics, or that I don't even read them, but I do, and they do upset or delight me. I think I keep it in balance now. When I was younger I was much more impressionable and I would get hurt more easily, but I'm getting like a dinosaur at this point, and Lord knows, I've had more than my share of very good reviews. I don't know whether critics are a necessary evil or what. Major critics in New York, for instance, have a country-wide influence, not only on the reading public, but also on other critics all over

America who read them and get swayed. It's amazing. You can pick up the Des Moines *Bullet*, or the Newton *Nugget* and you will see some New York critic practically sentence for sentence under the name of some kid who's been hired on the paper and who loves Pauline Kael of *The New Yorker*, or some other nut. That woman is *devoid* of any appreciation of humour and she is not a good critic, though she *can* write. Most critics can't write and they are also not good critics. That's what I think of critics! A few of them have been able to be constructive, so that you can read something and actually learn, but that's happened damn few times in my life. Most of them are extremely concerned about being read, and you find very often that you are being used, and abused, by people who really just want to entertain in their columns. There's also a number of them who can get vicious. What's that ass? . . . What's Simon's first name?

JM I don't think he has one!

JL I know what they call him, but what's his real first name?

JM John.

JL John! I think that really is a shame! That's an example of a man who really has lost any semblance of being a critic. Nobody with a brain in their head ever reads him to see whether or not something was good, or because they respect his opinion. They want to see how viciously he is going to slay somebody. He just spends paragraphs ripping somebody to pieces because he doesn't like the way their nose is, or because they've got a pimple on their face. Paragraphs on a pimple, believe me! There *are* critics like that, and we really should be damned grateful that they are employed as critics. You can imagine what would happen if Simon lost his job and didn't have that outlet for all that hatred. It would be no more safe to walk the streets than to fly to the moon.

Aud Have you ever made any films which you now think you shouldn't have made?

JL [*Laughs*] Let me tell you a Walter Matthau story. It's a beauty, because all of us in film and theatre are regularly faced with a terrible problem, and that is: what do you say when a friend does a real turkey? Well, just one of the films that I would love to forget was a thing called *Alex and the Gypsy* (1976). Oh God! I think it hit the fifty-cent houses in about an hour and a half! Anyway, it was a different sort of part for me (I was playing a tough bail-bondsman), and I thought, 'Oh, Goddamn! I'm going to kill 'em! This is a biggie! I can't wait for the first preview!' So I bring Walter and Carol Matthau and Felicia, my wife, and we go to the sneak preview, and we're sitting towards the back and I've got Walter sitting next to me because I want to watch his reaction, which I thought was going to be, 'Wow!' Well, he started snoring about halfway through, and then I noticed that people were getting up, I thought maybe going to the men's room, but they never came back. The place was half empty by the time the lights came up, and those that were left knew we were in the back and they just sort of snuck out without looking. So we're sitting there, and I said 'Walter, what did you think of the film?' and he thought for a second and he said, 'Get out of it!' That's the greatest line I've ever heard under those circumstances, and fortunately it kept me from committing suicide. *Luv* was another one that was a bomb. It was a delightful play, but it just could not transfer to the screen; it didn't work at all. And then there was the second film I did, which was called *Three for the Show*. That was another one which just disappeared down the thing. I was Betty Grable's husband, and the first day we met she said, 'You can call me Mom'! It was *not* a convincing relationship! It was a musical, and I was supposed to dance. Marge Champion and Gower Champion, and Betty Grable and me did number after number. Jack Cole tried to teach me how to dance, but I didn't even learn to time-step until Cagney taught me two pictures later in *Mister Roberts*. The funny thing is, though, that you can do films which are just terrible and they can be enormous hits. I was under contract at Columbia in the early 1960s and I had to do two films in a row, which I did everything except walk off to get out of. One was *Under the Yum-Yum Tree* (1963) and the other was *Good Neighbour Sam* (1964), and they made me number one at the box-office. I hated them! I thought they were the worst pieces of fluff ever made, and I still think it, but they were enormously popular with audiences. There's just no way of knowing. It's a crapshoot every time.

Aud You've only made one Western, and that was *Cowboy*.

JL I was thinking of the horse!

Aud Have you been offered any more Westerns?

JL Isn't it strange? I have not been offered any more Westerns! [*Laughter*] God's truth, I will never forget that picture for as long as I live, for several reasons. I did it with Glenn Ford, whom I love and who is a friend of mine, but Glenn had definite thoughts in his mind about who was the lead and what kind of an image he had, and he had not only done 150 Westerns, but also he was a great horseman. I had not been on a horse since I was about 6 and I had never ridden a Western saddle, and as I had to go directly from another film into *Cowboy*, I had no chance to learn how to ride. We started with some scenes where I was supposed to have changed from a tenderfoot into the wrangler, or whatever they call him, and I'm supposed to be running the ranch and riding up a storm. They gave me the fastest quarter-horse in California, named Sunday. He used to race and win! They put me on that damn horse and for eight weeks it seemed like I never got off. I split myself and I had to wear a Kotex every day and get back on that goddamn animal. So no, I have not done a Western since and I am not going to do another Western since! Glenn Ford took my boots and had the prop-man saw the heels off so that I had to look up at him. But it was fun, it was fun. I enjoyed it.

Aud My favourite Jack Lemmon moment among many is a scene in *The Odd Couple* which wasn't in the original play, where you are in a restaurant with Walter Matthau and you start snorting in an effort to clear your sinuses. Was that your idea or Neil Simon's?

JL Both. The script said that I had to make some kind of noise that would be loud enough to embarrass Walter in the cafeteria. What the sound would be was up to the actor, so the situation was Neil's, but the noise was mine. Neil is wonderful to work with. He's an absolute maniac about rewriting at the drop of a hat if a scene doesn't seem to work right away, or if the actors don't feel right. He'll go zipping off and in ten minutes he'll come back with a whole new scene. Neil is like Wilder in the sense that you don't need to change his writing when he's on his schtick. You find again that it is pared down, it flows, it's got its rhythm, and it's ruined if you add words, or take them out.

Aud Is it true that Walter Matthau wanted to play your part in *The Odd Couple*?

JL It's terrific that you bring this up! Walter created one of *the* great comedy characterizations of all time in *The Odd Couple*, not only in the film, but also on the stage. He walked off with every award and every review, and it was just brilliant theatre and magnificent acting. To the day he *dies*, Walter will regret playing that part! He always wanted to play my part; he *never* wanted to play his part. Art Carney did my role, marvellously, in the Broadway show, and the only reason that I did the film is that they wanted a name, because the property was very expensive and they felt they should try to insure the movie at the box-office as far as they could. Walter did not have a name in film at that point and nor did Art Carney, so they sent me to New York to see the play and when I got back they said, 'OK, do you want to do it?' I said, 'Of course, I think it's wonderful! I can't wait to work with him!' and they said, 'Oh yeah, you're going to love Art.' I said, 'What do you mean, Art?' and they said, 'Well, you're going to play Matthau's part, aren't you?' I said, 'Are you out of your mind?! Nobody in the world should even be *allowed* to play that part except Walter Matthau!' Walter got so mad at me. He said, 'They've got your name, kid!

You wanna sling your name out the window? What's the matter with you?' He was furious, and to this day he thinks that everybody was wrong and he should have played the other part.

Aud Do you have plans to make another film with Walter Matthau?

JL Not directly. Walter is like a brother to me and I love him dearly, and we also love working together, but it's very difficult, for two reasons. Number one, you don't want to overdo it: we certainly don't want to be Abbott and Costello! Secondly, it's hard enough to find a good script for *yourself*, but if you've got to get *two* parts, it becomes almost impossible to find the material. But hopefully we'll do it before too long.

Aud In the crying scene in *The Prisoner of Second Avenue*, were the tears real?

JL Yes, they were. It's funny about crying. I remember complaining to my bride years ago, 'There's one thing that some actors can do at the drop of a hat which I can't do, and that's cry. There are times in a scene when you want to, and I can't unless I try to make it happen.' She said, 'Why do you want to cry so much?' and I said, 'Well, because it's moving, I guess,' and she said, 'It's nowhere near as moving as seeing somebody trying *not* to cry.' And she was so right, so I've stopped worrying. If tears come, then they're honest and that's fine. If they don't, fine. Ultimately it's the playing that's going to do it, not the tears.

JM They often come from very strange sources, if I can just chip in briefly. When I was working with Laurence Olivier in *The Merchant of Venice* he had to cry at one point when he heard that he had lost his case, and he did cry with enormous convincingness. I asked him where it came from and whether he could identify with that situation, and he said, 'No, dear boy. I imagined all the foxes caught in traps all over the world.'

JL That's another tool that actors use all the time. It's called sense memory. You take something that you can relate to which may not have anything directly to do with what's happening in the play, and you use your reaction to *that* to achieve the emotion you need. It works.

Aud Of your many parts, which one have you most enjoyed playing?

JL This will sound self-serving, but I really don't know anyone who has been around as long as I have who has had more golden opportunities. The parts have been extraordinary over and over again. It goes back to my fifth film, which was *Mister Roberts*. Ensign Pulver was a part that I had wanted ever since the play opened on Broadway, when I couldn't get into the theatre to do a reading to be a member of the cast, and once I saw the play I said, 'Someday stock, somewhere rep, if I could just play Pulver!' Because the play was such a huge hit they didn't do the film for six or seven years after it opened, and they felt that David Wayne, who was so brilliant in the part, was just a tad too old by that time. I guess I'm four or five years younger than David, or I would never have got the part. After the elation wore off, I remember thinking, 'My God, this is a shame in a way, because you're still in your twenties and here you are with the greatest experience you're ever going to have!' Well, I thought that again when *Some Like It Hot* came along, and then *The Apartment*, or *Days of Wine and Roses*, or *Save the Tiger*, or *Missing*, or *The China Syndrome*. I think it's extraordinary, and any actor should get down on his knees and be grateful as hell and try to do the best he can. I really don't have a favourite. I have found that the last part that affected me that way is the one that I would tend to say, because it's the one that's freshest in my mind. But if I did have to pick a single part I would pick James Tyrone, even though it *is* the latest, not only for the part itself, but also for the overall experience. There has never been any experience in my life to equal the sheer joy of being part of this production. It is something which went beyond anything I could ever dream of in every respect, by which I mean not just the material and the character, but the people that I'm working with. It is 100 per cent of a fantasy. Not 90 per cent, but 100 per cent of it.

2

David Puttnam

David Puttnam was born in London in 1941. After working for a time in advertising and photography he became involved in film production in 1968, and in 1969 he joined forces with Sandy Lieberson to form UPS/Goodtime Enterprises, which rapidly became a focal point for the aspirations of British film-makers during the first half of the 1970s. In 1978 he established Enigma Productions, of which he remains the Chairman. He has been a member of several important organizations in the British film industry, including BAFTA and the National Film Finance Corporation, of which he was the Director from 1980 to 1985. He has also served as a member of the board of Anglia Television and as a governor, latterly the Chairman, of the National Film and Television School. In 1986 he moved to the United States to become Chairman and Chief Executive Officer of the Film Division of Columbia Pictures, but he resigned from this position the following year and returned to Britain in 1988. David Puttnam received an *Evening News* Award in 1978 for his services to British films, and in 1982 he was given BAFTA's Michael Balcon Award for outstanding contributions to the British film industry. He was awarded the CBE in 1983, and in 1986 he received the title of Chevalier, l'ordre des arts et des lettres from the French government. He has lectured on film in many institutions all over the world, including the Center for Advanced Film Studies in Los Angeles. His films as a producer include *Performance* (1970, Nicolas Roeg/Donald Cammell), *The Pied Piper* (1972, Jacques Demy), *That'll Be the Day* (1973, Claude Whatham), *Mahler* (1974, Ken Russell), *Bugsy Malone* (1976, Alan Parker), *The Duellists* (1977, Ridley Scott), *Midnight Express* (1978, Alan Parker), *Foxes* (1980, Adrian Lyne), *Chariots of Fire* (1981, Hugh Hudson), *Local Hero* (1982, Bill Forsyth), *The Killing Fields* (1984, Roland Joffe), *Cal* (1984, Pat O'Connor), *Defence of the Realm* (1985, David Drury) and *The Mission* (1986, Roland Joffe). His most recent production is *Memphis Belle* (1990, Michael Caton-Jones). His films have won countless international awards, *Chariots of Fire* receiving an Oscar as Best Picture and *The Mission*, the Palme d'or at Cannes. David Puttnam has also produced numerous films and series for television, including *The Memory of Justice* (1975, Marcel Ophuls), *Ptang Yang Kipperbang* (1982, Michael Apted) and the Channel Four series *First Love* (1982–3).

The following lecture took place on 12 September 1988. David Puttnam was interviewed by Anthony Smith, who was then the Director of the British Film Institute and is now the President of Magdalen College, Oxford.

David Puttnam

Anthony Smith David, you are the only Briton ever to run a major American media institution, and one of the Hollywood majors, at that. Let me begin by putting to you a quotation from Mark Lipworth's book, *Reel Power*. He says, 'Most of those who work in the industry are of modest ability and are only too willing to sell themselves for money, fame and an appealing life-style. Besides, they don't have much to say anyway.' Why go and work with them, or for them?

David Puttnam Well, if you're a European I think it's very, very difficult to be part of the film community within your country and not spend an awful lot of your formative years looking across the water and thinking that either things are just plain better in Hollywood, or that if only *I* were there they would be! It's a conceit, but I think it's a shared conceit: I don't think it's particularly something that *I'm* infected with. I remember that we went through several months at home deciding whether or not to go through with it, and my wife made the point (I think quite rightly) that she didn't, in ten years' time, want to hear me at 55 telling her how wonderful the industry would be if only I'd taken advantage of the offer that was made to me at 45, or how different my own life might have been. She felt it was something that we had to get out of our systems, and I think that would be true of just about any film producer, whether getting it out of your system means going there just to produce a film, or, in my case, attempting to run a studio. I think it's part and parcel of the ethic of being in the film business. You must also remember that I was coming off two things that definitely affected me. It may sound silly, but one dream I'd been pursuing for a long time was winning the Palme d'Or at Cannes. I'd been in competition eight times (seven times is a lot of times to lose!), and when *The Mission* won I was thrilled, and I felt that I'd cracked the one remaining thing that I'd wanted to do, and that it was a good moment to make a change. I'd also come away from the most terrible drubbing over the arrival of Cannon, where I had fought . . .

AS You were right!

DP Well, in hindsight, but I had fought a large part of my own industry to a standstill, and I was very . . . I wouldn't say bitter, but disappointed in many of my former colleagues who . . .

AS Yes, but by going to Hollywood you wouldn't be saying goodbye to Cannon, you'd be saying hello to Cannon!

DP I saw myself passing them in the middle of the Atlantic!

AS The answers you're giving are really answers about yourself and your life, but surely you knew what Hollywood was like. It always strikes people from Europe, who are used to power being concentrated in capital cities, that Hollywood is a terribly provincial place. After all, it's not the business capital, not the political capital, and not even the cultural capital of America, yet it has all this power concentrated in it. How does it wield that moral power over America when it doesn't have any of the realities that go with a great metropolis?

DP You're going to find that several of the answers or reactions that you'll get from me tonight will sound extraordinarily paradoxical, and I'm very aware that the attitudes I've *left* Hollywood with and many of the attitudes I took to Hollywood do represent sometimes irreconcilable paradoxes. I think one of the paradoxes is the role of Hollywood within the United States. People in New York and Washington know that Hollywood is really of zero importance culturally and politically, except when they're fund-raising prior to a presidential or senatorial campaign. At the same time it is of every importance, because there is a sense among sophisticated people in the United States that the tone of the country is, in some bizarre way, set in Hollywood. When there is a violent undertone in society, or when there is a new moral swing through the country, it's something which is either being created or exploited by Hollywood. I find that New Yorkers are particularly aware of this paradox. They know that Hollywood itself is a nonsense, and that it is something they should have nothing to do with, yet time after time they're seduced by it, and they acknowledge that it has this strange, almost unholy, power over Americans generally.

AS Were you given any information about what to expect when Coca-Cola offered you the job?

DP It was done the other way round. When they came to me they said, 'Under what circumstances would you come to Los Angeles and do this job?' and I laid out for them all the things I thought could be done. It wasn't just a question of money; it was to do with what one should try and achieve in order to make the job worth doing. That was the tone and tenor of all the conversations I had, and I can honestly say to you that it was almost too easy. On the other hand, it's not surprising that they were able to say to me, 'We don't want to be another Hollywood studio! We want something different!' because they had failed miserably at trying to be in any way similar. First they'd tried what's called 'the Tsar approach' with a man called Frank Price, who'd made very big-scale movies in a rather grandiose manner. That hadn't worked. Then they'd had an extremely nice man who'd been genuinely a best friend to agents and stars, and who worked on the packaging basis, and *that* hadn't worked. So they were coming off a series of failures, and it was perfectly reasonable to try and change their *modus operandi*.

AS What kind of power did you have, sitting behind that desk, to do work you couldn't have done in any other way, or to change the films of the world in the way you hoped to change them? Perhaps you could first describe the resources at your disposal.

DP The first resource was money, large volumes of money. I was responsible for a company the standing overhead of which was $55,000,000. That was to just open the door in the US. To open the door in the rest of the world was around $100,000,000. You've got one of the four or five world-wide distribution networks, and that is probably the most important of these resources; you've got the ability to take a film – a small film, a big film or a medium-sized film – and distribute it world-wide with whatever money is needed (within reason) to promote that picture. You can say we will make 5,000 prints of this film, or we will make 50 prints; we will spend $25,000,000 promoting and exploiting this film world-wide, or we will spend $25,000. So you have the power of life or death, not so much over the *making* of the film – where, interestingly enough, you have limited power – but over the manner in which the film is distributed, and the amount of money put behind it. You have approximately $100,000,000 worth of overhead, $180,000,000 in production expenditure, and something in the region of $220,000,000 for marketing and advertising support; a quick sum suggests something very close to half a billion dollars a year. That's a lot of money, and that power is controlled by the kind of relationship the head of the studio has with his backers – in my case, the Coca-Cola Company. I was enormously sceptical about how much freedom really existed with the job. I knew you had a great deal of notional power, but I wasn't at all sure how much *real* control you had over those enormous budgets, and my decision to go rested very largely on a series of meetings I had over an extended period of time. I found that I was constantly pushing against an open door. Every time I would question or challenge anything, they said, 'Well, of course we'll do that! We wouldn't have come to you in the first place if we weren't going to do that.' I feel on the one hand naive beyond belief that I accepted everything I was told. On the other hand, in fairness, I think I would have had to have been extraordinarily cynical *not* to believe it, because when they reached out across the Atlantic to me, they were very well aware of my views. I'd had a bad time in Hollywood ten years previously and I'd left, not so much in disgust, but certainly in disappointment. I was very clear about why I thought there was a job to be done with the studio and what type of studio could be evolved over a period of time, and so I think it would have been *very* cynical for me to say, 'Despite the fact that you reassured me on every single point I've raised, I still can't believe you.'

AS But was it practical for them to make the concessions that you asked for? Perhaps the people at Coca-Cola don't know the movie business in the way in which the Hollywood establishment does?

DP I've obviously given this a great deal of thought, and I think in retrospect that they believed what they were saying when they said it. I think that when I told them that the policies I wanted to put into place would meet tremendous opposition, they heard the words 'tremendous opposition', but they just didn't believe that the problems would come down on them personally in the way they did. I don't think they understood that at all. If you're the President and Chairman of the Coca-Cola Company, it's a fairly Olympian position in life: you don't actually deal with personnel problems a lot of the time.

AS But one of the things you just explained you were trying to do was to produce a wide range of films – small films as well as big ones. Is the small film as a *policy*, rather than as an occasional accident, practical for Hollywood? As you said, there is a huge overhead to be written off, and you have to have a constant, enormous return on the capital that's invested in the overheads. Isn't Hollywood now obliged, for the foreseeable future, to depend on vast-budget movies that make large profits?

DP That is a view. It's as complex as discussing the conflicting economic options as to what's right for this country. There is no one answer, there are just different views. I don't happen to share that view: I think it's the mega-budget pictures which have made the studios so extremely vulnerable. My plan was to strip back and start again with the studio, and to try to come up with a new generation of directors, writers and, in some cases, stars. Now, this was not quite as extraordinary or revolutionary as it seemed, because it is what, rather effectively, the Disney Company has put into operation. I know *Roger Rabbit* was an extremely expensive film, but prior to that, Disney had been making films which were significantly lower in cost than the rest of the industry, and one forgets that when they originally decided to build the company around artists like Bette Midler, she was not exactly at the zenith of her career: she was having a difficult time. So they bought into what might be termed extremely gifted, but comparative bargains as actors and actresses. They have yet to work with a big-name director outside Barry Levinson, and even Barry, when they started, was not at the peak of his career. What I was advocating – thought I didn't know it at the time – was not a million miles away from what Disney was successfully putting into place.

AS But you were trying to do it to a company which was owned by Coca-Cola and which was set in its ways, and you were therefore demanding a pretty substantial review and renewal of that company; and yet, as we read in the press here, you promised to do it all in three years! Can you go into an organization and say 'I'm going to change things substantially,' when, in effect, you're handing in your resignation on the first day, so they know when you're going?

DP The simple answer to that is no, and that's the greatest single mistake I made. My defence of myself, to the extent I feel I need one, is that *they* should have told me that. I'm not a corporate business man, I've never pretended to be. I'm self-employed, I've been working on my own for over twenty-five years. I think that's something they should have known and they should have advised me. Since it was, from my point of view, an absolutely fundamental condition of my doing the job, that should have been the point where we shook hands politely, expressed affection and parted. It was every bit as much their mistake, in my view.

AS But isn't that really a human mistake rather than a business mistake? You might conceivably change an organization in three years, but not if you say that's what you're going to do right at the beginning. It may well be impossible for business reasons, but it would seem to me to be impossible for human reasons.

DP I think that's half true. Part of the reason for this manic insistence on three years was that I felt a slight sense of self-betrayal, and I was trying to deal with the side of me that was saying, 'You've sold out! All of this doesn't quite ring true.'

AS I didn't dare to ask you this before, but when you made the announcement about three years, it *did* sound nervously patriotic, as if you were frightened that people in this country would think you'd raised two fingers to us all.

DP Looking back, of course, it sounds jolly naive, but I felt that in three years I could achieve something equivalent to what Mrs Thatcher achieved between 1979 and 1982: to strip back the company to the point where it could function properly. I wanted to get rid of these ludicrous (I thought) relationships they had with overpaid producers, directors and stars, and to create a different kind of ethos at the studio. I was also confident that during that three-year period I could employ and put in place the type of executive who would share the same belief about what could be done, and who would take over from me and allow me to come home.

AS But has Mrs Thatcher been able to do it? [*Laughter*] In any case, whether you were in business, or in the unions, ultimately they all gave in to her because there seemed to be, as the phrase went at the time, 'no alternative'.

DP I don't believe that. I'm certainly not a particular supporter, but I think that, looking back, she behaved extraordinarily courageously, especially during 1980 and 1981, and I hoped (though I never thought of it in those terms) to do the same. What I knew absolutely was that hell was going to break loose when we started to cancel these existing contracts and make the kind of requests we were going to make of the creative community. That was another thing I misjudged. I had listened for years to dozens of dinner-table conversations, and read dozens of interviews in which, one might term, the creative community let its hair down, saying, 'What we want is a *different* type of Hollywood! We *want* to make better films, we *want* to make more responsible films, it's not true that we demand these huge sums of money!' I believed all that, or wanted to, and while it's true to say that some genuinely important people were very good and did try to go along with what I was attempted at Columbia, I did get a rude shock when I discovered the reality of challenging the creative community with the very things they'd said they wanted. We said, 'Yes, you *can* make a different kind of cultural contribution, but I'm afraid we can't afford to pay you the sort of sums you've been used to.' Then they seemed to find themselves in some considerable difficulty.

AS So you went with a vision of creating a modernized and, perhaps, culturally more valuable institution which would have been a kind of beacon?

DP There were and are seven studios, and the reason I thought I might get away with it is that I was only tinkering with one of them. I was quite convinced that there was room for one studio that set out to do a different job.

AS But if you'd been right, the other six would have missed out!

DP I suppose that's true, but it absolutely hadn't occurred to me! I'm still convinced that the extraordinary, dramatic opposition that I encountered was for exactly that reason. It wasn't so much that they thought I was wrong, as that they were terrified of what might happen if I was right.

AS In doing what you did, it seems to me you were doing something you could have done in the Drama Department of the BBC or at Channel Four, albeit on a smaller scale. Don't we have institutions in this country which would have let you do what you were trying to do in what turned out to be impossible circumstances?

DP I would say not, with the possible exception of Channel Four under Jeremy Isaacs. If you work at the BBC, at whatever level, the truth is that your life is very trammelled by economic realities, and you are answerable to a bureaucracy. I wasn't moving into a job where there was a bureaucracy above me. In theory, my mandate was very, very clear. Even my financial programme was laid out for three years. I knew exactly how much money I had, to the dollar, so I didn't have to wade through syrup to get the resources.

AS So you had power over your own economy – going back to the Mrs Thatcher example – but you didn't have power over your society. Clearly there *is* a Hollywood establishment, and They, with a big capital T, couldn't take it. Who *are* 'They'?

DP There *is* a power grouping, and I got myself into even more trouble by describing it as rather like the Wizard of Oz: if you looked behind the screen, there was an old man with a tinny voice. I wouldn't want to put names to them because it doesn't really matter who they are as individuals, and also because I could be wrong, but they do exist. They are obsessed with what the Americans call networking: they speak to each other every day, sometimes several times a day, on the phone and compare notes. They offer each other stocks and shares to buy, and many of them allow their lives to be controlled by a negative trinity, composed of short-term financial gain, spurious prestige and a very, very paranoid attitude to adverse publicity. One of the things I like about this country is the hurly-burly you can get into, sometimes through the press, sometimes personally. You may get a thick ear or a black eye, but basically in the long run it's sort of fair. Michael Winner and I have for years enjoyed a ridiculous knockabout relationship through the press, where I pounce on every statement he makes and he does the same to me. It's good, there's something very healthy about it, and it allows me to feel alive and mischievous from time to time. That is not possible or permissible in the United States, where things are *far* more controlled, and I was seen very much as what they term 'a loose cannon'. For example, if an American executive were to do this lecture tonight, they would have rehearsed it thoroughly with you. They'd want to know every question you were going to ask, they would have discussed it with a battery of public relations people to determine what they should answer, what weight they should put on different answers, and what questions they should specifically avoid answering. They would also be in a terrible sweat about giving themselves and their company away, or giving an advantage to their competitors. I've never shared that. I have no particular problem about making a fool of myself. I think it's just part of being alive, and I don't take myself that seriously. I'm afraid that in some respects I was possibly unable to take Columbia that seriously, and I was certainly unable to take the Coca-Cola Company that seriously.

AS Do you have the right to say that, when you're dealing with hundreds of millions of dollars of someone else's money? There are shareholders who've got their investments and their future tied up in your stock, and you have a responsibility to them.

DP I think that's absolutely true, but again, it's just another reason why I was probably wrong to take the job. What I've described is what I am. I work hard, I like my job for the most part, but I cannot possibly reinvent myself, and I would cease to be effective in any terms at all if I tried to be, or behave like, someone else, and they *knew* that; I was very, very frank about all of that. However, I appeared on a fairly modest network television show about the influence of American cinema abroad, and I told the chap I worked for that I was doing it. He seemed fairly sanguine, but I discovered later that when the hierarchy in Atlanta turned on their TV sets during Saturday peak-time they became very exercised, not for what I was actually saying, but because I was there and they didn't know about it. They wanted to know who I'd checked it with and who had been my PR adviser – it all got a bit silly.

AS How do you feel about the choices you are making over movies when you've got that battery of investors behind you who are your real masters and mistresses?

DP I really didn't see it that way. I saw that here was a company which, in its wisdom, had made a decision to come after me as its Chief Executive Officer, and was going to take its chances with the choices I made, good or bad. I mean, I turned down *Moonstruck* because I didn't think very much of the script, and they had to live with that . . . It may seem trivial, but possibly it *was* my rather knockabout attitude to life, the public and myself generally, that threw them. They have been looking for a more serious-minded approach. I've never been that, and I wouldn't really know where to start. It's not machismo: it's twenty-five years of working one way and being too old, frankly, to reinvent the wheel.

AS Was there anything else you turned down?

DP I read the script of *Frightnight 2*, and it was so terrible that I felt that if I actually said, 'Yes, we'll make this film,' I would be abrogating any possible taste-factor in the decision-making process. We would have been just financing a title, and I felt that if I did that, I would also be creating an indefensible situation for myself. Having said that, which is quite high-minded, we also never reached a point where we could make *Ghostbusters* because we were always in negotiation: we spent our lives in negotiation on *Ghostbusters*. Where I let myself down very badly was in the decision to go along with the Bill Cosby film, *Leonard*, which was not as bad a script as *Frightnight 2*, but not much better. Bill Cosby was an important figure in the life of the Coca-Cola Company: he'd been a spokesman, he was a shareholder, and they were very, very keen to make the film. Frankly, I was swayed by the fact that things were going well early on, and I was winning more battles than I was losing, and the sense that I could do without a major row at that moment. I was persuaded – wrongly, as it turned out – that Bill understood his audience, an audience that I would probably never understand, and that he knew the type of comedy at which he excelled, so I put my own judgement into cold storage and went along with someone else's. With hindsight, it was the wrong thing to do. If I'd said no it would have been OK, I wouldn't have been fired, nothing awful would have happened to me; but it would have been a difficult battle at what seemed at the time to be a turning-point, and I decided not to take it on. It was a great mistake. It was one of the many mistakes I made.

AS Can I ask you about the role of the Hollywood agents? They seem to have risen to power since the decline of the old moguls, and you were really trying to come back and be a mogul as if the era of the agents had not arrived. Who are these agents, and why have they become so powerful?

DP First of all, there is no one group of agents who are villains. There are actually some extremely nice, benign and helpful agents, and then there are other agents who sometimes behave in a strange way, probably because they are, for the most part, more insecure. It's a strange job. I've *been* an agent, so I do speak with some knowledge. You don't *do* anything; you just talk on behalf of a group of clients about money and terms. Your job, really, is to ensure that your clients get a lot of money even if they don't want it, because you only get 10 per cent of what they get. An agent's livelihood depends on the financial success of his client, which may or may not have anything to do with the cultural success or satisfaction of that client, and I would have thought that it's difficult, and sometimes dangerous, for an artist to rely on someone for advice whose relationship with them is, for the most part, concerned principally with money. Unfortunately, we're also living in an era when people tend to take a very short-term view of their careers. I think it's true to say that twenty years ago many agents took a much longer-term view of their clients' success and were prepared to invest in their future. The industry today, sadly, doesn't allow for that type of career development. Careers are expected to last in many cases for not more than five years or so, and consequently there is tremendous pressure on both the client and the agent to grab the money while it's there. When I arrived, I believed sincerely that $20,000,000 as the average cost of a motion picture was too high, and also I believed that those costs weren't caused (as some people claim) by the ridiculous prices paid to Teamster drivers but, for the most part, by the ridiculous prices paid to actors, directors and sometimes even writers. I was attacking one of the fundamental shibboleths of the business, which demand that if you work jolly hard, one day or another you too can ask for $1,000,000 or more per film, and get it. I was denying the success syndrome of America, because their success *is* measured in terms of money. They don't really have Laurence Oliviers or John Gielguds, so they don't have a rule of thumb whereby you can say, 'My God, that man's had an extraordinary life and an amazing career! He may not be a wealthy man, but all things being equal I would like to emulate that career.' They don't have those role models. The role models they *do* have tend, for the most part, to be financially based.

AS Where did these astronomical salaries come from?

DP The studios made a terrible mistake six or seven years ago when they somehow allowed themselves to be talked into mega-salaries *on top* of a percentage of the box-office gross. It was the greatest single folly they ever got embroiled in, and you began to get these crazy situations where the actor takes $10,000,000 even if the film's a flop. Most of these salaries are set against the percentage of the box-office, so if the film is successful the salaries get jacked up anyway, but the thing went potty when the studios let themselves be trapped into these massive heads-I-win, tails-you-lose deals!

AS The agents presumably take 10 per cent (although I understand sometimes less) of their clients' earnings, but if they put a group of their clients together and create a package, they have done, in effect, what the producer does, and for that they take a much higher percentage.

DP Yes, they sometimes take what they call a packaging fee for having assembled the whole thing. To me, there was no point in running a studio – and again, I felt I made this clear to the Coca-Cola Company – if you were going to accept packages from another group of people. You might just as well become a bank, and as a producer I've always had an absolute horror of the idea of becoming a banker, either individually or as the director of a company. When you start as a producer the first thing you ask yourself is, 'Am I going to be the person who creates the financial infrastructure within which this movie gets made, or am I going to be someone who has something to do with the actual content of the film itself?' This is a career decision you make very early on, and since I took the second route I was on a collision course with some agents, not others. In fairness, I would say that I had a very good relationship indeed with about 75 per cent of the agents, and I came to grief with about 25 per cent.

AS But were they the large ones or . . .

DP In one case it was a large one, but in most cases not.

AS But what power do they have? Given the huge resources which you described at the beginning, couldn't you just ignore the ones who are making unusual demands on you and work with the others?

DP In fact, we did better than that. In the first ten months I was at the studio we actually did $8,000,000 worth of business with the agency with which I had the most publicized problems. That's not chicken feed, and it was significantly more business than that particular agency had done with the studio in the preceding year. So that fight wasn't about money, it was about control, and I was seen very much as a threat to the agency's ethos and status. That wasn't true of the other agencies at all.

AS What you're really describing is a situation in which a studio head is a deal-maker and doesn't have room for anything else because he's making deals with other people who make deals.

The film-making occurs, it would seem, at another level of those companies altogether. Was there room for David Puttnam in such a system?

DP With hindsight, almost certainly not, because having got to the studio, I discovered that while I was able to assemble, and in fact inherited, some very good people, we didn't have the human resources or, more importantly, the time to instigate material in the way that I dreamed we might. We just couldn't do it, so sooner or later I was going to become dependent on producers and on farming work out. My only solace was that these would be producers and directors whom *we* chose, and whom we could contract on fair and rather more sensible terms than had been the case before.

AS When you are in that position – when you're not just visiting Hollywood as a British producer collecting money and support, but are actually part of their system – what does Western Europe, and in particular Britain, look like? Do its manners, its ways, its stereotypes and images, play any part at all in the way in which you shape movies?

DP That's a very good question, but I'll have to break it up a little to answer it adequately. First of all, the bad news. Looking from over there, what you say to yourself is, 'Well, Europe! That's a place where *Rambo* does especially well.' That's the first nasty shock you get, that it doesn't have any cultural halo around it. Secondly, you say to yourself, 'It's somewhere where I'm able to judge more finely the creative capabilities of directors, and sometimes writers and actors, because they work on a better quality of material.' There may be some really first-class young directors in the United States, but it's almost impossible to find out because the calibre of material that they're offered to direct in their embryonic years is so appalling. Even more sadly, after they've been doing that type of material for three, four, or five years, *any* spark they might have had has been rubbed into the dust. In the UK and in other parts of Europe, we have the ability to spot quite early on directors who are able to make specific and interesting contributions to the work they are asked to do, and I think that's an important and underrated advantage we have. Thirdly, if you're cranking out movies that cost $20,000,000 apiece, then Europe looks jolly small, but if you are able to make films that cost six, seven, or eight million dollars, as we were trying to, then Europe becomes enormously attractive, because with the right film you can actually break even in Europe and use the United States as gravy instead of the other way round, which you could typify as the traditional situation. You have to remember that a successful small film is infinitely more profitable to a studio than a successful large one: the profitability of a film is enormously affected by its initial cost.

AS It might do very well in relation to its own investment, but it will contribute a smaller proportion of the general overheads.

DP That's half true; we've done our numbers differently. What I tried to do was work a different kind of average gross for a film. Most of the studios work on the assumption that they are going to have two big hits, a couple of break-evens and up to eight flops a year. What I tried to do was to cut down the flop rate by cutting down the cost. My only achievement the whole time I was at the studio was that we pulled down the average cost of a picture from almost $20,000,000 to $11,200,000. That's not bad.

AS Well, what about the revenue?

DP The jury's still out! The films that I was responsible for have only just begun to be released.

AS I was very interested in what you were saying about the extent of the contribution that Europe makes to the profitability of a film . . .

DP The profitability of a *small* film.

AS Does Hollywood try to read the changing attitudes of European societies in the course of choosing what movies to make?

DP No, I don't think they do at all, but they keep quite close track of American social change. They have a thing called VALS, to do with perceived values in society, and they research these VALS fairly thoroughly. They're supposed to indicate the type of thing the audience is likely to respond to in a year's time, and the way in which the demographics and attitudes of an audience are changing.

AS Can you give us an example?

DP Yes. By finding out what type of car Americans are becoming increasingly interested in, they believe that they can deduce other kinds of judgements from that information. They believe that once people have acquired a series of values, there is a great cross-over in these value-decisions from product to product, and films are looked at rather more closely than other consumer products because they're seen, very interestingly, as both value-setters and value-receivers.

AS But if you take something like, say, the ecology movement and concern about the environment, at some point or other, someone in Hollywood says, 'It's time to go green!' Are they looking at us in Western Europe or are they only thinking of America?

DP They're primarily thinking of America; they believe sincerely that we are one, two, three years behind these changing values in the United States. American film studios see themselves as domestic companies making films for American audiences, and the films then have an afterlife overseas. This is not always true – for example, *Out of Africa* made almost two-thirds of its revenue outside the United States and Canada – but they're right more often than they're wrong. What I wanted to do was to put together a smaller studio which didn't necessarily *have* to conform to that kind of judgement, and which could be enormously profitable specifically in Europe. One of the things that lead me to be very interested in the Coca-Cola Company is that it makes 62 per cent of its gross revenues outside the United States. Now, that's almost unique among the large

American consumer corporations, so you didn't have to persuade Coca-Cola that there was a bigger market outside the US than inside; they were made aware of that every single day of their lives. Most American studios would find that surprising, because only 38 per cent of their revenues – and even that's a recently increased figure – arise from outside the US, but I had a boss who absolutely understood the importance of the overseas market. That was another of those open doors I mentioned that I found myself pushing at.

AS They didn't *ask* you to leave Columbia, did they? What they did was sell the whole company over your head. Would you like to straighten the record?

DP I've tried to over and over again. They didn't ask me to leave because I think that when it came down to it, for whatever reason, the chap who was appointed as my new boss wasn't prepared to at that moment.

AS Do you think they sold Columbia to Tristar to create a situation in which you would feel you had to leave?

DP I have an ego, but even *I* don't have enough of an ego to believe that! I think that once they'd made the decision to sell to Tristar – which was absolutely a financial decision, and one which I genuinely believe had been addressed a significant time before I arrived – a number of people very skilfully rode the surf and saw it as a way of getting rid of me, too. So when I went with a series of what I think were perfectly legitimate and reasonable suggestions about how we might compromise (I'd said that I wanted to remain within the stockade, but that I'd like a smaller stockade with higher walls!), they found reasons, all of them contractual, why that wasn't possible; that's when I knew the jig was up. I said, 'If you can't do that, then the answer really is for me to go,' and I think something inside Victor Kaufmann probably went, 'Yippee!', though he managed to look mournful. [*Laughter*] Oh, he did! He did it very well! I would hope to do as well in similar circumstances.

AS What do you feel about it all now?

DP Well, I have no regrets at all about having gone to Columbia. It may have been very bloody sometimes, but I feel stronger, I feel a better-equipped person than I did before I went, and maybe it shook me out of something of a Little Englander attitude. I have to say it was a very difficult road, but someone else will go that route again and make a success of it. Someone tougher than me, someone more experienced who can learn from my mistakes, who will begin to alter things. I certainly know the *desire* to alter things exists among many studio executives, who are by and large a very decent and hard-working bunch of people. But they do find themselves – or they *believe* themselves to be – the victims of the audience, and until *that* alters, or until they shake themselves out of that belief, things will be difficult to change.

AS Do you think Hollywood does anything *better* than us?

DP Well, I don't know how to put this, because I don't want to offend every writer in the audience or anywhere else, but the one thing I can unequivocally say that the Americans do better than us is write movies. They *write* very good movies. When you're reading the scripts they're actually exciting, and they write *visually*. We don't. We write in a literary way, and we tend to write, I'm afraid, on a self-consciously small scale. I would say our writers suffer from suppressed ambitions. I can speak categorically about that. I read 400 screenplays during the year I was in the United States, and many of them did overwhelm me – admittedly, sometimes in a phoney way – with their power and imagination, and with a tremendous conviction that we find difficult to rise to in our work.

AS Speaking more generally now, aren't we watching, both here and in America, a narrowing of taste in general: in films, and perhaps in other art forms as well? The more diversified the systems of producing and distributing images become, the more video and cable and satellite we get, the narrower the choices seem to be.

DP It's true. It's a huge issue, and I see it as a direct result of listening too much to the market-place and not enough to the eyes, ears and dreams of the individual creator. The market-place will always want basically a version of whatever it's already had, so if you take too much notice of these life-style research modules that they throw at you, you will automatically get a narrowing of taste because what you're doing is feeding people what they've already told you they want. The truth of the matter is that the audience doesn't *know* what it wants. It only knows what it had and quite enjoyed. That's the great danger we're going to face in British broadcasting. People believe they're offering you a greater choice, but because they're tying that greater choice to purely commercial decisions about costs per thousand, and the number of advertising hours sold, and so on, they're really only going to be offering us back what we've already seen. Inevitably, I'm afraid, the more market forces play a role, the narrower our choices will become. We're likely to see more game shows, more soap operas, and less of the extraordinary, inspired programming that we've been lucky enough to get from time to time over the years.

AS So are you saying that the great pluralism that we thought was going to come with diverse channels is impossible if those channels are commercial?

DP Yes, because the pluralism you refer to has nothing whatsoever to do with plural decisions being made at the creative end. It's got to do with a pluralism in terms of the consumer. Good television programmes are the result of an individual vision – that's a corny, hackneyed phrase. Great creative decisions come out of the ether, and you pick them up magically because they're things you've never considered before. Marketing, even at its very best, is only subtly picking up and reflecting back to you what you already desire.

AS Is it conceptually possible for there to be between fifteen and forty channels in a society without a narrowing of taste?

DP Yes, it's possible in *principle*, but this isn't just 'a society', is it? It's a commercial society. That's the problem. What do you do when you're running this Dream Machine system and you've got Programme X, which only 400 of you tune in to, and Programme Y, which 22,000,000 tune in to, and the makers of both programmes come back and want to do a new season? Which one do you pick? It is not very hard to make that decision! Then again, the moment you decide to go with Programme-maker Y, are you going to have the courage to say to him, 'Well, you did wonderfully last season. Let's have something even more original this time'? Or will you just say, 'Can I have more of the same, but maybe with a bigger budget'? The metaphor I use is what I term the Wet T-Shirt syndrome. I have no doubt at all that if I put on the equivalent of a *Come Dancing* competition with wet T-shirts at 10.30 on a Friday night, people would pour out of the pubs up and down the country. The show would, at least for a while, be a phenomenon, there's no question about that. Now, how's the opposition going to combat it? It seems to me inevitable that they're going to be tempted to lose the T-shirt – that's the first thing that will happen. But now you've taken a very important step down the road for British broadcasting, and it's a dangerous road because the one fact that hasn't been taken into account about this ideal world of plural broadcasting is that the pressure on Rupert Murdoch or BSB[1] to do this is going to be absolute. If they really can get the bulk of the audience on a Friday night with wet T-shirt contests, then they will feel absolutely impelled to go that route.

AS If I were the Home Secretary, I'd say that the main institutions of broadcasting would still not be competing for income head-on in the way American channels are. The BBC will still have its licence fee, and ITV will still be there in some form with almost a monopoly on advertising in its area. It will be competing against satellites or cable companies which are selling on subscription, and that's another kind of money. So, although they are all trying to make commercial decisions, their money is generated slightly differently, and so they are not competing head-on in the way American channels are.

DP I'm sorry, I don't agree. I think the pressure on Michael Grade, and particularly on ITV1, if and when this happens, is going to be enormous. The advertising companies are going to turn around to them and say, 'Look, we're not going to book any more time on your channel between ten and eleven o'clock on a Friday night because, frankly, no one's watching it. They're all watching Rupert Murdoch. What are you going to do about it?' The ITV sector is dependent on advertising, and they will be forced, absolutely forced, to respond. The Home Secretary will have no grounds whatsoever to ban programming like that.

AS But there is the BBC in the middle of it all with two channels, also competing. It's got a lot of money – it's not like American public television, waiting for scraps to be thrown to it from the table – so it's really in the programme-making business and it can make its own decisions, it's not dependent . . .

DP You're agreeing with what I'm saying! The BBC *in its present form* is protected from that type of pressure, and ITV isn't. That's why it's so important to maintain the notion of public broadcasting as something quite distinct from television, whose principal pressure is commerce.

AS I was actually trying to make a different point. Surely if the BBC is providing very good drama and very good news, current affairs and documentary, that will also set a standard with which the others have to compete.

DP I'm obviously less confident than you are in the political will to maintain the BBC in its present form. I was a teenage deregulator, so that's possibly why I feel a little embarrassed! I'm a director of an ITV company, and the closer I came to looking at what's happening in television, the more I realized what a pernicious pressure, potentially, advertising pounds were, and that's why I'm saying that it's essential to make sure a *significant*, and not just a gestural, sector of British television is kept clear of that type of pressure.

AS Can I ask you, finally, what kind of work you think you will now be doing in Britain?

DP I spent a long time working out what kind of structure I wanted to work within, trying to benefit from the good and bad experiences I had at Columbia, and I've come to the conclusion that my natural taste is towards making relatively middle-class medium-priced pictures. There's no point at all, I feel, in competing with the wonderful work that has been done by Channel Four, partly because I see that work as a beginning rather than an end in itself, and I think those film-makers and writers, and in many cases actors and actresses, will eventually want to move on with the kind of work they're doing. Also, I've spent so much time abroad and I want to make films that have *genuine* international subject matter and appeal. I'm friendly with and admire a great number of international directors, writers and other artists, so I would like to make films which are not significantly or specifically British, but which are at the same time British-based. I've been working for a long time on a film with Istvan Szabo, who made *Mephisto* and whom I admire enormously, and I've been trying to work for twenty years with Jiri Menzel, who made *Closely Observed Trains* and *My Sweet Little Village*, and whom I think of as one of the world's great film-makers. I was was taught by my Dad to look for gaps in the market-place and not just to bang my head on the same wall as everyone else, and if there *is* a gap, it's in our relationship with Eastern Europe. There is a bunch of film-makers there who have wonderful films in them, but who for one reason or another haven't made them, at least not in the English language, and I'd like to be a conduit through which some of their work gets made. There's also a job to be done in the Soviet Union, perhaps as much in television as in features. Feature films are such an important thing in Soviet life that they might be quite fearful, but I don't think they're fearful about television co-production. I've already purchased the rights to a Soviet short called *Neptune's Feast*, which is a quite wonderful comedy. So I think my company will establish itself with a significantly different profile, working in a different price range from the normal British production company.

AS And will you have the same security of revenue to keep making the films?

DP For the time being I will, but more importantly I will have the security of distribution arrangements, so the films won't be last heard of in a small yet not uncritical piece in the *Guardian*. [*Laughter*] I will have the ability to make sure that the films we make do get seen by large audiences, hopefully throughout the world.

AS One is always reading that the British film industry is in dire need of cash and that it's incredibly difficult for British filmmakers to make films, and yet we see people like David Lean, Michael Winner, Richard Attenborough, Alan Parker and yourself, all able to make films, and if one looks at the way the Oscars have been divided over the last ten years, I think it's fair to say we've probably had more than our fair share. Is it true that when you want to make a film the funding is there?

DP I think it's really a question of which film. Let's take Mick Jackson as an example. He was able to make *Threads* as a semi-scientific programme for *Horizon*. You could never make a *movie* about the discovery of DNA, but fortunately the structure exists within British television to make a programme like that. I also think the people you mention would probably argue against what you're saying. I think they'll tell you that, yes, they're making a film, but nine times out of ten it's not necessarily the film they *want* to make, or they're not making it under the circumstances they would have liked. A whole host of very fine British directors have found it necessary to go to Hollywood in a state of semi-despair over the problems of trying to raise money to make films here.

AS But it seems to me that *you* make the films that you want, and Richard Attenborough does too . . .

DP Not true. Richard Attenborough desperately wants to make a film about Tom Paine, and he has found it more than difficult to raise the money to make it. I happen to think it would be a very fine film and could well be very successful. We would have made it at Columbia if I was still there. I know of three of four projects over the years that Alan Parker would like to have made, but which he hasn't been able to raise the money for. David Lean spent most of the last ten years trying to make *Nostromo* and has failed to raise the money.[2] What the film industry in Britain needs is three or four sources of permanent finance: three or four stable, forward-looking companies who own cinemas, who *rely* on being in the movie business in order to feed themselves with product, and who get their incomes (as EMI traditionally did) from the distribution and exhibition of films. We no longer have that. We have the apathetic Rank, I'm sad to say. I've admired them periodically, and I happen to like the people there, but they don't contribute to a sound British film industry because they are unaggressive and uninterested in British cinema. I'm lucky. One of the reasons I sit here and one the reasons I flog around the country making speeches is to try and make the point that I'm an embarrassing exception to the rule. I've been allowed for a number of years to get away with this lunacy! I'm always waiting for someone to tap me on the shoulder and invite me back into real life. I'm a very bad example of what is, in reality, a very real problem.

Notes

1 Rupert Murdoch's company, Sky Television, took over BSB in 1991.

2 David Lean started work on *Nostromo*, but died in April 1991.

3

Delphine Seyrig

Delphine Seyrig was born in Beirut in 1932. Her father, Henri Seyrig, was the director of the Lebanese Institute of Archaeology; her mother, Hermine de Saussure, was a distinguished Rousseau scholar; her sister is the composer Frances Seyrig. She began her theatrical career in Paris in 1952, and appeared in repertory at the Centre dramatique de l'Est and the Comédie de Saint-Etienne. In 1956 she moved to New York to study in the Actors' Studio, and after playing minor roles on American television she made her screen debut in Robert Frank's 16mm underground film, *Pull My Daisy* (1958). She decided to return to France when Alain Resnais offered her the role of the enigmatic heroine in *L'année derniere à Marienbad* (1960), the film which established her international reputation, and four years later she won the Best Actress award at Venice for her performance in Resnais's *Muriel*. Throughout the 1960s and in the early 1970s she appeared in a series of films directed by some of the most eminent film-makers in Europe, including *Accident* (1967, Joseph Losey), *Baisers volés* (1968, Francois Truffaut), *La voie lactée* (1969, Luis Buñuel), *Peau d'ane* (1971, Jacques Demy), *Le charme discret de la bourgeoisie* (1972, Buñuel) and *A Doll's House* (1972, Losey). Thereafter, however, the interest in the work of more marginal (or marginalized) directors, which had already manifested itself in such projects as *Comedia* (1965, Marin Karmitz) and *Journal d'un suicide* (1972, Stanislas Stanojevic), was to determine the course of her film career, and she now acted almost exclusively for film-makers, many of them women, whose names were notably lacking in kudos, but to whose work she was deeply committed. These later films include *L'atelier* (1974, Patrick de Mervelec), *Aloise* (1975, Liliane de Kermadec), *Reperages* (1977, Michel Soutter), *En route* (1978, Marta Metsaros), *Le chemin perdu* (1979, Patricia Moraz), *Le petit pommier* (1980, de Kermadec), *Orlando* (1981, Ulrike Ottinger), *Le grain de sable* (1982, Pomme Meffre) and *Dorian Gray sur le boulevard de la Presse* (1983, Ottinger). Of Delphine Seyrig's films since 1973, only those she made with Marguerite Duras and Chantal Akerman (for whom she gave one of her greatest performances in *Jeanne Dielman*) have been at all widely seen. Throughout her career she continued to act in the theatre, both in France and England, and her stage appearances include *A Month in the Country* (1964), *Rosencrantz and Guildenstern are Dead* (1967), *La chevauchée sur le lac de Constance* (1973), *La bête dans la jungle* (1981), *Letters Home* (1984) and *Un jardin en désordre* (1987). She also appeared regularly on television, and British audiences were privileged to see her in an adaptation of Henry James's novel *The Ambassadors* for the BBC, in which she gave an unforgettable performance as Madame de Vionnet. Her passionate feminism expressed itself not only in her films, but also in her work for the Centre Audiovisuel Simone de Beauvoir in Paris, an archive of films and videos by and about women which she co-founded in 1982. Delphine Seyrig died in 1990, after a long struggle against cancer.

The following lecture was given on 8 March 1987. Delphine Seyrig was interviewed by Sheila Whitaker, who was then the Head of Programming at the National Film Theatre and is now the NFT's Festivals Director.

Delphine Seyrig

Sheila Whitaker Just before we start, I think David Thomson says in his autobiographical dictionary that in that scene we have just watched from *Stolen Kisses*, the seduction scene, you actually ran up two flights of stairs beforehand to get the breathless effect. Is that right?

Delphine Seyrig That's the problem about giving interviews! You let out something very unimportant like this and then you hear about it twenty years later, it's still going around.

SW Is it true?

DS Yes, it's true, but I think all actors do that if they have to. If they want to be out of breath for some reason they have to find some way of doing it, and the point was that this lady was going up to this boy's room way up under the roof. I felt it was unreasonable to arrive there calm, cool and collected after climbing all these stairs, so I did what I would normally have done to go up and see him. I didn't think that was a detail of importance, but now it's become so. All actors do that.

SW It's interesting to know what an actor's secrets are. Now, you were born in Lebanon, in Beirut . . . Your father was an archaeologist . . . And I believe your mother was quite an independent lady as well, in her own way?

DS Yes, she was. She was sort of a sailor before she got married, but then she stopped sailing and went on to write scholarly books about Jean-Jacques Rousseau.

SW And then, during the war, you were living in New York – your father was posted there. That's presumably where you learned your English?

DS That's how I started, yes.

SW How did you decide to become an actress?

DS In the usual way it's done, I think – in the most banal way, in other words. When I reached the age of 17, I saw that I was good at nothing, and my father kept asking me, 'What are you going to do?' I happened to have an older brother who had friends who were in a young theatre company, and I saw them working and doing a performance and I thought that sounded like really fun work, so I decided that is what I wanted to do. They seemed to have a good time and to go to bed late, and to get up rather late too, and I thought that was a good idea. I didn't know much else about the theatre than that.

SW So how did you set about it?

DS My parents enquired about an acting school for me.

SW They didn't object to this idea?

DS No, they were glad that I wanted to do something. So that's how I started, that's really how I learned to work. I didn't know what work was about before, it just seemed to be a dreary word that I couldn't understand. When I actually started working for acting class I began to understand that work could be fun and absorbing and not necessarily repelling, and so it was a good solution on the whole.

SW And then you went to New York and you studied with Lee Strasberg at the Actors' Studio?

DS Yes, I did. I spent a few years in France and acted in one interesting company, which was Jean Dasté's company[1] – he provided very much the same upbringing in acting that Michel Saint-Denis[2] did in London. I stayed there a couple of years, and played Ariel in *The Tempest* and things like that, and then I went to the States because I had seen the films that Elia Kazan had made with people like Brando and James Dean, and I was fascinated by that. I don't know what happened to actors here when they saw those films, but in France we were quite amazed because it seemed like a magical way of acting which could not have been learned in any way, which seemed so spontaneous and unaffected, and with so little stress on words – in France, of course, we were taught to speak well. I suppose in England you have the same thing. We were taught to speak well, that was the main thing, and to be heard and to behave decently and nobly. Then we were actors – and *good* actors. Then suddenly, there were these ill-bred people, and you couldn't understand a word they were saying even if you spoke perfect English, and they behaved in such an extraordinary way – that was to me like a miracle! I didn't know how it happened, and I decided to go and see. I read a little paperback book about James Dean's life, and in this book they named his agent in New York, so I decided to go to New York and see the agent. She was very nice, but she couldn't guarantee that I was going to be the next James Dean! Then I went to the Actors' Studio and there I began to understand what it was all about, how they could achieve this seemingly improvised behaviour on screen. I still remember it was one of the very great moments of my life, the time at the Actors' Studio.

SW So obviously it radically affected your own approach to acting.

DS Well, I discovered that it *was* perhaps useful to speak correctly! . . . But in those days we were told in France that an actor should totally disappear behind the character, and that it was the character who was important and not us – and I believed that, but I still had some doubts. When I arrived at the Actors' Studio, what I understood – and I think that was the important thing – was that, if there is no personality behind the character, if the actor doesn't know himself perfectly well and cannot use all the qualities and defects that he has, then the character will be impersonal. The character will only be interesting if you bring your own experience into it. This was unheard of in France in those days, and now at last I knew what acting was about. That was how I began to trust myself to do something, because I knew it was *me* that had to do it and I didn't have to look in strange places to find what the character was. The character was *me*, it had to be *in* me.

SW But how does that relate to something you are quoted as saying, which is that if there is no history to a character you are playing then you have to invent one, because even the slightest gesture of that character has been informed by her history? Is that the sort of thing you learned at the Studio?

DS Yes, because they go together. One thing is to know oneself, and to know that one has certain reactions and certain types of gestures: we have to know our own behaviour in order to be able to use it in somebody else's story. But the actor also has to know the character's story so that the two can blend together. If you know nothing about the character you are supposed to play, and if you know nothing about yourself, then you produce impersonal behaviour on stage, which *I* didn't want to do, at any rate. You *do* have to invent a biography of your character, but it's *you* who's inventing it, unless you're playing Madame Curie, and then you have to read books to find out about Madame Curie's life. But if it's an imaginary character then you have to sort of create it yourself, so that when you arrive in the situation of the film you have a small idea of what has happened before, maybe a long time ago before the film starts.

SW Of how much use was that in your first film, which was a strange little film called *Pull My Daisy*?

DS None of that was in it!

SW I didn't think so, somehow! How did it come about?

DS Well, I was an unemployed actress in New York, and I had a friend who was at the Actors' Studio and she said, 'Do you want to play in this film? It's a short film, and my agent doesn't want me to do it because she doesn't think it's good for my image. Do you want to go up for it?' So I said, 'Sure, why not?' and it was *Pull My Daisy*, a film by Robert Frank, and the script was by Jack Kerouac. So I went in, and the other actors were Allen Ginsberg and people like that, poets and philosophers and beer-drinkers, jazz musicians . . . I was the only actress in it. I just went along with what was going on, though I didn't really understand it. What was interesting was that it was perhaps the first independent underground movie that was made in New

York in a loft. Now it's been done a great deal, but it hadn't then.

SW You actually went and did a couple of episodes of a CBS series, did you not?

DS I know what you're trying to get to! Yes, I was at long last hired to do a series for CBS television, and that meant going to Hollywood to do the pilot first, and I had never been to Hollywood or California at all. There's a funny story about getting that part. In my curriculum vitae it said that I spoke English without any accent and that I was bilingual, and this part was a French girl who was married to an American: the whole point was that she was French, so I had to have a very strong French accent. At that time I had a very strong *American* accent, and I thought, 'Nobody is going to believe my French accent!' So I went to see the producers at the Waldorf Astoria, and I said, 'How do you do, Mr Levy?' and I played the scene with a very strong accent, hoping it would not sound too fake. Then I handed over my curriculum vitae, and I saw the two of them chuckling about the usual actress trying to sound better than she actually was, saying she had no accent, and I thought, 'Oh, I should have scratched all that out!' But anyway, I got the part. It was a seven-year contract in case the series did well and was successful, and I went to Hollywood and did the pilot. It was very strenuous because I had to fake this French accent from morning to night, and finally I broke down and told my partner. He was the only person who knew that I didn't speak like that, so that at night I could have dinner with him and relax, and he kept the secret. This lasted for a month, and I thought, 'My God, how can I do this for seven years? Some day I'm going to have to tell them!' And then I had a month's vacation after the pilot was finished, and I went to Paris, which is when Resnais asked me to do a test for *Last Year at Marienbad*. I did the test and then he asked me to play the part, and I said, 'I have this seven-year engagement with CBS!' So they said, 'We will try.' There was a lawyer there – who, incidentally, later became the French Minister of Justice – and he would call

California on the telephone and Mr Levy would shriek in his ears everytime he said he wanted me to stay in France. Finally I got on the phone and said, 'Mr Levy, this is my country, this is a nice French film, I want to do it very much,' and I went on keeping my French accent while I was negotiating this. Finally they gave up and said, 'All right, come back and do the next three or four episodes and then we will write you out of the story,' which is what they did. I went back, still speaking like this, and they wrote me out and then I returned to do *Last Year at Marienbad*, which is what you wanted to get to.

SW Well, it's basically where it all begins, I suppose.

DS Yes, it's where it all begins.

SW What attracted you to this very strange film?

DS I think I am always attracted to very strange films to begin with! . . . I was very excited because this was an *ideal* story. It was not a realistic drama in someone's kitchen, it was every person's fantasy at one point or another in their life. It was such a real fantasy for me that I think it was my reality then, and probably still is in some way. I liked the idea that it was entirely a matter of imagination. I think I have no problem with that. I was asked very often afterwards, 'Did you understand what it was about? Did Resnais explain it to you?' and I said, 'No, I just loved it from the first time I read it, and I did not need any explanation.'

SW So what attracted you to *Muriel*, for which you got the Best Actress award at Venice? It's an extraordinary film.

DS Well, that is a very different story. First of all, it is the total opposite of *Last Year at Marienbad*, although at the same time it is not a typical realist film. It dealt with daily life and the life of this particular woman who faced her present and her memories of the past in a less imaginary context than in *Marienbad*. Also, it was interesting for me to play a woman who was much older than I was then, and I liked Jean Cayrol, who did the script – I liked his novels. I had very much enjoyed working with Resnais, and it seemed like a good idea to go on.

SW In fact you have worked with a lot of directors at least twice, if not three times: Resnais, Buñuel, Losey . . .

DS That is true.

SW Is there an explanation for that, other than that you have enjoyed working with them?

DS Yes, there's that, and I am also very faithful. Now that you mention it, when we were doing *India Song*, which we shot in two weeks, I remember saying to Marguerite [Duras], 'Why don't you sign us up for the next ten years? We will make a dozen films a year, or ten films a year, and it would be a happy life.' I would love working with the same family the whole time. I would love that.

SW Just working through ideas with the same group?

DS Right. I always envied people like . . . well, Ingmar Bergman is the obvious example, but also Jean Renoir – they had their sort of family, I would say. I would love that. Maybe that is the explanation.

SW In fact you worked with Losey twice, and on the second film, *A Doll's House*, you and Jane Fonda had some impact on the script, didn't you?

DS Yes. I had done a previous film with Losey, *Accident*. I worked on it just for two or three days and it went like a dream. All my scenes were with Dirk Bogarde, and it was really very lovely. So when Losey asked me to play in *A Doll's House* I was very excited, and I think Jane Fonda was too, because it is a very beautiful play and a play that, for women, was a very important one, and still is. So when we saw the adaptation, I think that she in the United States and I in Paris were both disappointed. Although it was written by David Mercer, we both thought that very important points were lost. Losey told us that we would rehearse for, I think, ten days in the real sets in a village in

Norway, and we would have the costumes and everything, and it seemed like perfection – really the best way of making a film. Then, just as the time came to do that, he said that the money couldn't be raised and we would have to do without those ten days' rehearsal, which was a big disappointment. I think Jane had typed forty pages of notes about the script, and I had underlined some things in my script, and we were counting on the fact that during rehearsals we would straighten all this out. Suddenly, we were faced with, 'We shoot tomorrow at eight o'clock!' so we had to say, 'Let's talk about the script for a while,' and I think that for two or three days the shooting was postponed and we tried to explain what we felt about it. I suppose it's an interesting fact that we felt this way about an *Ibsen* play: I don't think we would have felt that about most authors. It shows how Ibsen is acute and sharp, how deeply he explores women's problems – not always problems . . . his insight about women – that we should have felt so strongly about any departure from what Ibsen was saying.

SW You did manage to get some of it changed, did you not?

DS Oh, yes. Losey accepted that we were not making wild suggestions, we were just trying to stick to what Ibsen was saying, and he accepted it. I think it was difficult for him and David Mercer to accept that, but we were very keen about it.

SW You are also quoted as saying that you feel that actors and actresses don't have a great deal of power on film, not to the extent that they do on stage, where they can have a much greater input into what happens on the night.

DS Well, if you do one take and the director doesn't like it, he can say, 'All right, let's do another one,' and, 'Can you do this and that?' But once you have rehearsed for a month in a play and the director has told you what to do, nevertheless when you are in front of the public nobody can come up and say, 'Look, could you do that again?' So you *do* feel that you are in control of the end result. Also, your whole body is there all the time on the stage, which it isn't on the screen. You sometimes have this part or that part, depending on what kind of actress you are!

SW Your first woman director – and you have actually worked with a lot of women directors – was Marguerite Duras.

DS Yes, but she had a co-director because *La Musica* was her first film. I've done, I think, several first films with various people, but I've never seen them have a co-director. Perhaps it's a coincidence, but it was the first time I had a female director, and wouldn't you know that she had a co-director there to advise her and to make sure that everything was OK! Actually, they had very different ideas about what should be done. Sometimes Marguerite would say, 'Well, to me this film should be faces and words,' and we would say, 'Well, you know, that is not so, we're *not* doing just faces, and the camera goes and does all sorts of things.' Then she would say, 'Well, I can't see into the camera,' and we would ask, 'Why not?' and she would say, 'Because . . .' And it turned out the camera was too high for her and she didn't dare ask. We said, 'Why don't you ask for a box? You can stand on it and look into the camera.' She was really shy that first time . . . but she wasn't shy any more afterwards!

SW You presumably enjoy working with women directors?

DS You can't bunch them all up in one bag because they are all very different from one another, but I suddenly realized I had never worked with women before. I only realized when I started working with them, because before that there were just men, that's all. So I never asked myself what it would be like if the director was a woman, but when I *did* work with women directors I realized I was more familiar with them, but not as impressed as I was by male directors. It's probably the old thing. I think all girls are made to be impressed by the importance of the works of men, so you're automatically in awe, I think, at least when you're a girl . . . Then you remain that way, I suppose, through adulthood, and it's a discovery to find out that you can be on the same level as the director, that there is not necessarily a hierarchy. I do think that it is probably also important that these women were the authors of the films, that they had written the scripts, and that I was at one with the subject matter and the approach and the content of what they were talking about.

SW You also worked a couple of times with Buñuel. In his autobiography, he mentions that you told him while you were filming *The Milky Way* that, as a child, you used to sit on his lap during some meetings he had in New York.

DS I don't remember saying that. I know he says that in his book, so everybody asks me about it. I don't remember saying that.

SW You don't remember sitting on his lap, either?

DS I don't remember sitting on his lap at all, and I can't remember saying that I did. I don't want to blame it on Don Luis's slight deafness, but I might have said something else. Maybe I said, 'I would have loved to have sat on your lap when I was 3 years old.' I might have said that, but I don't remember saying it.

SW Perhaps it was wishful thinking on his part! How did you enjoy working with him?

DS Oh, it was wonderful, but very hard. He was very impatient if we didn't get it immediately. There was no discussion on how we should do it. 'No, no, no,' he would say. 'Go here, do your line, then come back here!' So you had to solve your problems all by yourself, and if you made a mistake several times in a row, he became very impatient and he would try and change the scene. He felt, 'Oh, she'll never get it! Lets try and change it around.' At one point he was a gag-man in Hollywood to make a living, and he was very specific about rhythms. I remember there was a moment when one of the actors was supposed to pour a cocktail for somebody while he was delivering some dialogue, and Buñuel had him rehearse, saying, 'All right, you take the glass first and then you take the bottle and then you put the glass down – you only put the bottle down after the glass.' The poor guy was trying to say his lines, but you felt as if you had to have a real experience in timing words and actions in a specific way, otherwise it wouldn't work. It was very interesting watching him do that. Directors rarely have that very specific idea of how they want you to pick up a bottle and pour a drink.

SW You are quoted as saying that you don't like the movie camera, and that this is why you prefer the theatre.

DS I don't like it, I am very afraid of the camera. I always feel as if it is judging me. I mean, if it could put on a smile, a warm expression, I might feel better once in a while, but it never has so far. Maybe one day cameras will speak with a gentle voice and say, 'Go ahead, love.' That would be very nice, but it hasn't happened yet. One person who was very aware of that was Fred Zinnemann. He wanted to do a whole scene in *Day of the Jackal* following me very closely, so he decided to use a long lens so that his camera was way back there, and I didn't feel that he was really following me. He did that to make me feel comfortable, and that was lovely of him because it *did* make me feel comfortable. I didn't think I was being trapped. When the camera is right here some actresses love it, I know that they do. They have a communication with this thing, and what they love about doing films is being very intimate with the camera. I have never been able to do that.

SW I think *I* would find it a bit strange!

DS Well, being an actress I probably should find *some* sort of arrangement with the camera!

SW You certainly seem to have done so, even if you don't *feel* you have! But, for example, *Jeanne Dielman*, where it really is just you on screen . . . sure, the son and the clients appear occasionally, but really it's just you. How did you get on with that?

DS Well, I was so concentrated on what I had to do in this film. *Jeanne Dielman* is supposed to be a very slow film, but all I did in it was rush around the whole time, and this is very strange: it shows how notions of time are really very artificial. Chantal [Akerman] wanted each activity of this woman to be filmed in its entirety, without cutting in on it to make it seem less long and tedious. In other words, if I was cooking she wanted me – in one shot – to open the fridge, take out the meat, open the cupboard, take out the salt, and have all the ingredients and finish the whole preparation of the food, all in the one shot. We didn't know how long this was going to take and there was just so much film in the camera, so we had to rehearse each thing completely in its real time to find out if we had enough film to do the whole sequence. Usually we overran by just thirty seconds, and she would say, 'Can you do it just a *little* bit faster?' and I would say, 'All right!' So I take the meat out of the fridge, I open the paper and the meat stays there, OK, and I take the salt out of the cupboard – oh, I forgot *this*! So we would have to do it all again, because going back to get the other thing would make it too long. Really, I had so much to do in this film! I was walking back and forth to the living room, to the kitchen, setting the table – I was extremely active – and so I was very surprised when people sat there and thought it was so dull, because *I* never stopped! I think they thought it was long and slow because they don't like to watch women washing dishes and cleaning tubs and preparing the dinner.

SW Which is really what the film was all about.

DS Which is what Chantal really wanted to look at, yes.

SW And presumably that is what appealed to you in doing the script. It must have been a very strange script to receive, or did she talk to you about it beforehand?

DS We discussed it. She had another script in mind before that, and it turned out to be an earlier draft of this one. Chantal's starting-point was: what is the difference between a normal, ordinary, married woman's life and a prostitute's life? In the earlier script, the action started in the morning, in the bedroom, and there was a photograph of the family, and the husband would get up and get dressed and put some money on the table and leave for the day, and then this woman began doing about the same thing that Jeanne Dielman is doing. Then Chantal decided that the husband had died, but the life of these women was pretty much the same. In other words, very often women get married in order to have a roof over their heads and to have something to eat, but not necessarily for other reasons. This then makes the link with Jeanne Dielman, who prostitutes herself for a few hours a few afternoons each week in order to exist and to feed her son and keep alive. For Chantal it was a sort of equivalent. That is why this prostitute looks so much like a housewife, because she *is* a housewife, except that she doesn't have a husband anymore, but that doesn't change much.

SW It must have been a very demanding role, quite apart from the rushing around to get everything in in the time of a reel of film.

DS Yes, it was, it was. I think one of the things that is very moving about Chantal's film is that to me it shows great love for all the daily gestures that this woman does and that she remembers seeing all her childhood – watching her mother, always from the back, either because she was at the sink washing the dishes, or cleaning the bath tub. For Chantal it was very sensuous, it was childhood remembrance, and I think that that is one of the aspects of the film which people don't really feel. Anybody who has had a mother has actually seen this, has had this vision of things when they were a child, but you forget it afterwards. You *want* to forget it afterwards.

SW You have actually played over here on the stage on two or three occasions, at the Young Vic and the New End, and in Edinburgh. How do you feel about acting in English? Are you comfortable?

DS Not very. Sometimes I feel that I am bilingual as I talk to friends, but when it comes to acting, you realize that there is a degree more. You have to be yourself even more when you act than when you don't act, because of this question of impersonal behaviour which is a tendency of all actors. The difficulty is to have *personal* behaviour, and when you speak a foreign language, even when you know this language well, somehow I feel that I learned it through listening to people. In other words, I am copying people, I'm copying what I always heard. It's a language I've copied like a mocking-bird or a parrot, and I don't feel it in real life, but when I'm acting I suddenly realize that it's not my real way of speaking, and that my real way of speaking is my French way. I can't really reach myself in English. I try to get as close as I can, but it's not really me.

SW So how do you feel that has affected your performances? Do you think it shows?

DS Well, in the theatre it's difficult for me to say because I can't see it, I can't hear it. But yes, I've had friends come and see some last rehearsals and tell me, 'My God, why aren't you yourself?' and I think 'Yes, I'm copying.' Generally I copy the closest person to me at the time; I start talking like my partner. I have a tendency to do that in French, too. I remember a long time ago I was playing Nina in *The Seagull* with an actor who was originally Russian, and like all Russians he still had a sort of Russian music about the way he spoke, although he spoke perfect French. Somebody came to see me at one of the first performances and said, 'Why do you speak with a Russian accent?' and I said, 'What do you mean?' Then I realized I had been copying my partner. The most difficult thing, I think, for an actor – in films and plays – is not to be influenced by the environment and actually to reach himself inside the part. *That's* the difficult thing.

SW Now, to go on to something quite different, you are a co-founder of the Simone de Beauvoir Audio-Visual Centre.

DS Yes, that was four years ago. Before that, in the 1970s, I bought three cameras with a group of friends. In fact, they were the first video cameras on the market: black-and-white video, no cassettes; it was reused like the old recorders. We filmed some events during the campaigns for the liberalization of the abortion laws in France, and there were a lot of goings-on in the streets in the early 1970s. We would film these demonstrations and these different things that we were interested in. To me, it was a great relief to be behind the camera and to see what it was like. I also did a long tape of interviews with actresses in 1976 – all with those first cameras, which don't exist anymore. We did so many tapes, and we knew that other women were doing some everywhere – in the States, in Germany, in Holland, everywhere – and we thought, 'What is going to become of these tapes?' So in 1981 we drafted a proposal for a Centre where all these tapes and works by women could be put in an archive to constitute a memory of women of our time. We got some subsidies from the Ministry of Culture and several other ministries in France, and it's been going on for four years, with very little funds. We have almost 600 documents now, mostly documentaries, but also fiction films by and about women, and we have also continued producing little films. We have a double task of maintaining the archive of women's work and also producing new works ourselves.

SW And why was it given the name of Simone de Beauvoir?

DS Because it seemed to us that Simone de Beauvoir had a meaning for anyone speaking any language – in Japan, everywhere. The connotations of her name are very strong and powerful, we wanted to honour her, and she was very happy when we asked her if we could use her name. She had been involved with us in those struggles at that time, and we had worked quite a bit with her since. During the 1960s she began concentrating on women's issues more than she had done before, and worked with the women who were in those struggles, and it was a very interesting evolution of hers. Before, I suppose, she thought that socialism would solve women's problems, and finally she decided that women had to fight their own causes, so that's how we got to meet her, and then decided to call the Centre after her.

SW She was quite a remarkable woman, I would assume.

DS She was an inspiration to us all.

SW Well, I think it's the turn of everyone else to ask Delphine some questions.

Audience It has always struck me as rather curious that right at the beginning of your film career, you and Alain Resnais worked together very comfortably and have never worked together since.

DS Well, you know, the general way it happens is that a director calls upon an actress, so I think the question should be put to him and not to me.

SW It is interesting, though, that he hasn't. Perhaps you should start your own project, and you could ask him to direct it.

DS But these French film directors are authors. Of course, Resnais has never written a script and he never will – he doesn't want to write scripts – but I don't think it's easy to suggest a story to him. He is open to reading them, but one that would really interest him? – that would be difficult to achieve.

Aud Could you comment on your new film with Chantal Akerman, *Golden Eighties*, which is very different in mood to her other films? It's almost frothy, very light-hearted.

DS I don't think it's that different from her other films. Her very first film, which she made when she was 18, was a short which she acted in herself: it's a comedy, and she commits suicide. It lasts thirteen minutes. She comes home, she opens the letter, she reads it, she climbs up the stairs, she goes into her kitchen, she hums to herself and she does all sorts of crazy things in a Charlie Chaplin way. She starts shining her shoes and goes on to shine her whole body, she starts mopping the floor, and then she empties the cupboard out and mops all the cups and saucers and knives and forks. It's very funny. Then, in the end, she turns on the gas and puts her head in the stove and suddenly it blows up: you hear, *boom!* – and that's it. I think she's always had this feeling about absurdity. *Golden Eighties* is perhaps the first time it's come out in a long feature, but in her short films it was already there. I wouldn't say that it's light-hearted. It has a kind of nervous, hysterical energy in it, and it's funny in a way where you're not sure how funny it is *really*. You're on the edge all the time, and I think that's an interesting way of saying very sad things.

Aud We seem to have lost touch with you lately because several of your most recent films haven't been shown widely in Britain. What of your work in the last twelve years would you most like to be seen by British audiences?

DS Oh, I don't like to make choices! I think that they should be allowed to see everything and then like whatever they like. This says a lot about the situation of film distribution nowadays. Audiences are made to see a certain type of film – the type where there is money to publicize the merchandise – and are deliberately cut off from all sorts of works which cannot find their way into a movie theatre, and when they do, there is no publicity about it so you don't even know what's being shown. It's very sad; it's the same in France, and everywhere else.

SW But if you had to chose one film . . .

DS I would hate to chose one film; they are all interesting for different reasons. Ulrike Ottinger's films, I think, are some of the most important being made in the 1980s, and nobody has ever seen her films, except a few privileged people who happen to be in such-and-such a festival. They've never been distributed in France, or Britain, or Germany – it's beyond me why. I can't chose, but I think all Ulrike Ottinger's films should be seen.

Aud Can I ask you if you are able to drop a character at the end of a day's filming, or do you find that you take the character home?

DS Well, I always thought I was in perfect control of that, and that this was a ridiculous romantic idea about the actor going home with the character. Then I was in a play about Sarah Bernhardt, and it seemed that I was behaving in the strangest way and I wasn't aware of it. When my attention was drawn to it, I had to recognize that it was really true and that I was becoming . . .

SW Were you limping all the time?

DS I still have problems from having done that play, because I had a wooden leg . . . Well, I won't go into the details, but I became like this woman in my everyday life; I didn't make the break fully. I wouldn't have known if somebody hadn't remarked on it, so I don't really know what the other characters have done to me!

Aud A number of the directors you have worked with have a remarkable visual sense. Is that something you're particularly drawn to?

DS Yes, it is essential to me, because very often it's the form that makes the contents so valuable. I have made films with people who did not have a visual sense. That's all right too – *sometimes* it's all right – but it's more exciting when the image is new, and is a revelation that goes with what is being said in the film. That's why I like Marguerite Duras's films.

Aud When you talked about *A Doll's House*, you said you were attracted by the idea of rehearsing. Is that something you like to do generally when you are making films, or do you prefer your first reactions?

DS But you never do that *generally*, this *never* happens – you never have ten days or two weeks of rehearsals before a film. I remember when we were making *Accident*, they flew me in from Paris for a reading of the script, and here we all were in a room a long time before the filming started, and we sat and read the whole thing. Already this was a miracle, and it was very, very wonderful, but it's rarely the case. Nobody can afford to have rehearsals before the shooting period. I remember Resnais got us together for both the dinner scenes in *Muriel*, to see how we worked as a group and how he wanted his camera to move, and I also worked with him on *Marienbad* for a long time. He took photographs and we had projections of films which we thought would help us with the character in the film. I loved that, I love to build up things, but you can almost never do that in films.

Aud Was it working with women directors that brought you, to some extent anyway, into women's issues, or was it women's issues that made you want to work with women directors?

DS Well, it was not women directors who raised my consciousness about women because it was raised long ago, but the question I ask myself is, how come I've made so many films with women? As I say, it's the directors who ask the actor and not the opposite, so how come so many women have asked me to act in their films? I've never advertised that I've wanted to work with women; it happens. Marguerite Duras was the first one, and then gradually others asked me, and in the last ten years I've worked mostly with women. If so many women hadn't made films, I would probably have been unemployed all this time!

Aud You obviously have a very close working relationship with Marguerite Duras. There is quite a big gap between *La Musica* and *India Song*, and I wondered if your friendship with her built up during that period, and how much she changed as she became an established figure.

DS Yes, she did change quite a bit between 1964, which was when the first one was made, and 1974, when we made *India Song*. She made *La Musica* with her co-director and, while I think it's a lovely film, it's a little bit impersonal, similarly to what I was saying about acting: she was not able to be herself completely. Then she worked through a period of making political films, and she asked me to do one at that point, but I couldn't see what I could do with it. Now, I think I was wrong, but at the time I couldn't visualize what she wanted from me and so I turned it down. She kept on writing; she is very prolific, but somehow I wonder if her fame didn't actually come more from her films than from her books. By the time she asked me to do *India Song*, she had found her masterly way of making films –

that freedom that she has, and that indifference to the way films *should* be made, which is great. When we started filming *La Musica*, I think we became very close immediately – I mean fairly close – but there are always long periods when we don't see each other because she is very busy, or I'm very busy . . . She always calls me up with these strange ideas. For *India Song* she called me up and said, 'Have you read the novel?' and I said, 'No, I haven't.' There was a long, shocked pause on the telephone, and I said, 'But Marguerite, I can buy it and read it! What is it? In fact, I would *love* to read it!' She said, 'Well, I'm starting Monday on a film version of that, and I was thinking of such-and-such an actress, but in the end I don't think that she's really what I want,' – the reason was that she was turned down by that particular actress! – 'so would you be ready to shoot? Can you read it?' 'Yes, Marguerite, I'll go out and buy it immediately.' So we started shooting the next week. She wanted me to wear a dress she had seen me wear in a play, and I couldn't fit into it any more, so I said, 'I can't wear this dress, we'll have to make one,' which postponed the film for about forty-eight hours. The next time she called me up, a couple of years later, she said, 'Do you know my play, *Vera Baxter*?' and I said, 'No.' Long, shocked pause. Then she said, 'Well, there is a part, a man's part, but I would like you to do it. Do you think you could do that?' So I said, 'Well, let me read it,' and I *did* play the man's part, which she changed into a woman. Nothing was really changed in the text – there was nothing much *to* change – and, in the end, I think she was disappointed: I think she felt it lacked something because I was playing a part which she had written for a man. That was my third experience with Marguerite, so I don't know . . .

Aud Do you think you might work with her again?

DS I tell you I'm all for it, and ready to sign up for a few years doing just films with her all the time.

Aud Have you ever worked with camera-women?

DS Yes, I have.

Aud Does it make a difference?

DS Of course it makes a difference!

SW It becomes a more friendly camera?

DS It's not a question of more friendly or less friendly, it's simply a question of sharing an experience, an untold but obvious . . . the same experience. What can I say? It *is* different, and I'm sure that men being filmed by a camera-woman would feel the difference too. In fact, I'm sure that men feel differently when they're being directed by a woman than when they are directed by a man. How can it be otherwise? You're being seen from the outside, somehow, and it's obviously a different point of view: you're being seen by somebody outside your own species, so to speak. But when it's female directors who write their own scripts, then it's even more strange, I think, because clearly men are not seen in the same way by women and it's apparent when you see the films. You can't help seeing that it's a woman who sees these women who see these men, and therefore the men must surely feel that they're being seen from a window, which is not the same as being seen from inside the house by another man. It *has* to make a difference; I don't see how it couldn't. In my case, I would certainly be less inhibited with a woman behind the camera.

Notes

1 In 1947 Jean Dasté became the Director of the Comédie de Saint-Etienne, one of a number of dramatic centres set up under a new policy of *décentralisation dramatique*, designed to renew the theatrical life of the French provinces with the support of both central and local government. He remained in this post until 1970, and was vigorously committed to encouraging the attendance of working-class audiences.

2 Michel Saint-Denis founded the Compagnie des Quinze in 1930. In 1935 he moved from France to England, where he

founded the London Theatre Studio for the training of young actors and directed many legendary productions, including *Noah* with John Gielgud and *Three Sisters* with Gielgud, Peggy Ashcroft and Gwen Ffrangcon-Davies. He worked for the BBC French service during the war, and then returned to France, where he became the Director of the Centre Dramatique de l'Est, another of the new decentralized theatres.

4 Satyajit Ray

Satyajit Ray was born in Calcutta in 1921, the son of Sukumar Ray, a writer, painter and photographer. He graduated from Calcutta University at the age of 19, and between 1940 and 1942 he studied graphic art under Rabindranath Tagore. In 1943 he went to work in the Calcutta branch of a London advertising agency and book publisher as a book illustrator and designer of book jackets. He co-founded the Calcutta Film Society with Chidananda Dasgupta in 1947. He visited Europe in 1950, and on his return he met Jean Renoir, who was then directing *The River* in India, and whose films were to have a profound influence on his own. It was while he was working at the agency that Satyajit Ray conceived the idea of writing a film version in his spare time of one of the books he had illustrated, Bibhuti Banerji's novel *Pather Panchali*. He bought the screen rights using his own and his wife's money, but the film was later taken over by the West Bengal government in return for producer's rights. The first screening of *Pather Panchali* took place at the Museum of Modern Art in New York in 1955, and its success initiated a series of films which now constitute one of the greatest bodies of work in world cinema, characterized by a profound and radical humanism which links Ray with Renoir, Rossellini and Mizoguchi. His later films include the remaining parts of the Apu trilogy, *Aparajito* (1956) and *The World of Apu* (1959), *The Philosopher's Stone* (1957), *The Music Room* (1958), *The Goddess* (1960), *Two Daughters* (1961), *Kanchanjungha* (1962), *Charulata* (1964), *The Adventures of Goopy and Bagha* (1968), *Days and Nights in the Forest* (1970), *Company Limited* (1971), *Distant Thunder* (1973), *The Middle Man* (1975), *The Chess Players* (1977), *The Kingdom of Diamonds* (1980) and *Home and the World* (1982). During the 1980s acute heart trouble largely restricted his activities to editing and illustrating the children's magazine, *Sandesh*, but in the last couple of years he has been able to return to film direction. *Ganashatru*, and adaptation of Ibsen's *An Enemy of the People*, appeared in 1989, and his most recent work, *Branches of the Tree*, received its world première at the London Film Festival in 1990. Besides writing his films,

Satyajit Ray has composed their scores since 1962, and he also wrote the music for James Ivory's *Shakespeare Wallah* (1965). He was the subject of a 1985 documentary, *Satyajit Ray*, directed by a fellow Bengali film-maker, Shyam Benegal.

The following lecture took place on 11 May 1982. Satyajit Ray was interviewed by Derek Malcolm, the film critic of the *Guardian*.

Satyajit Ray

Derek Malcolm Satyajit, I gather there has been a bit of a delay in the making of your new film, *Home and the World*. Why was that?

Satyajit Ray Oh, money problems – the producer ran out of funds for some reason. It will still be made, though not necessarily with money coming from the same man. We will do it in winter, and I'm much happier that way because that's when the story is set. Originally I was supposed to start shooting in April. It's from a novel by Rabindranath Tagore.

DM It's really quite a big film in Bengali terms. Will it be expensive to make?

SR Yes, it will; perhaps not as expensive as *The Chess Players*, but still an expensive film. It's a historical subject, it has a complex political background, it deals with an upper-class landowning family, so we will have to build big sets, the costumes will cost money and there's a lot of elaborate shooting on location.

DM Weren't you hoping to make this film about three years ago?

SR It was my first project, actually, before *Pather Panchali* – I think around 1949 or 1950. I had a screenplay, I had a producer, I had a contract, and then he suggested some changes in the screenplay and I was terribly cross and said no, so the film fell through. A good thing, too, because it's a terrible script, I've just thrown it away. Very amateurish, very Hollywood.

DM How do you actually start on a project?

SR First, of course, you have to find a story, a story which grips you, otherwise there's no point; a story which you keep thinking about, which gradually sinks into unconsciousness, and then you decide that you've found something that you badly want to film. The next stage is writing the screenplay. Sometimes it's not a very difficult process, as with *Home and the World*, where the film sticks very closely to the original. At other times there are certain elements in the story which you like and other elements you do *not* like, and you decide to make it for the elements which appeal to you; the rest you

have to discard. So there is a process of adapting which may
take a little time. When I get going, I always work with virtually
the same people. I've had two cameramen. I started with
Subrata Mitra, who photographed the Apu trilogy: I think he
photographed ten or twelve films in all. Then his assistant,
Soumendu Roy, took over, and I've worked with him ever
since. I've had the same editor right from the beginning, Dulal
Dutta, and I had the same art director for about fifteen years,
Bansi Chandragupta. Then he went off to Bombay, coming back
for *The Chess Players*, but he died suddenly in New York, and
I have been using his assistant, Ashoke Bose, since 1970.
Assistants keep changing. Most of them have directing
ambitions, you know, and at some point they want to branch
out on their own, so they come and tell me, 'I've got a chance to
make a film.' How do you react? I say, 'Go ahead, make it!' Two
or three of them have turned into film-makers, and some have
come back again – after a couple of failures, maybe. Of
course, the method of production varies from film to film. You
can have a simple film like my television film, *Deliverance*,
which I made in ten days, shooting every day on one location,
with a group of actors working very harmoniously and very
closely together. When filming is finished, you cut and do the
music (if there is any music to be done), and it's ready in
maybe a couple of month's time. But *Deliverance* was only fifty
minutes long, and if it's a full-length film, the shooting period
may vary between forty and, let us say, sixty days, depending
on the film's complexity. I don't shoot every day. I complete a
scene, then I cut it, then I do another scene, then I cut it: I keep
on cutting as I go along. It helps. It's something which I've been
doing right from the beginning, so I've stuck to that method.

DM So you don't actually shoot a huge number of takes?

SR No, never, unless I'm up against a really stupid actor. This has
not happened very many times, I can tell you that – only once
or twice – and then you may need half a dozen takes, but
generally it's one take. During *The Chess Players*, Richard
Attenborough was terribly upset when I would say, 'OK, no

more!' He would say, 'Don't you want a safety take? I won't be here if something goes wrong,' and I'd say, 'We can't *afford* a safety take!' Nothing went wrong, fortunately.

DM I know you've often found money very difficult to get. Has it become easier over the years to get enough money to make directing films less of a strain?

SR Yes, but costs have gone up during the last six or seven years, and it's becoming very difficult to make Bengali films of any dimensions. You can't afford to think big in Bengali anymore. *Home and the World* is a big film, but it's a famous novel and I have made two very successful Tagore films in the past, so the producers are willing to take the risk, but I think gradually we will find ourselves either making extremely modest Bengali films, or making films in Hindi. It may happen that way if costs keep going up, and there is no reason why they should come down again.

DM But you yourself can attract actors from all over India, can't you? I know that many Bombay actors who would normally not dream of going into what they would regard as an art film would certainly come to your call, and in fact did with *The Chess Players*. That helps you, doesn't it?

SR Yes, I am in a position of advantage there, I think, but of course, we have this excellent new breed of actors. Some of them are from the Poona Institute, some of them are from the acting school in New Delhi, and they are all very dedicated, intelligent and co-operative, and it's very easy to work with them.

DM They also appear in commercial films at other times?

SR They do it for the money. They will always be very willing to work in a serious film.

DM Do you think that the large number of new, young Indian directors who have sprung up over the last few years have appeared because there is co-operation from those leading actors, and from the government too? Do you think it's easier to start making decent films in India, apart from just commercial ones?

SR Oh, definitely, there is no question of it; one can really say that there is a concerted effort to make low-budget films. The problem is that once you've made them, they don't get shown! They go to festivals, they win prizes, but they don't get shown. This has happened with many films, actually, and clearly it's a crucial experience for the director for his films to be exposed to a regular cinema audience.

DM You had some very bad luck with *The Chess Players* in Bombay, didn't you?

SR Yes, but I could do nothing about it. They were a little worried because all these very busy, major professionals just left Bombay and came down to Calcutta to work for me, totally neglecting the other profession. Most of them were working on ten or twelve films at a time. I was certainly obliged to the two major actors that I used, Amjad Khan and Sanjeer Kumar, and they were very happy doing it, but the other distributors and producers in Bombay were not happy at all, and they were probably worried that, if this was going to be the pattern from now on, it would be disastrous for them.

DM So you think they didn't actually try very hard when it came to exhibiting the film in Bombay?

SR No. It was taken off after three weeks, although they had full houses every day. Just taken off, no reason given. Well, I know the reason because I know the distributor, and he didn't want it to succeed. His theory was that this was a film that cannot possibly succeed, and he could see that it was doing well and he was terribly worried because his theory was going wrong.

DM Do you think that commercial Indian films are improving, or are they just as bad as ever?

SR Do you mean commercial Bombay?

DM Yes.

SR . . . Because there is no such thing as a commercial Bengali film. Commercial Bombay films are very slick, the craftsmanship is often very good, even admirable. For instance, there is a lot in a film such as *Sholay* (1975) that I admire purely as a film-maker. Also, as I say, some of the acting is clever, competent, professional, stylish – there is a lot of that in Bombay films. But there is nothing in the films as such. There is no character, and the whole setting is so unreal. It's a kind of make-believe, fairy-tale world.

DM Now, you've recently made a couple of television films, haven't you? *Pikoo*, which was made for French television, and a Hindi film, *Deliverance*.

SR Yes. *Pikoo* is from an original story which I wrote about fifteen years ago, in the form of a diary kept by a small boy. The film has a different form, but it's still the same situation: one day in the life of a boy.

DM And that was entirely financed by French television?

SR Entirely, yes. It was screened in Paris almost a year ago. *Deliverance* is from a short story by Munshi Premchand, the writer of *The Chess Players*. Indian television wanted me to make a series of films for them, a series of six, but I said, 'Well, let's make it one to start with!' The idea was to make a film which would appeal to an all-Indian audience, so naturally I thought in terms of a Hindi film; and when you think of a short Hindi film, you naturally think of going back to Premchand. I found a remarkable short story – very powerful, very taut, very effective – and I decided to film that and they agreed. I made it in colour like my usual feature films, not really thinking very much of television, and I still hope to show it theatrically because I own the theatrical rights. As you probably know, we have black-and-white television in India still and the format is very small, and I decided perhaps not to make any more films for television until we have colour and a larger format.

DM They've been trying to get you to make films for Indian television for quite a long time, I imagine.

SR Yes . . . well, a couple of years, and I resisted in the beginning, but then, because I found this very fine short story, I decided to do it.

DM Did you change your technique for television in any way?

SR No, I think this film would work just as well on a regular cinema screen. You *do* have to be careful about the composition because a lot is cut off on a television screen, and perhaps you avoid long shots to a certain extent because you don't see very much on a small screen, but I don't think I avoided them to the extent that I should have done. I was watching it on television in Calcutta and I was really worried, because some of the shots don't come off very well. If the screens were bigger and if colour was there, it would definitely be better. I've been watching television here, and I find that on a larger screen you hardly lose anything.

DM Would you make television films for any other country if asked?

SR If they let me make Bengali stories. For instance, *Pikoo* was a Bengali film with Bengali dialogue, and French television agreed to put subtitles in French. I don't suppose every country would agree to that. If they do, I don't mind.

DM But you're not going to have it dubbed?

SR No, I don't like that.

DM Are there more television buyers for your films in the West than there used to be?

SR Well, I believe that theoretically it's possible to make good sales – for instance, in Germany – but nothing has been done, probably because of lack of enterprise on the part of my producers. What happens is that once they've recovered the costs from India, or let's say Bengal, they just lose interest. They go on to other things, other films, newer films. I can do nothing about it because I just work for a fee and have nothing to do with the profit or exploitation aspects.

DM You've never wanted to produce and control your own films in that way?

SR No. Then you have to run an office and keep files, and you need agents to be working for you in other parts of the world, because everyone cheats you. No, I'm happier the way I am.

DM If we could go back a little bit to your early days, what amazes me about a lot of your films is that the scenes we think are shot on location actually turn out to be sets.

SR We were very proud of that, and the credit goes to my art director, Bansi Chandragupta, and my cameraman, Subrata Mitra, who devised a system of lighting which for day scenes was incredibly good. *Pather Panchali* was, I think, 80 per cent location – except for the night scenes, which we shot in the studio – but for *Aparajito*, the second part of the trilogy, the house which was supposedly in Banares was a studio set. We had lots of shots of characters walking down the street, turning and entering the house, and when they're in the courtyard it's a studio, but the lighting is matched so beautifully that you can't make it out. We had a little conference – my cameraman, my art director and myself – and we decided to use a special kind of lighting. We were all great admirers of Cartier-Bresson at that time – you know, the idea of available light – so from that point of view, I think we achieved a great deal of success fairly early on.

DM How do you handle your actors? Do you tell them exactly what you want from them before they go on, or do you let them get on with it and make suggestions as they're working?

SR Well, once the script is ready and the casting is done, the major participants are asked to come along and I read the whole script, and if they're listening very carefully they would already know what kind of performance I want, because when I read I do a lot of acting. That's one stage. Then there are some actors who want guidance. Some of them might come and ask me to tell them a little more about the character – his background, this and that – and I oblige him or her, as the case may be. But in most cases, after the reading of the script, the actors just wait for the work to start. They know the part, they know the story (more or less), and they're given the dialogue, so they learn their lines, they come prepared. There is no pre-rehearsal, no rehearsing before the sets are ready. I can only rehearse with all the props in position, on a set which is ready for shooting. The rehearsal is on the day of the shooting, and it's maybe one or two rehearsals. Then I get going.

DM That's really very different from the way a lot of other film-makers work, particularly these days, with the endless takes, endless rehearsals. You don't really go in for that?

SR No. This idea of sitting and reading the lines in someone's house – in my house, let's say – makes no sense to me, because I want all the actors in position doing all the things we will eventually do at the time of shooting: getting up, walking, sitting down, handling objects, picking up, putting down . . . All that has to be there because the acting is affected by these movements, and requires a certain character through the movements, so without that it has no sense. They learn their lines at home – that's fine – but no rehearsal necessary, unless, perhaps, you're on location and there's a very long tracking-shot which involves two characters. There is such a scene early on in *The World of Apu*, where Apu and his friend are returning home at night on the railway tracks and Apu is talking about himself: what he is going to do about his future, about the novel he is going to write, and so on. For that we needed a rehearsal because I wanted to know precisely what distance he was going to cover for that long dialogue, and we needed enough tracks to cover the distance.

DM You also write the music for a lot of your films. Do you find that comes easily?

SR It didn't come easily in the beginning at all!

DM You use music pretty sparingly, too.

SR Now more than ever.

DM Why is that? It's very different from a lot of things that are happening now, especially in Hollywood, where music drums in every point three times.

SR I suspect that's because they need that LP eventually!

DM Do you always write it yourself?

SR Yes . . . well, not always: ever since *Two Daughters*.

DM Do you find it's easier doing it that way than engaging someone?

SR There are no film composers in India, really. The main reason I work with people like Ravi Shankar and Ali Akbar Khan and Ustad Vilayat Khan is that they are marvellous virtuosi and I wanted to use their instruments. I wanted Ravi Shankar to play the sitar and use as much of it as possible. They were not composers, really – except Ravi, who has written ballet scores – and also they were not prepared, or not happy, to write music which runs for, say, three minutes and seven seconds. They resented that, they wanted freedom, but you can't *have* freedom if you write film music. Up to a point, you must be limited to certain lengths, certain moods, certain tone colours. So it was getting to be very, very difficult to work with them, because I was getting ideas of my own and they resented being told to do certain things, or dictated to beyond a certain point, and it was threatening our relationship. In any case, Ravi Shankar was then becoming very famous internationally, so half the time he was abroad and was not there when I needed him, and I had to think of someone else. Then came Ali Akbar, who was a great sarod player. What really happened in the end was that I would ask them to record three-minute stretches of music in various tempos and various moods. I was then left with a number of fairly short pieces of mainly solo playing, and all the work was done eventually in the editing room. I had more fun working with Vilayat Khan on *The Music Room*, but it was not the ideal way to work and, as I say, they all disliked being told what to do. So, since there was nobody else, I decided to do it myself. Music had been my first love even before I got interested in films, and I had a certain degree of knowledge of western music and western notations because I had got into the habit of listening to western music with miniature scores. There was a time in my early college days when miniature scores would be my bedside reading: I would go to bed with a score. Composing was very difficult in the beginning, extremely difficult, but I persisted and now it's OK.

DM Have you composed any western music?

SR No, though in some of my contemporary urban films I write music which is a sort of synthesis of East and West, because classical Indian draga music doesn't really go with a city film. I'm constantly using Indian and western instruments in combination – trumpets, sitar, Indian drums, western flutes, clarinets, this and that – to get a new kind of tone colour which would correspond with the mixed kind of living of urban people.

DM Who are your favourite western composers?

SR Well, I suppose I could spend the rest of my life listening to Bach, Mozart and Beethoven, but I'm also very interested in the Baroque – Scarlatti, Rameau, that period, and even earlier. I love opera, I love Gregorian Chant, I listen to a lot of Brahms and a lot of Schubert songs. There was a time when I was listening a great deal to Sibelius. I like Bartok, especially the chamber music . . . That is a long list of names already!

DM Do you think there are more connections than we suspect between Indian music and western music?

SR They both use the same sequence of notes, but the *way* the notes is used is different. Western music has gone for counterpoint and harmony, and Indian music has gone for melody – not the vertical thing but the horizontal thing. All the same, just because Indian music is linear, it shouldn't give one the impression that it's simple, because the rhythmic aspect of it, the combination of melody and rhythm, makes it very complex. In fact, that combination amounts to a sort of counterpoint: the western kind is percussive; the Indian kind is melodic. I never had the slightest difficulty. I started listening to western music very early on, when I was 6 or 7. I don't know who bought them, but there were some records in my house, including a recording of one movement of the Beethoven Violin Concerto played by Kreisler, with the Berlin State Opera Orchestra – probably one of the earliest concerto recordings. I knew that at the age of 7, and it seemed a type of music I was totally familiar with; it didn't seem alien. I also had a toy gramophone which I got when I was a small boy, and which came with a lot of records – I think it was called Kiddiphone, or something. The records were marches, waltzes, all sorts of things, so I knew those too. The real study started later during my last years at school, and then, of course, I started buying records. At first I could only afford one movement a month, so it took three or four months to complete a symphony or concerto.

DM What about the influence on you of films?

SR No influence of Indian films.

DM None at all? Only western ones?

SR Yes.

DM Which directors in particular?

SR Oh, countless, countless directors, because I was a great film-goer in my college days – not yet a very serious student of the cinema, not even a film buff, more a film fan. I love American films of the 1930s and 1940s – a great period, don't you agree? I suppose Ford, Wilder, Capra and George Stevens taught me the craft of film-making, though I couldn't talk in terms of influence. Then I was exposed to the American films of European directors like Renoir, Duvivier, Clair – that was the next stage. By that time I was becoming very seriously interested in the cinema, and it suddenly took a new turn when I came across three or four books on film in the arts library where I was studying painting. How may books did you have on films in English in those days? About half a dozen in all. So I read Raymond Spottiswoode, Paul Rotha, the Pudovkin translations . . . and that's when I became conscious of the entity known as 'the director'. Before that, it was stars. If you are talking of *influence*, I think I was really more influenced by people like De Sica and Renoir than by the American directors. I love the 1940s Hollywood directors, but I don't think they have much in common with my work . . . but then, perhaps there *is* something . . . And of course, there is influence from other sources as well, from literature. I think I was greatly influenced by Bibhuti Banerji – the author of *Pather Panchali* – by his style of writing, his details, his dialogue, his portrayal of characters, his treatment of relationships. One is influenced by writers just as much.

DM And, of course, the Japanese cinema.

SR That came much later. Actually, *Rashomon* came to Calcutta at a time when I already had the script of *Pather Panchali*, in 1951 or 1952. We were absolutely bowled over by it, but that was the only Japanese film that we saw then. Mizoguchi and Ozu and others came much later.

DM Mizoguchi and Ozu must have been an enormous surprise to you, just as they were to us.

SR Oh, yes. Tremendous, tremendous!

DM Were you affected at all by the French New Wave?

SR I feel a great affinity with some of the best work of Truffaut, not that he, or anybody, produces masterpieces all the time. You have to judge from the best work of any director, and with Truffaut I often felt as if I knew exactly why he was doing certain things. But of course, I would never be called avant-garde. My story-telling style has been fairly simple. There is no question of using freezes and jump-cuts and that sort of thing unless there is a very special reason for it – like, for example, at the end of *Charulata*, where I think the freeze works. Perhaps it wouldn't be there without *Les 400 Coups*, so there may have been an influence. One person has done it, and then I do it in very different circumstances. It's become part of the language, so you can use it if you want to.

DM And early on in *Charulata* there's a very sharp, very obtrusive zoom-out, isn't there, in the scene where she is standing watching her husband?

SR That's what brings the scene to an end, actually. It was meant to be like a flourish at the end of a piece of calligraphy.

DM So you didn't go and see a lot of Indian films? There weren't any Indian film-makers who influenced you at all?

SR No, but even before I wrote that first screenplay for *Home and the World*, there was a period when I was toying with the idea of making films, and the first thing I did was to write screenplays of stories which had already been acquired for filming by some other director and I compared my treatment with what was on the screen, even trying to anticipate what the conventional treatment would be like. I had relatives in the cinema – an uncle of mine was one of the pioneers of Bengali cinema, and another uncle was a sound recordist – so naturally we all went to see their films. If there was something interesting we would go, but there was nothing that came up to any sort of reasonable standard.

DM Have you ever taken a risk in your work in the sense of making a film which was very much a new departure for you, or do you feel you know . . .

SR Oh, again and again! I feel that *Charulata* was a departure,

The Philosopher's Stone was a departure. *The Music Room* was a departure . . . I made *The Music Room* because *Aparajito* was a failure at the box-office and I wanted to do a film which would be popular, so I found a story where one could use song and dance, which I thought would be an ideal basis for a commercial film. But in the process of turning it into a screenplay – this very serious study of dying, decaying feudalism – instead of using the popular kind of film music, I used the cream of classical music, so that became a departure . . . I think my first original screenplay, *Kanchanjungha,* was also very much a departure from the norm, because the whole structure was new. I was not aware of the newness. I merely told the story which occurred to me: this is the situation, this is the family, these are the relationships, so what is the best way of telling the story? When I was watching the film with an audience I realized that it was terribly new, much too new for them. It was a mistake: now there is an audience for it; then, there wasn't. So you don't have to be very gimmicky and have lots of jump-cuts in order to be different.

DM I'm sure there are lots of people who would like to ask a question.

Audience Do you ever use your films as a political forum?

SR My God, no! Not a political forum! Though, of course, a lot of my recent films have a political background. I really don't know what a political film *is*, frankly; I don't know the definition of one. I *do* know that beyond a certain point you cannot make a political film in India because of censorship. You cannot make a radical film where you really attack the establishment or criticize the party in power. It simply cannot be done. But you *can* make films about political characters, and you can certainly have films where a political background is implied or established. I'm told that *Deliverance* is a very political film. Would you agree?

DM A very political film, yes.

SR But I didn't deal with it as a *forum*! Well, anyway, I've made a political film!

Aud Wasn't *Distant Thunder* a political film?

SR If you wish to call it a political film, you are free to do so.

Aud You say that you are very much a product of western culture . . .

SR I think East and West combined – fifty-fifty.

Aud Do you think there is a basic contradiction between these two elements of your life?

SR I don't think so. The fusion, I suppose, was already there. When I decided to become a film-maker, of course, one had to deal with Indian themes, and then you wanted to discover your roots – you became *conscious* of your roots – and I think that over the years I have come to know more and more of my country and my people and our problems. In order to be an effective and honest artist working in Bengal, working on Bengali or Indian themes, familiarity with one's cultural past, one's cultural traditions, is very, very important. But that doesn't obliterate the western aspect of my education. It's still there.

Aud I wonder how you feel about the relative merits of colour and black and white?

SR I still think of black and white as being a very effective medium, but unfortunately in India the black-and-white stock that we get these days is very poor, and you can't get all the subtle gradations that we could get in the days when we were using Kodak stock. Colour, on the other hand, has improved over the years, and the work of the laboratories has also improved. I think one big advantage of colour is that you can pack more information into a shot, but there is also this other, adverse aspect where colour has a tendency to prettify things. You have to strike a balance. That is why colour has to be used extremely cautiously, and that is why I design props and every piece of costume with a great deal of caution and care, so that nothing spills over, as it were, and everything is harmonized. I like colour very much now; I've got used to it, and of course, one obvious reason for using colour is that it's easier to sell a colour film.

Aud Can I ask you about your two films for children?

SR Oh yes, but those two films seem not to have gone down very well here. I'm rather unhappy talking about them here. I enjoyed making them, actually. The first one was *The Adventures of Goopy and Bagha*. My son, who was then 8 or 9, was complaining that I always made films for grown-up people – grim, serious films which made you cry – 'So why not make something for *me*?' So I wrote *Goopy and Bagha*, which is based on a story by my grandfather about two village characters: a drummer and a singer. That was a film for which I also wrote a lot of music, including some songs. It became an enormous success, and ran for 100 weeks in Calcutta. Then, of course, I got letters and telephone calls all the time from small boys and girls asking me when I was going to make the *next* film for them. This is something which it is very difficult to ignore, so I decided to make a sequel to *Goopy and Bagha* called *Kingdom of Diamonds*, which uses the same two characters, but puts them in a different setting. That again became a very, very big success, and both films are revived from time to time.

Aud I was thinking that you might mention the peace aspects . . .

SR Well, of course, *Kingdom of Diamonds* is the most outspoken political film I have made. I came close to using the cinema as a forum in that one. It is easier to be outspoken in a fantasy form rather than a realistic form, and I thought it was interesting, important and necessary to convey certain ideas about oppression, injustice and tyranny to the children at a very early age so that they get to know about these very fundamental concepts. I think it might help.

Aud I would be glad if you would tell us what is your own favourite of your films.

SR I think *Charulata* is the one that has the fewest flaws. I like *The Chess Players* very much too. It was a much more difficult film to make than *Charulata* because it was an extremely complex screenplay, and it was, again, a departure, because there are very few films where you have history and fiction running in parallel, and I think it works in spite of being in that form. The question of balance, of doing justice to both sides, was also very difficult. I also like *The Middle Man*, for very different reasons, and *Days and Nights in the Forest*. I think those three or four are the best. Still, *Charulata* is the film which, if I were asked to make it again, I would probably do almost exactly as I did it the first time.

Aud Would you ever consider making a film in English?

SR Yes, I have thought of making a film in English, but not outside India. I would like to make a film, not using English characters, but using a group of people who come from different provinces and who are forced by circumstances to use English as their language of communication. This is a very common thing in India, you know: you meet an Indian from the south, or a Punjabi, or someone from Bombay, and you use English automatically. I would very much like to make this kind of story, probably using English creatively in the sense that maybe one character will be very fluent, another not so fluent, and perhaps the third character would hardly speak English at all.

Aud When?

SR I don't know yet; I'm thinking aloud. In any case, if I were to make an English-language film, it would have to be set in India. I have no interest at all in working outside India.

Aud You started in graphic design before going into film-making. Do you still produce graphics for your films?

SR Not all films involve graphic design. I've done titles for a lot of films . . . for instance, in *Kanchanjungha* the titles have little sketches in them, and I devised a fusion of a Tibetan and a

Bengali typeface, which was quite an interesting exercise. I have often designed posters for my films. Nowadays I generally do sketches which I hand over to a commercial artist who produces the poster, but occasionally, if it's a calligraphic poster, I do it myself. I still do a lot of book work – book jackets, a lot of illustrations – and I have designed typefaces. I designed an English typeface also, which has never been marketed, but if I ever had the time to produce the finished drawings then perhaps it could be. It was an entry in an international competition, and I was asked to come up with the finished face. So I still do graphic work all the time, particularly for my children's magazine, which I edit.

Aud Have you ever thought of establishing a film school in Calcutta?

SR No, no. I know that the school in Poona is excellent, but I have never thought of either teaching in a film school or starting one myself. I think I am doing more useful work. I have made an open offer to the students in Poona to come and watch me while I'm shooting rather than me going to lecture them, and they have accepted. I think it's a much better way to learn.

Aud I understand that you wanted to make a film of the *Mahabharata*?

SR Yes, until I discovered that it was almost impossible. You would have to take an international audience into account, because it would be a very, very expensive film, and there are at least fourteen major characters. For an Indian audience there is no problem because everyone is familiar with who is who, but you also have to think of an audience which *isn't*, and to establish those very complicated relationships would be virtually impossible. It's very difficult to establish relationships in a film. Father, mother, son – that's OK, but uncle, mother-in-law, sister-in-law . . . The audience would be out of its depth in no time.

Aud Is it true that you wanted to make *A Passage to India*?

SR Yes, it's true.

Aud Were you disappointed?

SR Actually, Forster was alive at that time and I made a trip to Cambridge. I saw him, I spoke to him, but he didn't seem interested at all in the idea of his novel being filmed.

Aud What was it about the book that you found so fascinating?

SR Well, I must tell you that the fascination didn't last for a very long time! This sort of thing happens from time to time: you are suddenly fired with this desire to do something and you go quite far with it, and then the interest evaporates. I found Forster's observations very perceptive and very authentic, and I was intrigued by the character of Fielding – I found a great deal of identification with that. In general, I think it's the best novel about India written by a westerner. But Forster showed no interest at all. He said, 'I've written a book, I want people to read it,' and soon after that he died. By that time, *I* had lost interest. I never went back to it.

Aud Have you ever made a film which has really dissatisfied you?

SR Of course! There is one film which I don't even claim to be mine called *Menagerie*, which has not been seen here and which I was forced by circumstances to make. I had nothing to do, because I was supposed to make *The Adventures of Goopy and Bagha* when the producers backed out at the last moment, and my assistants had bought this story which they wanted to film. They themselves didn't have the courage to do it, they were not sure whether they could handle it, but they had already signed up an actor. It was a kind of salvage operation, and, as the money was there, I said, 'OK, I'll do it for you.' I don't believe whodunits make very good films, and this was not a very good story in any case, though I worked with a group of excellent actors. It was a fairly enjoyable process, but I knew that the film didn't have much substance, and it's not really my personal work at all. That's one film that dissatisfies me.

Aud What would you most like to make that you haven't made yet?

SR I would like to make more films about rural poverty, certain aspects of village life which I haven't done yet. To a certain extent *Deliverance* may be a beginning there, but I certainly would like to make more. It won't be easy, because our present Minister of Information and Broadcasting says in every other speech he makes that you should show the brighter, more pleasant aspects of India and that you should certainly *not* show poverty on the screen, especially when you are sending films out of the country. I also want to make a film about the Mogul period, though again, that's an expensive proposition. I would like to make a film about certain nineteenth-century characters in Bengal, particularly an extremely interesting Irish priest called Reverend Long. He knew Bengali, but the trouble with nineteenth-century themes involving the British is that the film would automatically have to be bilingual: there will be Bengalis speaking Bengali, English people speaking English . . . That is why I've been put off. It's not been possible to think of that in concrete terms.

5

Raymond Williams

Raymond Williams was born in 1921, the son of a railway signalman, in the Welsh border village of Pandy, and he was educated at Abergavenny Grammar School and at Trinity College, Cambridge. During the war he served in the 21st Anti-Tank Regiment of the Guards Armoured Division, and rose to the rank of Captain. He edited the journal *Politics and Letters* in 1947 – 48, and worked as an adult education tutor for the Oxford University Extra-Mural Delegacy from 1946 to 1961, when he was appointed as a lecturer in English at Cambridge and a fellow of Jesus College. He became a University Reader in Drama in 1967 and Professor of Drama in 1974, a post he held until 1983. His first published work was *Reading and Criticism* (1950), and during the next thirty years he produced a series of books which stand today as the single most important and distinguished contribution to the socialist theory of culture in the English language. They include *Culture and Society* (1958), *The Long Revolution* (1961), *Drama from Ibsen to Brecht* (1968), *The Country and the City* (1973), *Keywords* (1976), *Marxism and Literature* (1977), *Problems in Materialism and Culture* (1980), *Writing in Society* (1984) and *Culture* (1985). Raymond Williams was also a novelist, and his fictional works include *Border Country* (1960), *Second Generation* (1964) and *The Fight for Manod* (1979). He died in 1988.

This lecture was given on 21 July 1985.

Raymond Williams

The first audiences for cinema were working-class people in the great cities of the industrialized world. Among the same people in the same period, the labour and socialist movements were growing in strength. Is there any significant relationship between these different kinds of development? Many have thought so, but in interestingly different ways. One way that became common on the left saw film at an early stage as an inherently popular, and in that sense democratic, art. It bypassed, leaped over, the class-based, establishment theatre and all the cultural barriers which selective education had erected around high literacy. Moreover in a more sophisticated second stage of this argument, film, like socialism itself, was seen as a harbinger of a new kind of world, the modern world based on science and technology, fundamentally open and mobile and thus not only a popular, but also a dynamic, even a revolutionary medium. How does that argument look today after three-quarters of a century of primarily capitalist development of cinema? Is it simply to be dumped in that dustbin of history to which the left in that period was confidently carrying so many contemporary items, but in which today, and not always kicking and struggling, it finds *itself*, and so many of *its* ideas? It's worth taking another look in some reanalysis.

First, what is 'popular'? The key to an understanding of the cultural history of the last two hundred years is the contested significance of that word. It wasn't only cinema. It was, even more confidently, a century earlier, the press that was seen by democrats and radicals as *the* extending, *the* liberating medium, pushing beyond the closed and controlled worlds of state power and the aristocracy. In a directly related case, there was the long struggle to restore legitimacy to popular theatre as the State Act of the seventeenth century[1] had restricted the lawful practice of drama to a few selected fashionable theatres. What had come up strongly in the popular theatre, the 'illegitimate' theatre, and in the pub entertainments, the circuses, the music halls, was indeed a set of popular forms, lively and entertaining, though also limited by their exclusion from some of the older arts. When that Act was repealed in 1843, there was a contemporary removal of obstacles to that insurgent popular form, the newspaper. Difficult as it may now be to recall that history, in a time in which our labour movement and so many on the left cry angrily against the media, the facts are that these were seen and often feared as liberating popular practices, or at least, in the popular *interest*: indeed, the means, the media, of (though that phrase wasn't yet used) a cultural revolution.

But, what was often not noticed on the left, and is perhaps not fully noticed even today, is that there are others besides radicals and democrats who are interested in being popular. What was supposed to be a monopoly in one selected sense of the people fighting for their rights and their freedoms, turned out to be very different and was bound in those conditions to be different. Certainly radicals and democrats fought for the new forms and the new freedoms, but so did commercial entrepreneurs, capitalists in an unbroken line from that day to this. They saw their own versions of possibility in the new technologies, the new audiences which were being formed in the whole vast process, and they too, as again today at the leading edge of our own new technologies, were engaged in fighting the restrictions of state laws, fighting and manoeuvering for what *we* now call deregulation. They would not, it seems certain, have won in any single instance if they hadn't had behind them the evidence and the pressure of solid popular demand. What we see in the case of the early cinema is in that sense entirely typical of a more general cultural history. It had to fight its way through controls and regulations.

It didn't always fully succeed. Consider the United States Supreme Court judgment of 1915, refusing cinema the constitutional freedoms already guaranteed to the print media. 'It cannot be put out of view', they wrote, 'that the exhibition of moving pictures is a business pure and simple. They are mere representations of events, of ideas and sentiments published or known, vivid, useful and entertaining no doubt, but capable of evil, having power for it the greater because of their attractiveness and manner of exhibition.' It was because cinema was popular, in fact in several senses, that it was still to some degree controlled, as had happened earlier with the press and was to happen later with radio, television and video. Thus socialists are mistaken when they suppose that, in any post-feudal society, they have any kind of monopoly of the popular interest, or indeed that only they and their allies have contested both state and established capitalist power in the struggle for new freedoms. The honest way to see the real cultural history, which is in fact closely paralleled by that part of political history which concerns elections and parties, is that the new conditions and the new technologies made possible two wholly alternative directions of development. We can now see these alternatives more clearly, but for a very long time, and still in many cases today, they overlapped in practice because they seemed to have a common enemy: the old regulating powers of church and state, the relatively closed, constrained, often stuffy habit of a settled and traditionally hierarchical society, or the positive organization of received morality, represented in the case of the cinema by the characteristic report of the National Council of Public Morals in Britain in 1916. 'Moving pictures', they wrote, 'are having a profound influence upon the mental and moral outlook of millions of our young people. We leave our labours [people who serve on long committees often use that phrase, "we leave our labours"] with the deep conviction that no social problem of the day demands more earnest attention.' Familiar tones, familiar enemies. Perhaps too familiar, for while within that history there was bound to be overlap between the alternative new directions, nothing is to be gained – and indeed, much is to be lost – if we go on supposing that within the rhetoric of 'the popular' there is real common ground. On the contrary, we have to see how well placed this new and, at first, marginal capitalism was, both to develop and to exploit a genuinely popular medium.

We can see this in the case of film at once, as regards both institutions and majority content. The first cinemas were called theatres, after the early side-show phase, but a key factor of the technology soon gave them a transforming advantage. The indefinitely reproducible print, though structurally similar to the transforming technology of the press, could be used in new ways: to bypass the problems of literacy, to bypass in the silent era the old limitations of national languages, but above all to ensure rapid distribution of a relatively standard product over a very much wider social and geographical area. It isn't really surprising, setting *these* advantages within both earlier and later industrial history, to find a symmetry between this new popular form and typically capitalist forms of economic development. Nor is it surprising, given the basic factor of centralized production and rapid multiple distribution (so different in these respects from most earlier cultural technologies), to see the development of relatively monopolist, more strictly corporate forms of economic organization. Moreover, in the significant new phase which followed from the properties of the medium, these developed on a para-national scale. Many attempts were made, are still made, to preserve at least some domestic corporations, but the international, multi-national, para-national scale significantly overbore most of them. The road to Hollywood was then, in one sense, inscribed. And it's still important to remember that the only other organizational form able to make that kind of use of the opportunities of early film has been the comparable, concentrated state corporation of the countries we call 'actually existing socialisms'. But then we should never, when reviewing any phase of cultural history, suppose that the technology predetermined particular economic and social forms. All we can say at this level is that this available symmetry gave these actually developing forms an important, though not decisive, competitive edge.

Moreover, within the development of the capitalist version of the popular there have been, as people say, contradictions. We can understand some of these if we look at the majority content of early cinema. There is one difficulty in this, that very many students of film, understandably centred on the uniqueness and originality of their medium, know surprisingly little about the popular theatre on which, in that phase, it drew so heavily. Some people still compare the new medium of film with such older forms as the bourgeois novel or academic painting, when they ought really to be looking at the direct precedents, with the same urban audiences, of melodrama and theatrical spectacle. I often find it difficult to convince people that, well before film epics, there were naval battles in real sea water and train crashes with locomotives staged in London's theatres. Yet the record is quite clear. These staged spectacles were a central element of popular theatrical entertainment, on which the film camera and location shooting of course improved – in the end, remarkably – but not really as new content. Or consider melodrama, originally a play with songs and music, and created in order to get round the regulations about legitimate drama, which had been assumed to be confined to speech. Violent and romantic intrigue, long-lost heirs and dramatically revealed secrets, had been soaking into those old boards. Many early films were direct remakes of this material.

However there was also one element of melodrama which bears on our central question about 'the popular'. It's true of some, though by no means all, melodramas that a characteristic hero or heroine is poor, and that he or she is victimized by someone rich or powerful. The holder of the mortgage or the aristocratic officer are, in this tendency, typical villains. Thus it can be said, though often rashly, that melodrama was radical and that in the same sense the poor heroes, heroines and victims of many early films established a radical, popular base. But it is not as easy as that. One other key element of this kind of melodrama is that, after many twists and turns and seemingly hopeless situations, the poor victim is saved and the poor hero or heroine lives happily ever after. There is no problem in understanding why these resolutions were popular. But there *is* a problem in trying to relate these often magical or coincidental lucky escapes of individuals to anything that could be called, in the easy slide from 'popular', a genuinely radical or socialist consciousness. The resolutions are individual and, above all, exceptional. And even the wolves, at which we can all hiss, turn out to have relatives within the same system, who are good house dogs, or even guard dogs. A social pity or a social anger is at once centred and then, by the very mechanics of intrigue, displaced. Moreover, as time passed, that broad radicalism of early melodrama faded as steadily as the very similar radicalism of the early Sunday newspapers; the formula of the innocent individual victim could be reproduced, but with some new denominations of villains. I have lost count of the modern film melodramas in which various unspecified innocents are victims of socialist and trade union bosses and organizers, and they too still make their lucky individualized escapes. So this rough version of the popular is usually, at best, double-edged.

We then have to look at a very different kind of argument, at times swept up with this rhetoric of the popular, at times, and with some consequent difficulty, sharply distinguished from it. This is the interesting argument that film itself, as a medium, is inherently or potentially radical. Several propositions have been grouped within this. Firstly, there is the relatively simple argument that mobility as such, the most obvious element of the moving picture, has a necessary association with radicalism. Many traditional arts and traditional forms were identified as essentially static, the obvious products of unchanging or conservative social forms. Closely associated with this was the claim that film was inherently open as against the relatively closed forms of other media. These arguments eventually settled into the now conventional rejections of what is called naturalism or classical realism, and we shall have to come back to those muddled and muddling concepts.

But first we must look more directly at what it was in the

medium that suggested these initially reasonable arguments. A formal analysis of any new medium or form is in fact so difficult that we should not be surprised to find that, in relatively early phases, different people select very different elements as decisive. In fact, where the modernist critic sees mobility and openness in the medium, the Supreme Court justices saw mere representations of events, ideas and sentiments, published or known. It isn't useful to try to choose between these two views. In its new faculty of recording motion, the film camera could become either analytic or synthetic. To run a sequence of film in slow motion is to enter into a new way of seeing the most habitual movements, and this has always been an important use, as in the early experiments on how horses run, through the extraordinary scientific and spectacular sequences of cloud formation and plant growth, to the many and varied dramatic uses: the running of lovers, and the slow spin to death. At the same time, by cutting and editing the film material itself, the power to associate and combine different movements within an apparently single sequence made many new kinds of synthesis possible, offering quite new dimensions of represented action.

Always, that is to say in film, there were both frames and flows. How either were to be used was always, technically, open. This has its effects on the central question of reproduction, that term which is so critical to any socialist discussion of cinema. For it is, one might say, an obvious illusion to suppose that film is *not* an extraordinarily powerful reproductive medium in quite the simplest sense. Much more than ever in print, or within the evident and still visible mechanics of theatre, film can reproduce what can be widely taken as simple representation – indeed, seeing as if with our own eyes. It is, then, not only that millions of people have found pleasure in seeing what they take to be direct representations of distant or otherwise unknown places and people and events, but also it is in that extraordinarily significant cultural moment which began with photography that pleasure is found in the reproduction of wholly familiar people and places. Just as people still call excitedly to say that someone or somewhere they know is on the telly, or even, in the bliss of inexperience, that they themselves are on it, similarly many people make the point of going to see a film where someone or somewhere they already know perfectly well is to be reproduced in the magic of light. Of course, leaving aside induced ideas of importance or prestige being conferred by this selective reproduction, something else is happening in all this; it's basically the valued externalization of images. But what matters for the argument is how widely film has been valued as an accepted form of direct reproduction.

At the same time of course, and from the beginning, the properties of the medium could be used for quite different and even opposite effects. Simple illusions could be directly reproduced and, as techniques developed, marvellously constructed. Complex illusions could become commonplace. Moreover, and here a specifically socialist emphasis enters the argument, real but hidden or disguised, occluded relationships could in these ways be shown or demonstrated. Already, at the simplest level, a nineteenth-century theatre melodrama could show in successive scenes a poor miner's family, and the luxury of London to which the wife-and-mother has run away or been seduced. Eventually, the relative simultaneity of what are otherwise spatially distanced or separated actions could be, within the film medium, directly reproduced. But as what? As reproduction or illusion? For to see both these separated situations more or less at once is, in an everyday sense, an illusion. However, to see them as fundamentally related elements of a specific kind of society which otherwise could not be directly seen at all, is to reproduce in this new form a real but not ordinarily visible interconnection or contrast. Once constructive cutting and montage had become common techniques, this penetrative interaction of reproductions could be seized on as a modernism, even a revolutionary modernism. New concepts, it was argued, could be formed by the planned interaction of images. When I was a student, it was usual to say that montage and the dialectic were closely related forms of the same revolutionary movement of thought. To be sure, that was before we'd seen what looked like the same kind of technique used in a thousand films of every conceivable ideological emphasis. That was a period in which it was still widely supposed that 'the new' was inevitably 'the radical'. But as we shall see, this capacity to move beyond fixed spatial limits, to connect or to collide otherwise separated actions, to invest moments and fragments with the power of sustained or integrated imagery, this faculty of constructing a new flow, or of altering a known flow, is indeed in its whole range a major potential for innovation.

But then it is at this point that we have to look plainly at what has been called 'naturalism'. I'd be more impressed by contemporary radical rejections of naturalism if I didn't hear virtually the same rejections by the most orthodox film and theatre people who certainly don't know what it means. Naturalism, in fact, has close historical associations with socialism. As a movement and as a method, it was concerned to show that people are inseparable from their real social and physical environments. As against idealist versions of human experience, in which people act under providence, or from innate human nature, or within timeless and immaterial norms, naturalism insisted that actions are always specifically contextual and material. The purpose of putting a lifelike environment into narrative, or on to a stage or film, was to introduce and emphasize this authentically shaping force – the material, social and physical world in which people lived. The slice of life, that is to say, was no random helping. The analogy is much more to microscopy, where the intricate formations of life can be intensively examined. The leading principle of naturalism, that all experience must be seen within its real environment – indeed, often, more specifically, that characters and actions are *formed* by environments, as many socialists still insist – was intended as a radical challenge to all received idealist forms.

So what happened? It was what had already happened that was to prove decisive. Actually, the first lifelike, directly reproductive stage sets, like the thousands that were to follow them in cinema, were not constructed to explore the formation and development of life. They were constructed as one of the special forms of spectacle: lifelike reproduction; indeed, precisely *the set*, the setting, in which in the majority of cases human action is understood in quite different ways on the basis of innate or idealistic assumptions. In a bitter irony, naturalism came to be understood as the very thing it had challenged: near-reproduction, or reproduction as a setting, a cover, from the same old idealized or stereotyped stories. Now, in practice there were things which theatre naturalism, even in its own interests, couldn't do. The more it offered us everyday reality, the less it could move in two crucial directions, either towards unspoken thought or towards actions which were physically beyond its selected sights. Typically it became trapped in rooms in which people stared out of the windows or heard shouts from the street. Yet film, in the same interest, could at once move beyond these limitations; unspoken thought could be visually represented or could be given as voice-over. The camera could be taken and set up anywhere. All that then failed to happen on any sufficient scale was the intensely exploring diagnostic impulse which was the real naturalist project. Instead there was an appropriation of the term as a kind of inert external reproduction, and this is where the overlap between radical and establishment rejections of naturalism, loosely used, is so important. For the establishment, naturalism was the kind of boring, everyday reality which *must* be put down so that the self-centred voice, the leisured and talkative play-group, the bourgeois versions of legend and fantasy (passing, in the language of public relations, as 'the free play of mind') could expand without challenge, and even appropriate the whole name of art. So what are socialists doing inside that argument, in that company? Some of them are actually saying interesting if mixed things. The hardest problem for any of us is to distinguish between the radically different cultural tendencies which, within the whole formation of capitalist cinema, have come to overlap in practice.

Let me begin with just one of these distinctions: that in our time, the dissident bourgeois is not necessarily a radical, though that is often the self-presentation. The majority of the serious art of the past hundred years, in film as clearly as anywhere, is in fact the work of dissident bourgeois artists. But then it is like anti-capitalism: you can go on from it to socialism, or you can go back from it to variously idealized pre-capitalist social orders – hierarchical, organic, pre-industrial, pre-democratic. I don't know who first made the joke about the main characters in Soviet films being tractors, but he is quite as likely to be a dissident bourgeois, even what is called a modernist, as the more obvious kind of reactionary. Certainly, Soviet revolutionary cinema was stupidly and arbitrarily stopped in its tracks, but not because it had moved into a world in which men actually worked. Similarly, you don't get the socialist film by showing, as matter on its own, the idiocies and frustrations of bourgeois life, even if you go on to show, as in that classical dissident bourgeois formula of twentieth-century art, a selected individual getting out from under it and simply walking away. In the same sense, there is a crisis at that point in naturalist theatre when somebody is staring from the window at a world from which he or she is shut off. Dissident bourgeois art, including much of great interest and value, often stops at that point in a moment of exquisite nostalgia or longing.

But the more significant development is the growing conviction that all that can really be seen in that window is a reflection – a screen, one might say, for indefinite projections. All the crucial actions of the world are simply a play of psyche or of mind. The powerful images which result will, of course, be neither naturalistic, nor classically realist. When Strindberg, at just that point of crisis, changed his mind about what made people unhappy – he had thought it was the social order; he now thought it was something much more private – he began writing plays of great power, which in the 1890s were contemporary with the first films. In fact, as we read them now, they *are* effectively film scripts, involving the fission and fusion of identities and characters, the alteration of objects and landscapes by the psychological pressures of the observer, and symbolic projections of obsessive states of mind. They were all, as material processes, beyond the reach of even his experimental theatre, but as processes of art, they would eventually be realized in film – at first as expressionism in an exploratory cinema, later as available techniques in, among others, routine horror and murder films, and in that kind of anti-science fiction commercially presented as SF.

Within these powerful developments, as well as those of majority cinema, which was reconstructing narrative in even more powerfully reproductive and closed forms, taking up as always new themes and issues from social life, but showing interesting, pleasurable, even exciting or moving ways of accommodating to them, realizing how these things must be – within all that, socialists, it can be unsentimentally concluded, are rather likely at times to feel lonely. The whole pressure of a social, and then a cultural, order is even better than it used to be at persuading us that we are probably mistaken. But then, what would it really mean in practice *not* to be mistaken? What would it mean to celebrate the socialist films that we have and to find ways of making new ones? There are different levels of answer. My main point in re-emphasising the historical meaning of naturalism was to prepare for saying that, over a much bigger area than we usually recognize, there are social realities that cry out for its kind of serious, detailed recording and diagnostic attention . For after all, the central socialist case in all matters of culture is that the lives of the great majority of people have been, and still are, almost wholly disregarded by almost all arts. It can be important to contest these selective arts within their own terms, but our central commitment ought always to be to those areas of hitherto silent, or fragmented, or positively misrepresented experience. Moreover, we should not, as socialists, make the extraordinary error of believing that most people only become interesting when they begin to engage with political and industrial actions of a previously recognized kind. That error deserves Sartre's jibe that, for many Marxists, people are born only when they first enter capitalist employment. If we are serious about even political life, we have to enter that world in which people live as they can, as themselves, and then necessarily live within a whole complex of work and love and illness and natural beauty. If we are serious socialists we shall then often find, within and cutting across this real substance, always in its detail so surprising and often vivid, the profound social and historical conditions and movements which enable us to speak with some fullness of voice of a human history.

I don't want to be understood as saying that only naturalism can do this. In many situations there are different and often better ways. But I do want to say that after three centuries of realist art, and after three-quarters of a century of film, there are still vast areas of the lives of our own people which have scarcely been looked at in any serious way. It's sometimes said that we can't make socialist films within any naturalist convention until we have socialism and can show it. Isn't the mere reproduction of an existing reality a passivity, even an acceptance of the fixed and the immobile? But first, this is to overlook the long histories of our peoples in which movements and struggles, particular victories and defeats, reached their own moving crises. So large a part of our histories has been appropriated or falsified by enemy artists and producers, or by the indifferent who have converted them to spectacle, that there is enough work in that alone for several generations of socialist film-makers. Within our own time there are also these moving crises, these victories and defeats, and it should be one of the particular qualities of a serious socialist, including serious socialist artists, that these can be looked at as they are, not in the brief enthusiasms of despairers, of mere supporters, but in the unalterable commitment, in and through any argument or diagnosis, to the lives of the working people who continue as real men and women beyond either victory or defeat. This hasn't been and will not be the whole content of socialist film, though for many countries it has been a rich and enduring tendency.

There is at least one other important area which is particularly relevant to those of us who live (often ourselves making images) in what are called the advanced, but are actually also the image-soaked, societies. It is here that the most creative tendency in modernist art, often at its best in film, can find connections with the kinds of social commitment to which, often under pressure, it has become opposed. I mean that the central process of image-making itself – which, as against the enclosing flow of orthodox art, modernism emphasized, and deliberately cut across – this central process is now in itself a major factor in consciousness and in gaining consciousness. There is some real social basis for this cutting-across the processes of image-making, in the widespread contemporary distrust of what are called, too simply, the media. Many people now see and know that they are being misrepresented, but too few, and none of us all the time, really know how this happens. A merely sullen distrust of contemporary stereotypes is at best defensive and often disabling. A shouted anger against them is better, but nobody can go on shouting all the time. In fact, all the way through from the simplest forms of labelling, through plot manipulation and selective editing, to the deepest forms and problems of self-presentation, self-recognition, self-admission, there are processes of production in which we *can* intervene. Here the special properties of film, most notably the bringing together of otherwise separated areas of reality and of fundamentally different ways of observing it, have already been evident and could be developed much further.

This work can be done at either root or branch. It is one of the tragedies of modernism, in revolt against the fixed images, the conventional flows and sequences of orthodox bourgeois art, that it was pressured and tempted by the very isolation that was its condition, into an assertion of its own autonomous and then primarily subjectivist and formalist world; a world of autonomous art. It wasn't always like that. It needn't go on like that. The revolt against the fixed image and the conventional sequence can find connections with those areas of shared reality where we are all uncertain, crossed by different truths, exposed to diverse and shifting conditions and relationships, and all these within structures of feeling – *not* formed ideas and commitments, which, of course, also continue – which can be reached as common. We so often see, in the past, that otherwise separated or isolated people found their minds forming, their feelings shaping, their perceptions changing into what to them seemed quite personal, but were also, when they could be looked at from the necessary distance, common historical ways.

But in the practice of film, as also I think in the novel, there are available forms which are already part of that long composition of the popular, which is too easily dismissed as merely commercial art. Who, for example, could find a readier form for exploring misdirection – that concealment or contradiction of truths from sharply opposed real interest – than the apparently known form of one kind of crime story, or spy story, or thriller? The fact that the truths commonly exposed by the usual mechanisms of these forms are arbitrary or trivial, or are safely plotted to arrive simply at the dangerous foreigner or the enemy agent, shouldn't be seen as an obstacle. For all these forms came through in a radically dislocated culture which was concealing most of the truths about itself. The false hero who reveals all, but actually reveals nothing except his own presumed sharpness, and who temporarily restores what can pass for an order, is simply the accommodation of the form. He needn't be – and indeed, at the most serious level – *cannot* be – it's real definition. There are crimes and disloyalties now happening everywhere around us which really need to be tracked down, not in the enclosing rhetoric of an already known political statement, but in the complex and surprising ways in which they actually happen, and within a social order in which any serious investigator would come to know he's a participant, as well as the idealized all-seeing observer.

These are among the branches we should occupy. I know of course that it is much easier to say than to do. We have all seen the material realities of that long capitalist appropriation of the popular, and its scarcely less disturbing indifferences to the genuinely different, but we are in a very strange and perhaps hopeful situation. All the big things just now are against us, but within what is not only a very powerful, but also an exceptionally unstable social and cultural order, there are forces moving of which nobody can predict the outcome. A strong and active generation of actual and would-be film and video-makers is more alive and eager in what it is beginning and want to do than in any earlier and perhaps more congenial time. The response to an action as evident and overwhelming as the coal strike is already at this early stage more encouraging in film and video than in any other of our arts. Meanwhile, the economy of cinema had radically changed and, in its coexistence with television and with new forms and institutions of distribution, is now far from being the old monopoly, though the old and the new oligopolies still hold most of the ground. Yet there it is: only a few of the films that have been shown in this festival of socialist films at the National Film Theatre were made in simple, supportive conditions. What socialist, anyway, would expect in our kind of world that it should be easier for him or her than for our brother and sister predecessors? It's understandable that all those short cuts I discussed were seized on – that the popular was inherently *our* own territory, that the medium was inherently open and mobile – before we learned that most dislocations and contradictions, those once magical words which would destroy bourgeois society, would with great power be used as dislocations and contradictions of *us*. The exploratory, the experimental and the innovative, we thought, were predetermined to be on our side. None of that is now true, yet when we have got to know about it, we are in a position to have learned something and to go on encouraged – in that sense, to find our own ways.

Audience Professor Williams, you seem to be implying that there is no reason at all why cinema should be socialist or be dominated by socialism.

RW There is no inherent reason why it should be. But it is one of those media that can be used by socialists – taking socialists in a broad sense – though at first people thought socialist cinema would just happen because it was that kind of medium. At least we've learned that *that* isn't so. The thing is, then, not to get depressed about it; I mean, it would be rather sad if socialists were always having to write off each medium in which they had once placed great hopes and hang on to the new one. It isn't like that. The technology doesn't decide which kind of use it's going to have, or which kind of feeling or commitment it's going to make possible. It's open in different directions and I was trying to argue that there were very good reasons in the whole economy why film could be easily appropriated by a particular kind of capitalist. But equally, if you've seen that happening, it's no reason for saying that therefore it can't be used for other political positions.

Aud The idea that the more people know, the more we shall move towards socialism doesn't seem to be actually borne out by a long way, does it?

RW Well, it's always asserted that people now know a great deal by comparison with their ancestors, you know? One would have to have a long discussion, though, about what is meant by 'know', and this is indeed one of the things in which these technologies are very relevant. People have the impression that they know all sorts of things they've seen on film or television, when they really know nothing which is necessarily different from what would once have been the real claim, 'I saw it with my own eyes.' That is the whole problem. It was most interesting during the miners' strike that people didn't say, 'I am disturbed by this violence,' – you know, the common position. They said 'Night after night *on our television screens*, there is this violence.' In other words, it was precisely its framing in that particular technology that gave people the sense that they were seeing what was happening. But the most elementary examination of how film of actuality is made shows that everything depends on the position in which the camera is set up, the way the film is edited, what commentary is added to it, and so on. So that when people now say we know so much more than our ancestors and yet it hasn't moved us towards socialism, we must remember that the knowing is of a very particular kind, and some of it is false knowing and some of it is simple confusion. I believe as a socialist that the more people know, the more they will understand the need for socialism, and obviously I could prove it to my own satisfaction, but I don't think of it as an historical law. What I *am* concerned to say is that there is no basis for concluding that people now know so much, and have seen socialism and have decided they don't like it, because I don't think that's the history at all.

Aud In the late 1930s, I saw some of the Russian films which were, in those days, supposed to be glorifying socialist Russia, and basically all they really showed was the glorification of work. I remember one film in particular where the leading character operated a loom, and she started with one loom and a bit later on in the film she was working three or four, and it finished up that they built a whole factory and she was working all the looms. It wasn't socialism, it was enslaving, and I think that really it gave everyone a bit of a knock, you know? It wasn't very enlightening, really.

RW Well, of course, yes, there are many cases. There were films which were consciously made to induce the new spirit of labour and the dignity of labour and so on, and this was often falsely done by people who were not going to do it themselves. There's always that lovely story about the Dovzhenko film, *Earth*. A new tractor was being delivered to the commune, and the peasants were to look delighted, but he couldn't get them looking delighted enough. And anyone who knows peasants confronted by something new would understand this – they would naturally have a long look at it, and they'd *use* it before they expressed an opinion. On the other hand he could hire a conjuror, and have people watching a conjuror and looking delighted and amazed, and that's one of the things about film. You can intercut this delighted audience watching a conjuror and in the film you are seeing with your own eyes that they are delighted and amazed by this new machine. Now a lot of that was done, and of course it's part of the whole complex history of socialism being attempted in that desperately poor and backward and disrupted country, literally a place of famine and total dislocation. There was an ideological purpose in saying work is the highest duty, and it could very easily be abstracted from its real social forms – decisions about what work should be done, and how, which are real socialist questions – and it often was. You could say the same thing about some of our own left documentary films of the 1930s. I had something of that in mind in repeating that joke of Sartre's, that for one kind of Marxist people are only born when they enter the factory; their existence as human beings before and through and after that is not seen from that narrow perspective as real human existence at all. These are emphases which at certain times you can understand, though you always have to replace them in the real history. But of course, they must never be allowed to appropriate the name of socialism, because if that's done, then there are far too many people who know about work in rather more direct ways to be as easily bowled over as a visiting film-maker.

Aud If one of the aims of socialist film-making is to present people with alternative ideas and views, what about the difficulty of actually getting backing for making films, and the whole problem of state censorship. I heard a talk a couple of weeks ago by Ken Loach about various films that he and other people wanted to make about the situation in the north of Ireland, for example, and he said that state censorship had intervened in various different ways and stopped those films being either made or shown. So isn't that, for a socialist, one of the really big problems about film?

RW Yes, of course, it is an enormous problem. As I was saying towards the end, the history of socialist film-making – for that matter, the history of socialist intellectual work of any kind – is that it has very rarely been done in supportive conditions. And in that sense I don't think we should be too pessimistic about the present or immediately recent situation, because the fact that many things are blocked is true and obvious. You could be equally surprised how certain things get through. Loach, for example, has made films of considerable significance, although never at any time was there some social order set up which said, 'You're a socialist film-maker, please make some socialist films.' It's achieved by a complex negotiation of the system. There are periods of relative openness and relative closure in this. There is, in one sense, insatiable demand, in that there are problems in any culture which professes liberalism in operating the kind of control which would be simpler and more direct in other kinds of society. None of this is to say that the opportunities are simply there, or that there aren't blocks, but it *is* to say that there are certain times – and the important thing is to be able to see them and seize on them – when certain things can be done, often by combining something with something else which has a different kind of leading edge. Indeed, I think that the history of the last twenty years in Britain has been much like this. You could describe it at one level as a highly centralized state which is out to control what people think and feel, and obviously at certain times this is quite explicitly so, and then you'd have to say, 'Well, how is it that in the last twenty years there is a significant body of work which has entered these hitherto silent or forbidden areas, and has achieved something of substance?' This is where the relatively insatiable demand of the current distribution system for material does create some of these opportunities. It simply is an expansion, above all. There's always been room for some work of an unorthodox kind.

Aud You talked about popularity and entertainment value, and I wanted to say something about accessibility, because one of the major problems for socialists making films is to get across things that may not be accessible to most people. For example, you have films like *Reds* (1981) which put in a lot of romance and everything else in order to communicate to a wider audience. I'd like you to say something about those films, and also what you think about the possibilities of soap opera, which is very popular in discussion at the moment. Do you think it's a form that can be used in radical ways or not?

RW Well, to take the last point first, I've been arguing for twenty years that serials are an area that radicals ought to look out for, because one of the things that is often missing from radical art, particularly modernist radical art, is precisely continuity, precisely consequence, what happens after what happens, which, after all, is the basic construction of that kind of serial. As against many sophisticated modernist forms, people *are* intensely interested in what happens after the person walks away on their own, disgusted by everything. We know they're going somewhere, we know they've got to live, and the form which gets it down to a fine formula is the commercial soap opera, the form which says, 'Well, you know, nobody's life is dispensable.' You *do* follow them through, you *do* see what happens, and moreover, from a socialist point of view, understanding relationships and the consequences of human situations is often only possible if you do follow it through in time. Now, on the more general point, it's then a question of what you mean by 'romance'. To take a simple situation, Orwell wrote *1984*, in which a man and a girl are in love but, because there is this cruel state, they are put under threat, under danger of their lives, and they betray each other; under the spreading chestnut tree they betray each other. This is the awful conclusion that Orwell came to. Now, what I always remember is that when Orwell was wounded in Spain in the Civil War, his wife Eileen, who had got out of Spain – and it was a fairly dangerous time for people who had been in that tendency – went back. She went back because she loved him, she went back because he was ill. Now, that is a human situation that people call 'romance'. I mean, we've seen films which would turn up the music for the girl going back to the man she loves, who is dying in a hospital bed. But, it happened. And in that sense it is a profoundly socialist idea, because it is about the sense of comradeship, of people who *do* put themselves in danger, and this is at once both personal and political. Now I don't think we should feel that, because that would have some superficial similarities to certain kinds of Hollywood romance, we've therefore got to say, apologetically, 'Well, as socialists we shouldn't be touching that, we should be explaining the inadequacy of anarchism as against the socialist line, we should be studying conditions in the industrial regions around Bilbao.' No, why *should* it be that? That's where a socialist experience is either denied or confirmed. And it can be denied. Some people don't go back. Some people rat and betray, and so on. In the same way (I know I'm just speaking of my own poor efforts in this!) you can use things like investigative reporting, you can use things like tracking down the truth of a particular crime, you can even use this whole abstract interest in espionage. People say, 'Well, it's just a love story, it's just a crime story,' but that's an extraordinary error, and since I criticized Orwell, I'll now redress the balance by agreeing with him. He said that, if socialists abandon these forms and let them all be written by the enemies of socialism, they have only themselves to blame if people drift away from their ideas. These are forms that we can use. Soap opera, for instance, was developed to get people watching so that a sponsoring soap company had a definite captive audience for its adverts, and that is the way they've appropriated the human interest in continuity. But that is no reason for giving up the human interest in continuity. What one has to say is that there is only one answer to misrepresentation, and that's another representation. I don't think we must get in the position where all we do in this culture is say how rotten it is. We're not going to be short of evidence, but it's not a very constructive thing to confine ourselves to doing. Anyone who gets the slightest chance of working in those ways ought to take it, even if mistakes are made.

Aud Wouldn't it be possible to introduce certain radical themes into soap opera if the right sort of people were writing it? You mentioned the miners' strike, for instance, so you could have a plot about the miner who loses his wife when she runs off with somebody else because he's in the nick, or because she doesn't agree with him coming out on strike and they're going to lose their home . . .

RW I don't believe, of course, that one should *avoid* the great industrial and political crises, and I hope that in ten years' time we have a hundred novels and a hundred films of that extraordinary period, more or less directly. But there are ways and ways of exploring it, and you begin and end with the commitment to the people, not to recognizable political or industrial event; the people who are there before and after it, and these people not simply as heroic figures of the abstract action, but in this kind of diversity. All I *would* say is that those whom I with some deliberateness called enemy artists – I don't just see them as different, I see them as enemy – endlessly harp on the failure of relationships, the dislocation of communities, the defeat of noble efforts, the end of idealism. This really is the only thing with which they can defend this social order: not that it's good, but that it's inevitable. People aren't good enough to live in better ways – this is the heartland of their system. They don't any longer try and say it's better. They just say, 'We understand people, we know they're out for themselves, we know that if they try something good it fails.' And because of that there is what I called a bourgeois dissident form of art which shows all this with great power, and what happens is what poor Brecht saw happening when he wrote *The Threepenny Opera*. He wrote this play about eighteenth-century highwaymen and whores, not for the interest of the eighteenth century, but to say what capitalist society is like. It was put on in a bourgeois theatre, and the precise people he was writing about went and said, 'What delightful low-life! What lovely songs!' What comes out nowadays of the enormously self-approving majority culture of the United States? Idealized pretty pictures of life in the streets and happy suburban parties? No. What comes out is people who are at each others' throats almost continuously and who endlessly do each other down. Now, that's not because some radicals have secretly captured Hollywood and the networks and are showing how disruptive and criminal American life is. If you're shown often enough that nothing will work, that people aren't decent enough to make anything better, then that becomes the one really clinching argument. You go along and you hear somebody saying we could all live differently, and at the back of your mind you always know, because you saw it on television, that there are always these bad people who bust it up. So although I think that socialists have got to explore defeats and failures and the cases where people aren't strong enough to carry the strain – we've got to do that, otherwise we're just in the fantasy business – it's not enough, because it has persuaded us so thoroughly that we're not up to much, that it actually becomes entertaining to be shown that we're not up to much, and that is a bad condition to be in. You have to enter that same process and say, 'Look, this went wrong this time for these reasons; we're going to track it through, we're going to understand it, and we're not going to accept the conclusion that it was inevitable.' At that point you stop being a dissenting bourgeois, which is, after all, the easiest thing to be now, because you can appear to be separated from that world of power and money while you're actually providing all the feelings that obstruct any challenge to it. I mean, I have the greatest respect for the serious people who did it first, but not for the people who do it now, as formula, because they have some need to say that failure is inscribed in the human condition. Everyone who has lived in this actual world already has enough doubts, has enough knowledge of weakness and of how often things fail. It may be some kind of therapy to see it endlessly replayed, but the moment when people feel the break from the possibility that at least something can move, something can be got right, something different can be felt . . . I think that at the moment, that kind of celebration of possibility is the most profound need.

Aud It seems to me, if you look at television soap operas nowadays, twenty years after they first appeared, the social level has been pushed up very considerably. They've all got higher standards of living, they're all drinking gin and tonics, which wouldn't have happened when it first started. What are the pressures that are making that happen?

RW I wish I altogether knew. There is a very curious management, I think, of the mixed feelings people have about wealth. That is to say, people simultaneously enjoy its display and enjoy disapproving of it. It is very significant about *Dallas* that the central tycoon character is an out-and-out villain, about the lowest kind of human being that you could imagine within that world. This is very skilful manipulation, and you see the same in these constant images of royalty. What looks like unmitigated creeping of the most gross and slobbering kind is, at another level, rather spiteful and malicious: every opportunity is taken to do down the very people you're also idolizing. So without being too solemn about it, I think that one of the ways of handling people's intense irritation with the idea that there are people much wealthier than they are is to let them enjoy the fashions and the sense of mobility and all the talk about millions, and at the same time to show that they're a dirty lot and that you probably wouldn't be happy if you owned an oil company. I think this has happened, but it can't be the only reason . . . This has become a gawping culture, and in that sense very different, I think, from the twenty years or so after the Second World War, when it was continually pretended that we all lived in much the same way and that what would interest us were people not too unlike ourselves. The glitter has been put on since then.

Aud You acknowledge the importance of interesting and entertaining an audience, but when you're actually portraying real events, like news items, and there's still this insatiable desire to interest and hold the audience, aren't you running the risk of misinforming them? How could you reconcile still entertaining people and yet presenting the facts?

RW Well, it depends very much on how it's done. I mean, nothing is ever going to compete with song and dance for entertainment: Law One. But if you're moving beyond the self-evidently entertaining and pleasurable, which is not going to have much of this other content – although it can be real in its own terms – then I think we don't always know what is going to interest people until it's been tried. I think if people insist on inserting preformed theoretical positions into some observation of what is going on, or if they simply think that recording for its own sake is bound to be interesting, then things often go wrong, but certain things entertain in the sense of engage, interest, satisfy our feelings in a different rhythm. This is all I would say – in a different rhythm from the more obviously exciting. My main position on that, as I said, is that there are the things that almost everybody enjoys, like the intensely examined love stories, the mysteries, the crimes that have to be unravelled, and none of them are in any sense incompatible with the most serious political attention. We've been afraid, because those forms have been what we regard as stereotyped commercial entertainment, to use the forms. It's as if people being socialist means that they never get involved in anything exciting – or, for that matter, romantic – which is more than we can afford to concede, especially as it fits *their* image of the sort of people we are.

Notes

1 England's theatres were closed from the beginning of the Civil War in 1642 until the Restoration in 1660. Intensely aware of the political dangers of an unrestricted revival of drama for the still-fragile Stuart monarchy, Charles II established a monopoly of 'legitimate' theatre in 1662 by granting royal Charters, or Letters Patent, to two companies: 'the King's servants' at Drury Lane (who were technically part of the Royal Household) and 'the Duke of York's servants', who occupied a theatre in Lincoln's Inn Fields. This second Charter devolved on Covent Garden in 1732. The Letters Patent rendered the two companies independent of the licenser of theatre buildings, the Lord Chamberlain, and while they changed hands many times in the next 200 years, the monopoly they conferred was reinforced by the Theatres Act of 1737. They were finally abolished in 1843, largely because the growth of various forms of 'illegitimate' drama had long since made them obsolete in practice.

6

Robert Mitchum

Although he might well be the first to deny it, Robert Mitchum is undoubtedly one of the greatest actors the American cinema has produced. He was born in Bridgeport, Connecticut, in 1917, and after spending his youth on the road and doing a succession of odd jobs, he went to California and joined the Long Beach Players' Guild. He made his first film in 1943, and in the next two years he appeared in more than twenty movies, beginning with small parts in Hopalong Cassidy Westerns and such films as *The Human Comedy* (1943, Clarence Brown), *Dancing Masters* (1943, Mal St Clair) and *Thirty Seconds Over Tokyo* (1944, Mervyn LeRoy), and then graduating to leading roles in B Westerns. His big breakthrough came with *The Story of GI Joe* (1945, William Wellman), for which he received what has so far remained, predictably, his only Oscar nomination as Best Supporting Actor. He went on to become a major star at RKO, and his position as the definitive post-war leading man was rapidly established in a series of extraordinary films, including Raoul Walsh's Freudian Western *Pursued*, Edward Dmytryk's *Crossfire* and Jacques Tourneur's masterly film noir *Out of the Past* (all 1947). Working regularly with Hollywood's finest directors, he contributed admirable performances throughout the 1950s to such films as *Macao* (1952, Josef von Sternberg/Nicholas Ray), *The Lusty Men* (1952, Nicholas Ray), *Angel Face* (1952, Otto Preminger), *River of No Return* (1954, Preminger), *Track of the Cat* (1954, William Wellman), *Night of the Hunter* (1955, Charles Laughton), *Heaven Knows, Mr Allison* (1957, John Huston), *The Angry Hills* (1959, Robert Aldrich), *Home from the Hill* (1960, Vincente Minnelli) and *The Sundowners* (1960, Fred Zinnemann). In 1958 he formed his own production company to make *Thunder Road*, for which he also wrote the screenplay and a number of songs. He remained a top star throughout the next three decades, and his later films include *Two for the Seesaw* (1962, Robert Wise), *El Dorado* (1967, Howard Hawks), *Secret Ceremony* (1969, Joseph Losey), *Ryan's Daughter* (1970, David Lean), *The Friends of Eddie Coyle* (1973, Peter Yates), *Farewell, My Lovely* (1975, Dick Richards), *The Last Tycoon* (1976, Elia Kazan), *The Big*

Sleep (1978, Michael Winner), *That Championship Season* (1982, Jason Miller) and *Maria's Lovers* (1984, Andrei Konchalovsky). Robert Mitchum also appeared in the television mini-series *The Winds of War* (1983) and its sequel, *War and Remembrance* (1988).

The following lecture took place on 24 June 1984. Robert Mitchum was interviewed by Derek Malcolm, the film critic of the *Guardian*.

Robert Mitchum

Derek Malcolm Bob, it's really great to have you here, and I'm very, very glad that your wife, Dorothy, to whom you've been married for forty-six years, is also here. When you first met her you'd been, I think, on Chatham County chain-gang previously. What did she think of you?

Robert Mitchum She thought I was very dashing – I was on crutches, so she has a little sympathy for me. She had a date with my brother and I just aced him out, and we rode around and I told her I'd be back. I had a minor infection on my ankle from a chain collar, and when I met her parents I told her mother I hurt my leg hopping a freight train. I didn't want to tell them I'd been on a chain-gang because that was not socially acceptable, but I thought, 'Freight train? Everyone does that.'

DM Tell me, why were you on the chain-gang? I believe it was about six days before you escaped?

RM I was a dangerous and suspicious character with no visible means of support. A common charge of begging, for the crime: poverty. 'Trespassing on railroad property', that was it.

DM Did they think you were a thief?

RM Well, I was in jail. I went in on Sunday and I had a hearing on Friday, and when I finally got into the courtroom they read a description – which was me – and a description of a burglar who had robbed a shoe store on Wednesday. I'd gone to sleep and I asked for a rereading of this charge, and I said, 'Well, I've been in jail since Sunday', and the courtroom broke up and the judge hammered on the desk, and he was a little miffed by that. So he said, 'You look kind of thin and poorly, Robert Charles, I think about 180 days on a state farm should straighten you out.' And that was it, off I went.

DM How did you escape?

RM I just walked away. They didn't miss me.

DM You lost your own father when you were very young, but you had an amazing step-father, Hugh Cunningham Morris, who was an Englishman, wasn't he, and who had thousands of adventures?

RM He was from Land's End, yeah, and he ran off when he was about 14 and went to Australia. He sailed windjammers and then travelled with a circus for a while, and he held simultaneous commissions in the Royal Flying Corps, the British army and the British navy; we had pictures of him in the Camel Corps. He jumped out of an aeroplane that was torn up over Europe in World War I and picked up a lot of shrapnel; it took away half his liver. He was tattooed all over and ran a newspaper in Canada, and when he met my mother he was Features Editor of the Bridgeport Post in Bridgeport, Connecticut; my mother was working for the newspaper. The first time I went in an aeroplane he took me up: Fairfield, Connecticut, open cockpit, leather helmet. When World War II broke out, he began to itch and perspire, and he finally sent a letter to Winston Churchill, and he got a reply. Churchill said, 'Things are tough, but they're really not that bad.' So he joined the Merchant Marine and shipped out to Okinawa when they were blowing that place up, and I used to hear a lot of stories from returning airmen. He had a garden growing on the deck of this freighter, and they'd say, 'There's some crazy Englishman there shooting at the Japanese with a rifle trying to protect his leeks and cauliflower.' That was the old man.

DM I think you left home at the age of about 14?

RM Well, I kept coming back until finally, when I was 16, I left and went to California.

DM But you must have travelled thousands and thousands of miles before you were 17.

RM No. I went to California and I made a total of nine trips back and forth across the country on freight trains, but it was the accepted mode of travel at that time. It was during the great Depression. There were bankers and university professors, all sorts of people travelling. Also some legitimate people.

DM What sort of jobs did you take on the road?

RM None. I just kept travelling.

DM But you were a boxer for a bit, weren't you?

RM Well, that was when I got to California, and if you fall off a train, or they pull you off, they ask you what you did. Down south, in the south-east, they'd look at your hands, and if you had callouses they would pretty much let you go because you were going from one job to another, but if you didn't, they figured you must be some kind of a mountebank or thief, and they found work for you to do. They could feed you for about thirty-eight cents a day and they'd rent you out to the county for two dollars a day and make a tidy profit. Out west, you could always find work as a fry-cook or a dish-washer, but your arms got marked up with hot fat spattering over them, and your hands would wrinkle up washing dishes. So I told them I was a fighter and they just threw me in with some gorilla on Wednesday night, and that was it.

DM Did you get a bit more money if you won?

RM No, you just got another ride out of town.

DM Having been a boxer and a dish-washer, all sorts of things, how the hell did you get into movies?

RM Well, it was the obvious thing to do. I was working at Lockheed[1] and that wasn't going to get it. I was there for a year and in a year I slept once for four hours. I had terrible reactions to not sleeping, so the company doctor suggested that I quit. I said, 'Quit? I've got eighteen dollars,' and he said, 'Things have come to a pretty pass when a clown like you has to go on to the street and starve to death.' So I quit, and I went to work in a shoe store where I was fired about once a day. These girls would come in and try on thirty-six pairs of shoes, and I'd finally holler, 'Beaver!' and I'd get the axe, and the guy would tell me to get back into the storeroom and smoke a cigarette or something until she'd gone, and then he'd hire me back. But it was good because I was working on commission and I could go on interviews. I think it was about the third interview, I went out and met Bill Boyd at the old 'Pop' Sherman[2] Company, and that was it. They put me on a horse up in Kernville, California and I never looked back.

DM Didn't the horse throw you off?

RM He did indeed.

DM I believe you were a substitute for an actor who died in an accident: Charlie Murphy?

RM No, no. I went up there and we went from Bakersfield to Kernville on a little bus that wound round the river. We got there, the sun was shining brightly and everybody was sitting out on the hotel veranda, and I thought that that was strange because on those cheap pictures they used every available ray of sunshine. So I hopped out, went out on the veranda and said hello and smiled at everybody, and they were all very sombre and gloomy. I learned then that somebody had just been killed that day, an old guy named Charlie Murphy. He was driving six horses and he had the reins wrapped around his hands and around his wrists, and he bounced off the wagon seat, he went back and forth under the wheels and it just cut him to pieces. So I was sort of chastened. That evening I went into the Wardrobe Department and a fellow called Earl Mosier stuck a hat on my head and said 'I think this will fit you, kid,' and he took a knife and scraped the hat out; he scraped out the dried blood from Charlie Murphy's head.

DM You also appeared with Laurel and Hardy in a film called *Dancing Masters*. Do you remember them well?

RM Quite well. I was surprised. They were very droll in front of the camera, but off camera Oliver Hardy was concerned about his legs. He had phlebitis, or something like that, and he was not at all happy. And Stan was sort of dazed and just sat in the corner and talked to his secretary. The funniest guy on the set, I think, was a guy called Doug Foley who became a great friend of mine, and I've worked with him several times since then. We worked on the Hopalong Cassidy films a lot together. It was not my place or privilege to engage in long conversations with Mr Laurel or Mr Hardy, but they were not antic performers off-stage.

DM What do you reckon was the film that really started you off?

RM I suppose it was *The Story of GI Joe*.

DM And I believe that was a bit of a fluke, your being chosen for that, because a lot of other people must have wanted that part, bigger names than you at that time.

RM I don't know that. I just know that I went over and did a test with Buzz [Burgess] Meredith for Bill Wellman, and Bill wanted to use the test in the film, and he *did* use part of it. That was it, I just got the job.

DM It was obviously a big step up for you. Were you nervous about it at all?

RM No, I wasn't nervous about it, and it wasn't until people started looking at me and began to recognize me that I realized I'd made a horrible mistake.

DM You got an Academy Award nomination for that part, and then, I presume, the films came thick and fast. You always referred to yourself as the RKO workhorse.

RM Well, I went to work at RKO. I don't remember what I did there first, but they had the old Zane Grey series, the Westerns, and it was bruited about the studio that I was going to do them. Tim Holt had done them, but he'd gone into the Air Force. I told them I couldn't ride a horse, and they came back with all these Hopalongs and the other Westerns I'd done. They took everybody from the studio, all the contract players, and put ill-fitting clothes on them – hats that came down to here, boots four sizes too large. Finally, they came out with a set of tailored clothes for me, and that was it; they had them *tailored* to me, so obviously I was the chosen one. I did *West of the Pecos* and *Nevada* and I think maybe one other, and in between I did other things.

DM And you did war service briefly, didn't you? What happened there?

RM Nothing. I went into the Infantry. I told them first I was homosexual, and they said, 'Prove it!', but I couldn't find a willing partner. Then they said, 'Bend over,' and I said, 'I can't – my back,' and they said 'Ah, ha! IA Infantry! Headaches?' 'Yeah.' 'IA Infantry!' So that was it. They sent me out to Camp Roberts, and the first night – it was about three o'clock in the morning – I heard some close-order drill being called, and I look out the barracks window and I see these guys, and the platoon sergeant stuck his head out the door of his room and I said, 'Are you leaving or just coming in?' and he said, 'What the hell's the difference?' So I was there in cadre for several months. Then I went down to Fort MacArthur and I was training men there; I was a drill instructor. The general had decided that there would be no relaxation of discipline on this post, so everybody had to drill with the incoming group and the outgoing group. So I'd go into the officer's quarters, ask who was in charge and say, 'OK, so sign here, you've just completed two hours' drill on a hot, dusty parade ground.' So one day there was a light colonel from New Orleans, a Medical Officer, and he said, 'Is that the way you fulfil your duties, soldier?' and I said, 'Every chance I get, sir.' So he signed it, and I had orders then to report to the Orderly Room the next morning and fall out. There they told me to report to the Medical Office, and there was the colonel, and he kept me at attention the whole time, and he said, 'I think your talents are being wasted in the army, Mitchum.' I said, 'I'm perfectly content, sir,' and he said, 'Well, anybody with a pair of lungs and a copy of the field manual can call drills. How would you like to be an assistant to the Chief Orthopaedic Examining Surgeon?' I said, 'I cannot *stand* the sight of blood, sir,' and he said, 'With any luck you won't see too much blood.' I tried to demur, he kept me at attention, that was it – this was an order. I was dismissed, and I went to report to an old Kentucky abortionist who was sitting in a room with no furniture. I went out and got a detail of recruits to go to the loading dock, and we brought in a chair and a desk, and the chap sat behind the desk, and I went outside and knocked on the door and he said, 'Come in.' I went in, reported very smartly, turned around, went out, came back in and said, 'Sorry, we have to take the desk and the chair.' So he said, 'As you see, Mitchum, nothing is very organized around here. As soon as I find out what we're doing I'll let you know.' So he did, and from that day forward I told 900 men to turn around, bend over and spread their cheeks. I could prognosticate the future, I could diagnose all your ills, I became an expert, and if anybody questions that I will be happy to demonstrate.

DM After your tour as a rectum inspector . . .

RM Keister Police, we called them.

DM Keister Police, I'm sorry . . . you went back to movies straight away, did you?

RM Immediately, yes. I came out of Fort MacArthur, I had a suit and a bottle of Scotch in my locker, and I put on both of them. The next thing I knew I was down at the Marine Corps base in a Marine uniform, and we were up to take twelve, and a guy nudged me and said, 'If you quit goofing up, those numbers wouldn't be so high,' and I was in the middle of a picture with Guy Madison called *Till the End of Time*.

DM You used to work in several films at once sometimes, and I believe on one occasion you did actually work in three films simultaneously for RKO and MGM.

RM I was doing a picture with Laraine Day, *The Locket*, and they called me over to Metro on a film called *Undercurrent* with Bob Taylor and Kate Hepburn. I was just leaving the office and they called me to Arthur Hornblow's office, and I went there and they substituted me – if you'll believe this – for Walter Pidgeon on a picture with Greer Garson.

DM Called *Desire Me*, wasn't it?

RM Nobody desired anybody. They had five directors; none of them would put their name on it.

DM George Cukor started it, didn't he?

RM I believe so, yes. Mervyn LeRoy finished it, Victor Saville was somewhere there in the middle. There were, I think, five different directors all told.

DM So you were working on one in the morning, one in the afternoon and one in the evening for three weeks?

RM That's right. I'd finish at five o'clock in the morning at RKO and I'd have to be at make-up at Metro at seven o'clock in the morning, and I never slept for three weeks and never had a chance to eat. Also, I had to fly up to Monterey, about 400 miles or so, for the first shot after lunch, then I'd fly back to go to work at night. It was a nightmare. I became completely unglued eventually.

DM One of the movies we've seen in this season of your films at the NFT is *Macao*, which you made for von Sternberg with Jane Russell. What was von Sternberg like as a director?

RM He was very short and sort of arty, and he was from Weehawken, New Jersey, but he had a German accent – he was very German. I said, 'Where did you get that accent, Joe? You're from Weehawken, NJ,' and he said if I wanted to know anything about anything, any artistic matters, to come to him, because he *knew*, he was the omniscient artist. He had a junk shop in Weehawken. He began, I think, in Astoria, Long Island, in the old studios there, and finally got tired schlepping those cans of film back and forth, and he went to Germany and heralded himself as a great American director. He got a job, and then he returned from Germany and came to the States as a brilliant *European* director. He had suede trousers and scarves and things like that, and he used to stand on an apple box. We had a cameraman, Harry Wild, and when Harry lost patience he would jump on his hat or kick the apple box, and one time he kicked the box and von Sternberg fell on his behind because he was standing on it, and I think Joe lost heart at that point. Finally, when the picture was done, there was no way they could glue it together – I kept meeting myself – so they turned it over to Nick [Ray]. Nick, Jane and I just stood and looked at each other, and then Jane handed me a piece of paper and some pencils and I wrote one line and we just ad libbed from there. They'd said that the picture needed three days' work, but they didn't say *what* three days, and we worked about three weeks – but at least finally they could release it.

DM So you had to make up a lot of your own lines, then, did you? Did they allow you to get away with them or were some of them too much?

RM Some of them. I remember meeting Jane on a stairway and decided to kiss her, and she said, 'Before breakfast?' and I said, '*For breakfast*,' and they said, 'No, you can't say that.' I didn't see anything wrong with that. I still don't.

DM Well, it looks a pretty good film now, despite all that. I suppose another person everybody will want to know about is Marilyn Monroe, who was with you in *River of No Return*. How did you get on with her?

RM Very well.

DM She was a hard worker, was she? She didn't come up late or anything like that?

RM No. We were working up in Canada, by a river that comes right off the glacier, so there were a lot of round stones which were all covered with a very fine powder from the grinding of the glacier, and she was supposed to trot down to the river and cut the raft loose that was tied to a tree. I said, 'Don't *run* down there, if you run you'll break your leg.' She was standing by the camera saying, 'It is the flight of considered panic, it is the flight of considered panic,' and I said, 'I don't care about that, but if you run down there you're going to break your leg.' She said, 'It is the flight of considered panic,' and Otto [Preminger] said, 'Action!' and she ran out and broke her leg. She was a very funny girl, she had a great sense of humour, and was a very nice girl, a very *generous* girl – unfortunately, because people took from her a great deal and gave very little in return. When I was working at Lockheed, my partner on the shaper was her then-husband, Jim Dougherty. That's when I first met her. Dougherty was built like a brick— you know, big red Irishman. Marilyn was a child bride, about 15, I think.

DM But she wasn't a nuisance on the film at that stage, then?

RM No, not at all.

DM So what happened to her, then? Why did she . . . ?

RM I don't know. She was never terribly confident, you know. She didn't think she was the prettiest girl in the world – not very sexy, she thought, and she didn't *present* that. She became more and more withdrawn. I would see her occasionally, but I really don't know what happened to her. She was very shy.

DM I reckon one of your greatest performances, for which you certainly should have got an Oscar, was in *Night of the Hunter* for Charles Laughton. I'll always maintain it was ridiculous that you didn't even get nominated for that. How did you meet Laughton? How did that come about?

RM Well, I had known Charles, and he called me one day and he wanted me to read a book. He said, 'I have this book, and there's this real *bastard* in it!,' and I said, 'Present!,' and he said, 'Well, I'm *not*. I'm making my living reading the Bible, you know, and I can't even consider admitting knowing anyone like that.' So he brought the book over, and I called him up and said, 'I'm ready!' and that was that. I met Paul Gregory then, and we formed some sort of joint production arrangement, and they got Shelly Winters. When they came to Lillian Gish, I said, 'Charles, she's a little frail, isn't she?' He said, 'I'll show you frail!' and he ran some of *Way Down East* – the scene on the ice flow – and it didn't just *look* dangerous, it really *was* very dangerous, so I said it was good enough for me. She was as strong as a Belgian mare, man! I thoroughly enjoyed it, because pleasing Charles was our pleasure and he was a delight to work with. He should have been directing the whole time.

DM But the film wasn't a box-office success, was it?

RM I don't know. When I clock out I forget all about that part. [*Applause*]

DM I know that sometimes you don't see your films, but did you see that one in particular?

RM I eventually saw it, yes. I've seen bits and snips of it on television to remind me it's there. I'm sure I *must* have seen it, I'm sure Charles would insist.

DM You wouldn't say that was one of your favourite films, or would you?

RM Yes, I enjoyed it, and I enjoyed doing the character. I wanted to do it in West Virginia but I was outvoted and we shot a lot of it in the studio. I remember there was a scene of me riding on a donkey in the background, and actually it was a midget on a tiny pony. We had all these stylized sets, and Charles thought that my character was so despicable that he was afraid that women would snatch their children off the streets when I came around, so he put in all those bits with the owls and all those animals along the river in order to lighten it a bit. I think I was still fairly despicable.

DM Another of your best films, I think, is *The Lusty Men*, which Nicholas Ray directed. You had some trouble with the script there, I believe?

RM We didn't have a script when it started. We had a letter from Tom Lee – it was about a seven-page letter – and we had something like twelve or thirteen pages of ideas, and sort of a beginning. Susie Hayward came over and we were sitting there and Nick was explaining the whole thing to her. He was a bit like a librarian: very pedantic if he chose to be, and a bit cerebral. So he went through the whole thing, and Susie sat there – she was knitting – and she said, 'I'm from Brooklyn, what's the *story*?' So he said, 'Tell her, Bob,' so I got up and started walking back and forth and told her a story. She said, 'That's all right, is that on paper?' and Nick said, *'Of course!'* and he dragged out toilet paper and all sorts of things. So he convinced her, I guess, that we had a script. Arthur Kennedy was also highly doubtful. He was dubious about the whole procedure and we couldn't get him to come into the studio – we had to meet him across the street at Lucy's – but we finally got the thing underway. They had assigned Horace McCoy to us as a writer, the guy who wrote *They Shoot Horses, Don't They?* Horace came in one day – he had undergone some strange metamorphosis and he was sort of jiggling up and down – and he had a paper, and he said, 'Now, *she's* standing there in front of the mirror at the exercise bar, and she's stretching out like this, and *he* walks in the door, and the miner's lamp is still burning in his hat, he's got his coat over his shoulder and a lunch box . . . ' He read us this scene, and we didn't know what the hell it had to do with a Western! Nick said, 'What's that?' and Horace said, 'Only the greatest damn scene ever written!' and he turned around and walked out. We couldn't disagree, but it had nothing to do with the project in hand, so we figured we were in some sort of trouble, and I guess David Dortort came in and helped out, and somebody else. We would call him down to the set and he would write down whatever we had conjured up, and we got on very well until finally we were working on location, and Susie was very concerned about *my* character and she said, 'I want to know what happens to him.' So again Nick said, 'We've got to go to work on it,' so we rode back to the studio and we talked and sent out for something to eat and we nattered back and forth. Finally I said, 'Nick, I can't do this night after night. I can't work all day and come back here wrestling with the script at night.

My wife says, "What do you *mean*, working late? What do you *mean*, writing?" ' So I said, 'Let's kill him!' Nick said, 'They'll never hold still for that!' because we had just been through that on *They Live By Night*. The studio wouldn't let me play the bank robber because he gets killed. They said, 'No, you're our hero, we can't kill you off.' So Nick said, 'They won't go for it,' and I said, 'What can we *do*? I can't just walk off into the sunset with Susie Hayward. Let's just kill him,' and he said, 'OK.' So the next day Nick went over and said, 'Susan, I'm very pleased to tell you that he gets killed, he dies,' and she said, 'How?' and he said, 'I don't think that's any of your business!' We hadn't figured it out yet . . . but it worked out pretty well.

DM It did, it's a lovely film. The other two Westerns I love very much are *Pursued* by Raoul Walsh and, of course, Howard Hawk's *El Dorado*. They must have been fun to work with, both of them.

RM Well, both of them were great individual characters. Raoul was a tough character, really. He would set up a scene and say, 'OK, roll it!' and he would turn around and walk away. He only had one eye, and he would roll cigarettes with one hand on the blind side, and as he was walking away from the set the tobacco would fall out, and he would light it and – phew! Roll another one, light it – phew! He would do about five of those, just fire the paper up on his blind side. Finally there would be a protracted silence, and he would say, 'Is it over? OK, cut it! How was it?' and you'd say, 'Well, a lamp fell off,' and he would say, 'Well, was it natural? Did you pick it up again? Right, OK! Rip the page out! Next take!' He never even watched . . . but he was marvellous, he had great confidence in everybody, so if you told him it was good, that was fine. As for Howard, I was living in Maryland then, and I got a call from my secretary who said, 'What about a Western with Duke Wayne for Howard Hawks?' and I said, 'Fine.' Howard called me later and I asked him where he was going to shoot it, and he said, 'I thought I'd do it in Tucson, Bob.' 'Fine, that's a good location. What's the story?' 'Oh, no story, Bob, just the character.' So we went to

Tucson and did it. I had to be shot in the right leg and I put the crutch under my right arm, but Howard said, 'No, no, no . . . ' So I said, 'The crutch substitutes for the injured member.' Then Duke said, 'Goddamn it, I used to break my leg every Saturday afternoon! Put it on the left side!' and Howard said, 'Besides, it leaves your gun-hand free, Bob.' So I said, 'OK,' and I hippity-hop around with this bad leg. Now, we get to the studio and we have to re-shoot the wounding of the leg, and we had a doctor there actually playing the doctor. I had the crutch on my left side, but the doctor says, 'No, no, no, the crutch substitutes for the injured member.' So now I have the crutch under my *right* arm. Then one day the associate producer comes back and he says, 'Oh, my God!' and I say, 'What is it?' They had just been to see the rushes, and he said, 'As you go through the door, the crutch goes – phew! It changes side from the exteriors to the interiors!' So I say, 'What are we going to do?' and he says, 'I don't know, it's about half the picture! Half is outside, half inside!' Then Howard comes along swinging his cane, and the associate producer says, 'Mr Hawks, we have a problem.' 'What's that?' 'Bob's crutch is under the left arm when he's outdoors, but the minute he walks through the door it's under his right arm.' So Howard said, 'Why, they'll never notice that! Think nothing of it,' and that's the way it went. Finally, we were shooting the last scene, after Duke has been shot in the leg with buckshot, and he picked up his crutch and started out, and I said, 'You've got it under the wrong arm,' and he said, 'How the hell would you know? You've been switching it back and forth ever since the picture started!' So we just stuck in that line and it solved the whole thing. Howard was a real character, you know. There was a scene with four or five guys at a table, and I'd say, 'Howard, *he's* already dead, we shot *him*' 'Might want to use him again, Bob.' He switched the scenes back and forth . . . A peculiar form of genius, we never really figured it out.

DM Why were the films so good despite all this?

RM Well, he would take them out and preview them, and if he didn't like the response he would take this scene and put it here, and that one there, and he would do it thirty or forty times until it was right. I guess he did it with all his films. I talked to Cary Grant about *I Was a Male War Bride* (1949) and Cary said that's exactly what he did in that. Howard would let the film run on at times when they ran out of dialogue, and Cary and Ann Sheridan would just ad lib. It turned out beautifully.

DM Speaking of *El Dorado*, why did Duke Wayne wear lifts in his shoes? He was a huge man . . .

RM He wasn't that huge. I was passing his office one time and he was goddamning and laying everybody out, really going for the place, knocking the chairs over. He beckoned me, so I went in and he brought out a jug and poured two drinks and he said, 'Got to keep them Wayne-conscious!' That was his business, being Duke Wayne.

DM So he had to be bigger than everyone else?

RM Damn right.

DM Did you get on well with him?

RM Very well. He used to talk about directing me in a picture. We were working at nights in old Tucson and Duke was sitting outside his trailer putting his wig on and he said, 'Goddamn it, Mitch! When are you going to let me direct you in a picture?' and I said, 'Duke, that's all you ever do anyway.' Duke couldn't help directing. We had a lot of fellows in the film who were in their first picture and Duke would pull them around, and I'd say, 'Duke, would you for God's sake leave those kids alone, you're scaring the bejeesus out of me!' and he said, 'I know I ought to keep my mouth shut, but Jesus Christ!' He just couldn't contain himself.

DM What about Joseph Losey, who directed you in *Secret Ceremony*? There was a bath-tub scene, wasn't there? You were *in* the tub, you *weren't* in it; nobody knew quite what was happening in the tub. Did *you*?

RM No. I was supposed to be in the tub with Mia Farrow, but then I was replaced by Elizabeth [Taylor]. I guess I just didn't fit in the tub with Mia, and Elizabeth was a lot smaller. I guess they couldn't get a bigger tub, so they threw Liz in. I never did figure that out.

DM Did you enjoy making that film?

RM Sure, I enjoyed working with Elizabeth and Mia.

DM Was Losey a director you admired?

RM We didn't hear much from him; he was just a presence, he was there. We worked here in England and then over in Holland for a while, but I don't remember Joe as particularly obtrusive.

DM I think he was very busy photographing the rooms in that house as much as the actors.

RM Yes, that was a weird place. I found it was a home for demented nuns or something like that . . . people streaking through the halls.

DM What about David Lean? You made *Ryan's Daughter* with him, and it took months and months to shoot. That must have been a pretty boring business.

RM Not at all. I enjoyed the Irish countryside, and I had to accept it and get used to it because I was there for the better part of eleven months. There were times, weeks on end, when I never worked, and the crew would say, 'Why don't you come out on the set? It's like death without you there.' So I'd come out on the set and David would say, 'Who's that laughing? Why are they laughing? Are they laughing at *us*? Are they with us or against us?' And if I didn't come, the crew showed no interest in this film at all. It was a strange experience . . . and David found it very difficult to speak my name; he would say, 'So-and-so.' You had to wring it out of him.

DM Wasn't it Robert Bolt who phoned you and asked you to do the film in the first place? – on rather peculiar terms, I seem to remember.

RM Well, I unwittingly answered the phone one Sunday afternoon and it was Robert and David calling about the film, and I said, 'I'm sure you can find somebody else, there must be a lot of Irish actors out of work.' They said, 'No, we particularly want you,' and on and on. Finally Robert said, 'Did you have anything else in mind?' and I said, 'Yes, I had planned suicide. No further questions.' So he said, 'Well, if you would do this film first, then I'd be happy to stand the expense of your burial,' so I said, 'OK, I'll be there', and I went.

DM Lean has been very copious in his praise of you subsequently, and I'd be interested to know what you thought about him.

RM Well, David is a master visualist, and I don't know that he has enough time or scope to fulfil himself completely – or enough money. I've never seen anyone as devoted to the medium as David Lean, it's a wonder to watch him work, and it's most rewarding and gratifying to see the results that he achieves through his devotion. I think he's a master – mad, but a master.

DM One of my favourite films of yours is *Farewell My Lovely*, which was directed by Dick Richards. Did you enjoy doing that?

RM Yes I did, very much. Dick Richards we called 'Itchy McGinnis', he was like this all the time. When Jack O'Halloran first came to work . . .

DM Jack O'Halloran was the heavyweight boxer who plays Moose Malloy?

RM Yeah, and we were at the top of the stairs of this saloon. Dick would say, 'Roll it! Wait a minute, could you move that lamp over? OK, roll! No, cut! Are you going to be *there*? Roll it! Cut!' This went on and on for twenty or thirty minutes, and finally Dick said, 'Roll it, roll it! Are you rolling? Cut!' – so they cut. O'Halloran said to me, 'Is that the way they do it?' and I said,

'No, usually they say "Action!" or something like that,' and he said, 'Yes, I thought so, I've seen it in the movies. Do you think we're in trouble?' I said, 'We're in trouble,' and we were. But he got himself together every now and then to get the picture done, and we enjoyed it.

DM What about the remake of *The Big Sleep* which you made in London with Michael Winner?

RM That's another character, isn't it? Michael is so outrageous, I think he's very funny. He went his way, he blew up the trees, he set fire to the house. I said, 'But the poor woman who *owns* the house!' and he said, 'Nonsense! I can keep it out of court for years! By the time it comes to court, it'll all have grown back. Silly bitch won't get a penny!' Blew the whole joint down.

DM He likes to have the action going one way and then another, doesn't he?

RM Yes, he does, in close quarters especially. When everything is going *this* way, he puts the cameras and shoots *that* way, and then *this* way, and everyone is crashing into each other, and he falls down in hysterics with laughter and says, 'Idiots! You stupid, clumsy idiots!' He gets a great joy out of it.

DM You think he actually likes being a film director just for that?

RM Oh God, he wouldn't have it any other way, would he?

DM And I think he stands there, doesn't he, waiting for a pencil?

RM He has a boy at his left shoulder, two steps to the rear, half a step to the left. He puts his hand out . . . the boy needs to be psychic: it's either a cigar, a pencil, a scratch pad or the script, and this guy has to know or he gets a reading off. 'Idiot!' He doesn't even turn around to score him out, just shouts it over his shoulder. He has to have a chair at the ready, everything, and he loves that he has a cabin boy whom he whips constantly all day long.

DM Well, I don't think that would be a very good description of

DM Peter Yates, with whom you made another very good film, *The Friends of Eddie Coyle*.

RM Oh, no. Peter is a gentleman, a very charming man, a very nice smooth, easy fellow.

DM Did you enjoy doing that?

RM Yeah. We were surrounded by all the teamsters, all the thugs of Boston. George Higgins, who wrote the book, was the Assistant US Attorney General for that New England area, and he said, 'Some of those characters you are associating with are criminals, they *are* really!' I said, 'What do you want from me? Those are our technical advisers!' They were all safe-crackers and hijackers, and he'd been trying for a long time to get an indictment on them for gambling fixing and the fixing of sporting events. He finally quit in frustration, and I guess the man who succeeded him eventually got it done because I get letters from a couple of them from Leavenworth Penitentiary – they'll be out next year. I enjoyed it very much. I'm sure a lot of the dialogue which was very authentic, must have come from inadmissible tapes. You know, being a US Attorney General, Mr Higgins had taken all these illegal tapes and listened to all the cons' conversations and transferred them to paper. Very effective; I liked it.

DM You had your own production company for some time, and I think the first film you made with it was *Thunder Road*, which has become a cult movie now. The director is almost unknown, a very shadowy figure called Arthur Ripley.

RM Well, Arthur was not commercially well-known, of course, but he had made a film called *Voice in the Wind* (1944) with Francis Lederer – an excellent film, which he shot in three days. He was a very gifted man and a drinking fellow – a tall, sonorous, big-nose character from Brooklyn – and he was teaching at UCLA when we nailed him. The same scripts had kept turning up and they were not very exciting, and someone said, 'Why don't you do one of your own stories?' So I dragged one out and I got a friend, Jim Phillips, to work on it with me, and he went back to Washington and did a lot of research with the Treasury Department and then the North Carolina Alcoholic Beverages Department. As a matter of fact, a lot of our special effects we sold to the original Bond film – all the car stuff, damn near the whole of our budget. When I first went to United Artists they said, 'How much is this going to cost?' and I said, 'It will cost us between $350,000 and $750,000.' They asked why the discrepancy, and I said, 'The more we screw up, the more it's going to cost, obviously.' In the end it cost about $400,000. When they got it back in the projection room they said, 'What the hell *is* this?' They couldn't figure it out. I did a couple of the songs and some of the music, and we ferreted out a lot of people and ruined their lives by putting them in the picture. I think there was only one real survivor and that was Mitch Ryan, who has done fairly well. The rest of them became unglued, fell apart.

DM Besides writing music you've written poetry too, haven't you? . . .

RM Yes.

DM Do you write any poetry or music now?

RM No.

DM Why not?

RM I'm otherwise occupied. I just don't find the time or the inclination, really.

DM You wrote some of the music for an oratorio that was performed in Los Angeles – I think Orson Welles produced it. That was in aid of Jewish refugees, wasn't it?

RM Yes, it was the first Israeli bond rally, in Hollywood Bowl. A dialectitian named Benny Reuben did it. He had red make-up on, and he went through all the characters and changes of lights and then, at the very end – I think the line was, 'Hear me, brother, hear me say I was *born* a refugee' – we turned a green light on him and suddenly he was in black-face. Very clever, it brought the house down. He was delighted.

DM What about *The Winds of War*? Was that a bore to do?

RM At times, sure, because you read the travel posters and it sounds very exciting and engaging, but when you get there, not quite so. We finished in LA just before Christmas, and when we arrived in Zagreb in Yugoslavia it was minus twenty and still falling. We went out in the country, and you're eight miles from the toilet and when you get there it's frozen. Lunch or dinner was bean and barley mash, that was it – you could set a telephone pole in it – and a slice of bread that thick to make a sandwich you have to be a crocodile to get your mouth around. There were no amenities at all. Then, when we were working in Yugoslavia and Vienna, there was no snow. When they went there on location scouting in October or November there was snow, but not in January or February. They used that ground-up plastic and everybody behind the camera had a mask on, but in front of the camera we were sucking it up.

DM I think we might open this up for some questions from the audience.

Audience What are your hobbies and interests?

RM That's a very difficult question to answer. Unfortunately I have some horses, and I breed and raise them. I pay the bills, when they win my son owns them, and when they lose I own them. That's about it, really.

Aud Do you do a lot of reading?

RM A lot of dreary scripts, yes.

Aud Would you consider doing a stage play in London?

RM I doubt it, I really doubt it.

Aud Why not?

RM It's a lot of hard work.

Aud Many of your contemporaries, like Burt Lancaster and Kirk Douglas and John Wayne, have got around to directing one or two movies. Have you never been tempted to try your hand at directing?

RM Well, the director usually has to get there in the morning before the actors do, he has to stay there after they've gone, he has to go to the projection room and watch the rushes, he has to talk to the producer . . . I don't think so, I think I'll stick with what I've got.

Aud Which is more important to you in choosing a project: the script, or your fellow actors and actresses?

RM The script, really.

Aud Mr Mitchum, you've been a hero to many people for many years, is there anyone whom you yourself have particularly admired through your life, may we know who this is, and may we know the qualities in them that you admire, please?

RM Well, I really never thought of that, you know, but after being in Israel through the winter and walking the Via Dolorosa, I began to have a great respect for Jesus Christ, because I tell you, if *I* was packing that cross I'd have said, 'Fellas, do what you have to do, but I'm not packing this cross another foot.' Really, I'd just sit down and quit right there.

Aud Which films are you most proud and pleased with, Mr Mitchum, and are there any performances you feel have been unduly neglected by critics and film historians?

RM Some of them have been over-remembered, I would say, I don't think any have been neglected. I should think *Night of the Hunter, The Sundowners, Heaven Knows, Mr Allison* . . . I really can't say. I think *The Friends of Eddie Coyle* was a decent film. Usually when I think about films I just hark back to a pleasurable location and how easy it was to make.

The quality of the film itself is out of my control; it has nothing to do with me.

Aud Mr Mitchum, one of the most notorious events in your career was a very early conviction for pot-smoking.

RM It was for conspiracy to possess.

Aud What influence did it have on your career?

RM It didn't have much influence. It prohibited me from playing boy scouts and nuns, choirboys, things like that. The charge was resubmitted, thrown out for lack of evidence and expunged from the record. I was in the place for seven minutes.

Aud So you were innocent?

RM That's what the judge said. I would say morally guilty, factually innocent. I regard myself as morally guilty of almost anything you can conjure up.

Aud You've always been extremely relaxed, not to say laconic, about the films in which you've appeared. In your long career, are there really no projects about which you feel in retrospect genuinely angry, or mad that you made them or about the way in which they emerged?

RM No.

Aud Could you tell us a bit about working with John Huston, and also with Deborah Kerr, because the co-starring of you and Deborah Kerr seems very unlikely, but in fact produced marvellous results.

RM That's the first time I ever heard that – I thought it was ideal casting. Deborah is a delight. She could be anywhere in the world and I could be here and we could get the whole thing done through clairvoyance; she is absolutely a delight for me to work with. John is sort of a legend . . . Again, its like working with Laughton – you look behind the camera to see how John is reacting and you wait for that and it's very rewarding. I think in all the time working with him the only thing he said to me was, 'Even more, Bob! Even more!' I said, 'Really, John?' and he said, 'Even more!'

Aud You mentioned *The Sundowners* . . . Did you really shear all those sheep?

RM I sheared a number of them, and I found out what hard work it is. I was appalled because I kept nicking little pieces off; I would nick off a little tit or something. Didn't bother the other guys at all – they just put some tar on it, and if it was a big gash they would just stitch it up and chase them out. Very cavalier treatment of a woolly.

Aud Mr Mitchum, I presume you do your own stunts . . .

RM I *did* my own stunts, and as a result I no longer do them because I've had a lot of close shaves and a lot of broken bones.

Aud Two questions: firstly, did you ever work with Ronald Reagan? and secondly, has his performance improved in the last four years?

RM I've never worked with him, no, and I think his performance has improved. He was a friend of Robert Taylor, and we occasionally had dinner with Robert and Ursula and Ronnie Reagan, and you never wanted to tell a joke or anything because he really was the supreme eagle scout. I think the Oval Office has loosened him up a little, he jokes it up a little more now than he did before.

Aud Could you tell me something about a film which no one has ever mentioned, and which never got a theatrical release over here? You played a father who had been inside for murdering his wife . . .

RM The film was *Going Home* (1971) with Jan Michael Vincent and Brenda Vaccaro. There was a script going around about a bunch of washed-up jazz musicians in San Francisco and I kind of liked it, I thought it would be a pleasant exercise, and I talked to the people who were involved in it. They came back to the office a week or two later, and I thought it was the same people, and we agreed on everything without being too specific. When they were leaving I said, 'I'll see you in San Francisco,' and they said, 'Wildwood, New Jersey,' so I thought, 'Well, they've changed the location, that's all right.' A couple of days later I asked my secretary, 'Why did they change the location to Wildwood-by-the-Sea, New Jersey?' and she said, 'They didn't.' I said, 'I signed for the wrong picture?' 'Yes,' she said. That's how I happened to do *Going Home*.

Aud You've shown us this afternoon what a wonderful mimic you are, and you've used accents in *The Sundowners* and in *Ryan's Daughter*. Do you wish you could have had more outlet for using accents in your films?

RM No. It's like . . . I have horses, and people ask me if I ride, and I do if I have good cause for it, that's all.

Aud Mr Mitchum, do you think you might like to be in a soap opera?

RM I don't know, I've never thought about it. As a matter of fact, up until last night I'd never seen one. I saw Joan Collins last night shaking her head, but prior to that I'd never seen a chapter of a soap opera.

Aud Since you obviously have all the vocal, physical and intellectual equipment to do a classical part, is it because you don't want to, or does no one ever think of you for Shakespeare, or Molière, or any of those?

RM Well, they don't do too much Shakespeare and Molière on film.

Aud Some.

RM Some? It's never come to my attention.

Aud Well, there's *Henry V* and *Hamlet* . . .

RM It's been done, hasn't it?

Aud There's always television.

RM Yes, unfortunately there is.

DM I think John Huston said that you ought to play King Lear, but perhaps you could double up as the clown, too.

RM Yeah.

Aud You once said you've learned two things about being an actor: one was that you couldn't act, and the other was that it didn't matter. Well, some of us think you're a very great actor . . . [*Prolonged applause*] You obviously go to great pains to underplay your talent. Why is this?

RM I never said I couldn't act. I've always had a horror of doing a turn, of standing back there and trying to draw attention to myself. I figure that if the director wants you, he'll move in to get you, and if one hair moved on that giant seventy-foot screen they'll see it, really. I told someone the other day that if you look at someone like Spencer Tracy when he's playing a big close-up, and he just moves like that, you say, 'My God, what control!' because . . . well, it's all there. His head is sixty feet high and his eyes big enough to drive through, and everything becomes apparent. I don't think it's necessary to go through the whole thing in profile. If directors want it, they'll get it. That's what they're paid for.

Aud In view of your laid-back attitude to your job, does all your success surprise you, or is it something you were consciously working towards?

RM Well, it was something gradual, not like you suddenly walk out of the door and – pow! there it is. I remember the first time I saw myself on the screen in a public theatre. My wife and I were sitting there behind three women, and I appeared on the screen and one of them grabbed the other and said, 'My God, who *is* that? That is the most *depraved* face I've ever seen!' The word spread.

Aud What is your attitude to the new generation of actors who take hours exploring their motivation? How do you rate those people compared to your own attitude to your work?

RM I've seen three films in the last ten years, so I haven't seen very many of them, I'm just glad I don't have to finance them. Other than that I know very little about them.

Aud If you hadn't been an actor, what might you have been instead?

RM Oh God, I don't know. I don't think I would have survived. I probably would have been a writer – you know, a lonely, crippled writer. But this was a Godsend to me. It just came along – playing cops and robbers, cowboys and Indians, free lunch, getting paid for what you like to do.

DM Well, Bob, it's been going now for nearly two hours, so I think we ought to let you go. You know, someone said to me, 'Are you *really* interviewing Bob Mitchum? That's going to be difficult!' But it's not been difficult, it's been very easy. It's been a great pleasure to me and to everyone here, and I hope you'll come back.

RM Oh, I bet you say that to all the girls.

Notes

1 Robert Mitchum was employed as a sheet-metal worker at Lockheed, Burbank, in 1941–2.

2 Harry 'Pop' Sherman, an independent producer who made the Hopalong Cassidy Westerns.

7 Margarethe von Trotta

Margarethe von Trotta was born in Berlin in 1942. She studied German and Latin literature in Munich and Paris, and then took courses in Dramatic Arts in Munich, Stuttgart and Frankfurt. In 1968 she began to work as an actress in film and television, and during the following eight years she appeared in nearly twenty productions, including two films by Rainer Werner Fassbinder, *Götter der Pest* (*Gods of the Plague*) (1969) and *The American Soldier* (1970), a French TV movie directed by Claude Chabrol, *Une invitation à la chasse* (1973), and seven films directed by Volker Schlöndorff, whom she married in 1971. Her first film with Schlöndorff was *Baal* (1969), and thereafter she became increasingly involved in the production of his films, first as a writer and then as a collaborating director. They co-wrote the screenplays of *The Sudden Wealth of the Poor People of Kombach* (1970), *Strohfeuer* (*Summer Lightning*) (1972), *Coup de Grâce* (1976) and *Die Falschung* (1980), and they co-wrote and co-directed *The Lost Honour of Katharina Blum* (1975). Margarethe von Trotta made her solo directorial debut with *The Second Awakening of Christa Klages* (1978), and rapidly established herself as one of the most distinguished European film-makers of her generation. Her later films include *Sisters, or the Balance of Happiness* (1979), *The German Sisters* (1981), *Friends and Husbands* (1983), *Rosa Luxemburg* (1985), the episode entitled 'Eva' in *Felix* (1987), *Love and Fear* (1988) and *Die Ruckkehr L'Africana* (*The Return*) (1990). She also wrote the screenplay for *Unerreichbare Nahe* (1984), directed by Dagmar Hirtz, and in 1984 she made her only acting appearance in recent years in Zanussi's *Blaubart* (*Bluebeard*). *The German Sisters*, which remains, perhaps, her supreme achievement to date, won the Golden Lion at the Venice Film Festival.

The following lecture was given on 26 August 1986. Margarethe von Trotta was interviewed by Sheila Johnston, a film critic and journalist.

Margarethe von Trotta

Sheila Johnston Since so many of us have just seen your new film about Rosa Luxemburg, I thought that we could start by exploring some of the background to that, so I'd like to ask you to begin with how you became involved with this material.

Margarethe von Trotta My first meeting with Rosa was in the late 1960s – 1968 and 1969 in Germany, during the student rebellion. They carried around all these portraits of very important revolutionary men, like Lenin and Marx and Ho Chi Minh, and the only woman amongst all these portraits was Rosa. I looked at her, and I felt she was not just a type to be carried around in the streets, because her portrait was not just an activist face; she had such a very interiorized and rather sad face that I was fascinated by her. I bought some books and some letters and some political writings, and I went on reading her, but without knowing that one day I would do a film about her. I was still an actress and I didn't see that one day I would have the *possibility*, even if I'd already had the wish, to become a director. This was still the time when, for a woman, it was not so easy to go into directing, rather than being a script girl, or a costume lady, or the other jobs that women used to get in the cinema. Then in 1982, Fassbinder wanted to do a film on Rosa Luxemburg – it was his very last project – and when he died, the producer came to me and asked me to take it over. In the first place I was a little bit horrified, because I was so fond of Fassbinder and he was a friend of mine and he had just died, but then I thought that it might be not only a chance to rehabilitate Rosa, but also a sort of homage to Fassbinder. A script had already been written for him by Peter Märthesheimer, who also did *Lola*, *Veronika Voss* and *The Marriage of Maria Braun* – though, of course, Fassbinder used to change the scripts a lot. He assigned the scripts to Peter, but then after that he altered them according to his needs, though this time he hadn't had the opportunity to do that. So the producer gave me this script, but . . . well, it had been done for somebody else and I said, 'I have to go my own way and find my own vision of this woman.' The writing and the shooting of the film took me three years, and there were financial problems, because in the beginning the producer said he had all the money, but then he hadn't. So I had to find it myself.

SJ How useful did you find Rosa's own letters and writings? How relevant were they to your project?

MVT There are five volumes of her letters now edited – that's about 2,500 letters – and they were very, very important for me, because her political writings are brilliant. I read them several times, and if you know them you will also know that she had very much her own special language, and I tried to preserve that in the film. That was my main criticism of the script by Peter Märthesheimer, who didn't have one speech or one sentence of hers in the script, because he thought that the speeches might be too difficult for audiences. But I think her personality is so linked to her language that you can't just invent your own speeches and put them in her mouth. Therefore all that you hear in the speeches are her own words, though in the English subtitles it's perhaps a little bit reduced. She uses very poetical and very sensitive language in her letters, and if she hadn't been a revolutionary, she could have been a novelist or a poet.

SJ You spoke of the need to rehabilitate Rosa. Can you explain what you meant by that, and why you felt it was necessary?

MVT Well, in Germany there are two clichés: the right-wing cliché that she was only the bloody and cruel Rosa, and the left-wing cliché that she was only the political martyr. But in between there was nothing, and when the students were carrying around Rosa's portrait, I felt that even they didn't know exactly what she was. In the early 1970s a stamp was issued bearing her face, and there were postal employees who refused to frank it because it was Rosa Luxemburg, and there were even people who were getting private letters with this stamp on them and refusing to take them! So I had the feeling that she was one of the most important women in German history – actually, she was Polish, a Polish Jew, but she did her main work in Germany

– and I wanted to give her the chance to speak to people now. The film is not complete; it's really a fragment of her life, a fragment of her thoughts. In two hours you can't give the complete universe of such a brilliant person. But I tried to make a balance between her political thinking and her personal life, because I think she's one of the very few politicians who lived her private life according to what she said in public. Politicians always have big programmes and they say big words, but if you look closer, then you see that they are living in a quite different way, whereas Rosa lived very authentically. Her thoughts and her programme entered her personal life, too.

SJ Could you say something about the difficulties you had in finding someone to play this role?

MVT I think that's the last question I will answer from the stage, and then I think it's better if we go into a public discussion – it's more vivid. In the beginning, I wanted to have a real Polish–Jewish actress speaking German, and I went to Poland and I spoke with several actresses, and also with directors, but then I realized that, in Poland, Rosa Luxemburg is more or less hated because she was a communist and an internationalist. Some actresses told me that they couldn't play the part because they would be lynched in their country if they did, and there was a theatre director who said to me, 'But why do you want to get her out of the canal? Let her stay there!' At first I found that very cynical, but then I understand the situation of Poland, and I think that they were judging on the basis of what Poland is like nowadays . . . Perhaps they no longer feel that Rosa is a great personality of their own. Daniel Olbrychski, who plays Rosa's lover, Leo Jogiches, was very against the film in the beginning, but then when we worked together and spoke about Rosa so much, and he changed his mind, and afterwards he said that it would have been impossible to bring this film to Poland and discuss it there. So I didn't find the actress, not only because they were against playing the part, but also because I didn't find the *right* one. In the beginning I always thought that there must be some resemblance physically, but when I found an actress who resembled her a little bit it was *more* annoying, because it was always *not quite* the face – near it, but a bit wrong. Then I had the idea of casting Barbara Sukowa, who does not look like Rosa, but who has the temperament and the character, and a convincing way of speaking and behaving. So because I had already worked with her on *The German Sisters*, and we knew each other, and I knew that she was very, very involved in our political situation in Germany, I asked her to do it.

Audience Did you ever think of doing it in black and white?

MVT No. I would like to do a film in black and white, but not a historical one – it was too obvious for me. It would look like a real documentary then, and I didn't want to pretend it was a documentary. It's fiction; it's very authentic, but it's still fiction, and it's a very subjective selection of things on my part.

Aud Having the same actress play both Rosa Luxemburg and Gudrun Ensslin could almost be a political statement in itself!

MVT It was not supposed to be, but now it is. In the film, when Rosa and Leo are in Poland, he reads a text about terrorist actions, and she was very against that. She was opposed to that kind of political individualism, so she would not have agreed with the actions of Gudrun Ensslin. In fact, in my film *The German Sisters* I had a portrait of Rosa on the desk of the *older* sister, *not* the sister based on Gudrun Ensslin, and at that time I said to Jutta Lampe, who played the older sister, 'One day we will do a film about Rosa.' I thought then that Jutta would play the role. In *The German Sisters* I tried to demonstrate to some extent the roots of this so-called terrorism in our country, and to show that it came out of the disasters of our history and out of Fascism. Rosa for me is the first victim of the Fascists, because the people who killed her, in the end, became Fascists and followers of Hitler.

Aud Who *was* responsible for Rosa's murder? Was it the government in power, was it the Social Democrats?

MVT Well, the Social Democrats came into the government because the right-wing General Ludendorff[1] saw that Germany would lose the First World War, and he didn't want to take the responsibility. As you know, Germany had to sign the peace contract with the American President, and the military wanted to put the blame on the Social Democrats and and make it look as though *they* lost the war. The right-wing Social Democrats, like Ebert and Scheidemann,[2] were very proud to be finally in power, but they were not very revolutionary; they were very bourgeois already, and for them Karl Liebknecht and Rosa Luxemburg were a danger. They knew about the plan to kill both of them, and they didn't interfere. The actual killing was carried out by right-wing officers and soldiers, but Ebert knew about it, and so that's the guilt of this time for the Social Democratic Party.

Aud You're not going to be popular with those people, are you?

MVT No! They think that's just history; they have nothing to do with it.

Aud Did you get a reaction from them about the film?

MVT No, I don't know the reaction. I only know that in the Vorwäts, the ex-main journal of the Social Democratic Party, there was one critic who wrote that there is a trail of blood from Ebert, who knew about the killing of Rosa and did nothing about it, to Schmidt, who knew about Stammheim[3] and did nothing about it. That was speculation – nobody knows if Schmidt really knew about it or not – but Schmidt was very angry, and he managed to throw out the critic and the editor. So that was a reaction!

Aud Did you have trouble getting finance for the film?

MVT I *always* have trouble, with *every* film, but then in the end it works. *Rosa* was the most expensive film for me till now.

SJ What was the arrangement with Fassbinder, then? Had he set up a production deal with somebody when he died?

MVT Yes, It seemed so, because when Fassbinder died, the producer came to me and said he had twelve million Deutschmarks, but then he turned out to have nothing. He believed he could get the money on Fassbinder's name, and then he believed he could get it on *my* name, but it was much more difficult to do that. But we have a production company of our own – Volker Schlöndorff, Reinhard Hauff and Eberhard Junkersdorf, who is a producer – and so they took over the project and tried to get the money.

Aud I'd like to ask if one can see a train of thought about the relationship of the state to women in the series of female characters you've portrayed in your films? I'm not interested in the feminist side of it as much . . .

MVT Why not?!

Aud Well, yes, that as well . . . but in a more general political sense, in the context of Germany?

MVT In fact, Rosa didn't think of herself as a feminist, though I think she was, in her way. She wanted children and a family and love with her friend Leo, and on the other hand she wanted to work and to be a political being. That's the important point, I think, for every woman who wants to work and express herself outside the home or the personal relationship. Rosa wanted so much to have both things, and I think that's very legitimate, but the man was not on her level. He only accepted that she was a revolutionary, and when she said she wanted to have a child, he said, 'But your children are your ideas.' I think that's a very crucial moment in her life, when she sits down with the cat at the table; it's very sad, the cat's like a substitute for this child she couldn't have. I met a woman who knew Rosa personally. She was 92 years old, and she was Rosa's student when she gave lessons at the Social Democratic School in Berlin, and she told me about this scene with the cat. It's not in any of the biographies; that's not a scene for the historians! She told me that she was invited once by Rosa to have lunch with her, and she went to her home and there were three plates on the table, so she thought perhaps the third plate was for the housemaid, but it was for the cat. The cat was really sitting like an adult person at the table and eating very correctly, and I thought that that was such an extraordinary image – this woman who is supposed to be the most brilliant and intellectual person sitting there eating with the cat. That shows her solitude so much that I had to put it in the film. It was very difficult to domesticate the cat to do it.

Aud Do you think she represents anything specific about women as revolutionaries?

MVT Well, as I said, she is really the only person I know who was politically involved at that time who really lived in the way she proclaimed you have to live, and I think *that* is probably a woman's behaviour – to really stay with what you are thinking. The last time we had a change of government in Germany, the Liberals sided first with the left-wing, the Social Democrats, and then they changed to the right, because they thought that the right would come to power, and the only members of the Liberal Party in our country who stood out against this change just for the power were women. I found the same behaviour in Rosa.

Aud Are you more concerned with individuals or with politics?

MVT But what's the difference between individuals and politics? I don't see much difference. I think we are all living in a certain society, we are all very constrained by its ideologies and its power, and we are all suffering by it. So if you are an individual and you are suffering in your family, for me that's political too, and it's political to show it. In some films I speak openly about politics, like in *Rosa*, and in other films I show only individual relationships, but they are all political as well.

Aud *Rosa* has been criticized in this country in a review in *City*

Limits which says that the film undervalues Rosa's politics and shows them as not being relevant for today. What would you say about that?

MVT Judge for yourself. I don't want to defend myself, though I *do* think her politics are relevant for today, especially what she is saying about militarism, and about peace and war. For example, her speech about forty years of peace – you could give the same speech today . . . I mean, it's a whole life, and she wrote so much – what can you put in two hours? Everybody has a chance to go on and read her, and that was my aim with the film: to create an interest in her person and her ideas, and then people can go and look more deeply into her thoughts. I think that's the only thing you can do in a film.

Aud While I can see that you can't include Rosa Luxemburg's whole life, I was a little bit surprised that there's really not much mention of the 1917 Revolution in Russia. When she was in jail and the date kept being shown on the screen, I kept thinking, '1917 – surely this will show her being revitalized, even though she's still in prison,' but the Revolution isn't mentioned until one of her comrades in the Spartacist Rising talks about it. You *did* mention the Revolution of 1905, and I wonder why 1917, which was obviously much more important and successful, didn't come into it as much?

MVT Yes, she first *was* revitalized by the October Revolution, and then she was very soon disappointed by Lenin and by his strategy, and she wrote an article where she criticized this authoritarian, elitist way of handling the Revolution. I tried to include it at first, and I had actually shot some scenes about it, but then I felt it was too superficial simply to jump in and then leave it, and that if you were going to deal with the Russian Revolution, you would have to do it very much more seriously and give much more space to the discussion of what she was thinking about it. So I left it out, and I just illustrated her work and her way of thinking with German history and the German revolution. But in fact it *is* a lack, and there are also flaws in the way I show the German revolution, because that was much more complicated and had many more nuances than I showed. I would like to make a film only about those two months one day to show everything that really happened. As for the 1905 Revolution, I put it in because that was, for her, the really big hope, and she came back to Germany and thought that now, all the German Social Democrats would be enthusiastic and would follow in that direction. Then she realized that they were already much too conformist or reformist in their thinking, that they were not willing to go this way, and for her whole life in Germany that was the main point of her struggle.

SJ To what extent was what you were able to show in the film dictated by your financial limitations? I'm wondering about the emphasis on the intimate aspects of Rosa's life . . .

MVT No, that was not a question of finances, that was my choice. I wanted to show them both.

Aud Your previous four films all gave us a little hope at the end; *Rosa* is the first one where you haven't done that.

MVT You feel that the film is pessimistic? Well, that's history! It's a sad end, and I couldn't show it in another way. I mean, the fact that she was killed three times – that was *very* important for me. In all our fairy tales, in the Grimm stories, there is always this magic number three – you have to do something three times to make it true, to make it real – and here she is killed, in a way, three times. They shoot her, then they shoot her again, and then they throw her in the canal. They had to kill her three times to make it real, so you can imagine how afraid they were of this very small, physically very weak person; they were so afraid of her ideas. That's very German behaviour. So that was the end, but then you see the canal, and the water of the canal, and it goes on – until now. For me, the last image means that it's really history that is going on, and it's always a little bit like that. It comes to us and it's still our guilt. I think that somebody like her could be killed in this way now.

Aud I would like to say thank you very much for your wonderful films. I really enjoy them, I think they're wonderful . . . [*Applause*]

MVT That's a good end! [*Laughter*] No? No? OK!

Aud . . . and I wanted to say that a sad ending doesn't necessarily mean that a film is pessimistic, because I think that what comes through in Rosa Luxemburg's political writings is the idea of never giving up and the idea that revolution is possible. If you go away with that feeling, it can help you to do something.

MVT That's true. It's a pessimistic end in the historical facts, but her behaviour and her attitude, her patience, her courage, her belief in history, her refusal of resignation – that's something very encouraging. She had so much patience with herself and with history. Nowadays you throw away products and ideas very quickly. When they are not effective in one or two years, then you throw them away, and I think it's very important to look at a person who does *not* throw away her beliefs and who really stays with it, even in prison and even if she is killed by it. I think that's something important.

Aud I don't know whether there has been a mistake in the translation, but in the English credit at the beginning of the film it described Luxemburg as a pacifist. Now, of course, her opposition to militarism is not an opposition to revolutionary war, and I don't believe that Rosa Luxemburg *was* committed to non-violence; she was committed to the use of arms, if need be, in the revolutionary movement. I thought your film was extremely exciting and beautiful, but I did feel that you'd erred by presenting Luxemburg as a pacifist, or someone who believed in the peaceful road to socialism.

MVT You are right. The expression 'pacifist' in the opening credit is perhaps not very well-chosen, because she *was* for the struggles of the working class, but she was also against violence. She was for the working people taking over the power, but only in a moment when they are strong enough to take the power without bloodshed. That is in her testament, in the manifesto she wrote for the foundation of the Communist Party, and Liebknecht confirms this too. They were not for blood and for violence, but for the real revolutionary movement, and therefore, in the end, Rosa was against the uprising in 1918, because she felt that it was not yet the moment. It was a moment where it would end in a bloody struggle, but not in the taking of power, and therefore she says, 'We have to wait.' I think that towards the end of her life, that was her main problem. She saw that at this very moment of taking power people would be killed, on both sides, and yet she liked animals and she liked flowers, and she found it extremely difficult to reconcile liking these things with being in favour of a bloody revolution. That was the point for me. Perhaps that's my own interpretation, but it *is* documented that in the last two weeks of her life, she fainted several times a day. I show that, and I think that was the very moment she realized that it is a problem to love the whole of mankind and nature and all that, and at the same time to continue in a bloody political struggle.

Aud But she never excluded the armed struggle if it came to that . . .

MVT No, no, she never did, intellectually or in her writings, but . . . you know, there's one letter where she talks about her cat catching a bird and killing it, and she had a heart attack because of that; she had to take pills, because she loved birds and yet she loved the cat . . . You have to read this letter – it's really very, very impressive – and that was one part of her character. She wanted to take the power with arms and with struggle, but in her other personal feelings she was just not able to accept that you have to kill people to have the power. She said that, on the one hand, you have to be a very energetic revolutionary, but on the other, going into a revolution and killing a worm because you are not attentive enough is a crime. That's a real breath of socialism, to have the most revolutionary energy and the greatest humanism.

Aud I was just wondering why Rosa Luxemburg didn't really try and communicate with the other prisoners when she was in jail, which might have been a good chance for her to communicate her ideas.

MVT She couldn't because she was kept isolated.

Aud Oh, I see, I got the idea that she chose it . . .

MVT No, no. She was not a real political prisoner; she wasn't imprisoned for an actual political or criminal act. She was in preventive detention so that she couldn't speak against the war outside, so they had to isolate her in the prison, too.

Aud The music in *Rosa* is very beautiful. Can you tell us how you work with your composer Nicolas Economou?

MVT *Rosa* is already the third film for which he did the music, so we work very closely together. I always said to Nicolas, 'You must compose a requiem,' because for me the film was a requiem, and when I was shooting I kept on thinking of the Requiem of Verdi. For me, the film was more a lamentation for a dead woman than a very activist sort of film, so I wanted to make my lamentation clear in the music. I don't know if you felt it, but that's what I meant.

Aud What did you find out about Rosa's relationship with Clara Zetkin? Was it a very close relationship?

MVT Yes, it was. She had two main women friends: Luise Kautsky, who is in the film too, and Clara Zetkin.[4] With Luise it was much more a sort of classical woman's friendship, but Rosa and Clara were comrades, they fought together. Both of the women, and all of the other characters around Rosa, are a little bit too weakly drawn for their real personality, I think. I didn't do enough justice to the other persons. Clara Zetkin was a very strong and very important woman in her own right.

Aud I was surprised that you can do a film about Rosa Luxemburg without mentioning her most famous remark, that freedom is always the freedom of others. Was that on purpose?

MVT Yes. That's a very famous phrase and I had a scene with this phrase in it, but then I cut it out, because it's so cliched, you know? The only thing everybody knows about Rosa is this sentence, and it's just . . .

Aud So it *was* on purpose?

MVT On purpose, first to put it in and then to put it out. [*Laughter*]

Aud Do you think Rainer Werner Fassbinder would have liked your version of the film?

MVT Well, he certainly would have done it in a different way, but he was very fond of my films, so I don't think he would be very opposed.

Aud You're a great director, but you're also a marvellous actress. Are you planning to do any more acting, or are you now working full-time as a director?

MVT Mainly I look at myself as a director now, because it was always my wish to be a director in the first place and becoming an actress was only a detour, to learn about it. At that time there was no possibility of becoming a director, so I ended as an actress . . . but now Zanussi wants me to act on one of his films, and I think I will do it.

Aud Can I ask how you feel about East Germany and about the two Germanys?

MVT Well, that would be another film! I want to do a film about that with Christa Wolf, the East German novelist. It's easier for me than for her, you know, but one day we will do something on that. I love her work very, very much. I showed her my script for *Rosa* and told her all about my adventures during my research, and she said, 'But why don't you put it in the film? You must show the very subjective way in which you encountered Rosa.' I said, 'But I have only two hours for the film! If I put one hour on me and only one hour on Rosa, that's not fair!' Then she saw the film at the première in Berlin and she liked it very much. I think she was afraid it would be a bit like an East German film.

Aud It's interesting that the theme of the two Germanys is much more a preoccupation of East German artists. I feel that to the West German . . .

MVT No, West Germans don't pay attention to the fact that there are two Germanys. They live too well, so they don't bother so much.

Aud But it does concern you?

MVT Yes, I have many friends in East Germany and I often go to visit them. It's very strange, you have to wait and to pay and to be observed . . . It's not easy.

Aud In *Friends and Husbands* and *Sisters* you made a great deal of use of dreams and hallucinations, and I wondered if you could say something about that, because you seem to use it a great deal as a technique.

MVT Yes, I believe that life is only partly the reality you're living. It's also your thoughts, it's your visions, your past, your dreams – for me they're all on the same level. Perhaps you may ask why there isn't a dream in *Rosa*, but she only mentioned one dream. She was not very aware of dreams, so I didn't want to invent some!

Aud I think that *Friends and Husbands* is one of the most erotic films . . .

MVT I didn't feel that it was so erotic, but I'm glad if it's . . . [*Laughter*]

Aud . . . There's one scene especially where the husband is coming home and comes round the corner, and the audience is led to believe that he's going to see something from the window, something going on between the women. Are you intentionally teasing us there, or is it just a way of showing him up?

MVT But it depends on what you are expecting to see. It was just that they were sitting there and laughing and being very relaxed together, and for him that was the point. If they had been lesbians, that would not have been so disturbing for him; it was just that they were such good friends together.

Aud Absolutely, but I thought that because we came round the corner *with* him, we were also being led on, in a way. Did you do that on purpose?

MVT Yes, I did.

Aud I want to ask about a much earlier film of yours, *Summer Lightning*, where you seem to say at the end that remarriage is necessary for a divorced woman in order to make some kind of life. That's not still your view today?

MVT No! – but that's not what I meant then, either! You always have these happy endings with a marriage, and this time it was very ironic: it was a sort of happy ending which was, in reality, a sad ending. It wasn't meant as a real solution.

Aud How difficult is it to provide alternative images of women to those found in Hollywood films?

MVT There are not so many women in Hollywood films, I think. [*Laughter and applause*]

Aud There are a number of great American actresses who are . . .

MVT Yes, but that was in the past, not nowadays! Look at the films today! . . . Anyway, I can't consider that – it's not my problem. It's the Americans' problem if they want to have strong women or not, and in the films even the men are not very . . . [*Laughter and applause*]

Aud You've always worked within a German context in your films. Have you ever wanted to work with non-German subject matter?

MVT No, because I think there are so many things to say about my country, and also I am very dependent on my language in my work with actors. Even if I turned my back to them, only hearing them speaking, I know if they are right or not, and I wouldn't have this feeling in another language. So I have to stay with more or less German subjects . . .

Aud But Rosa Luxemburg isn't a German subject!

MVT Well, OK – she has influenced people all over the world and she was an internationalist in her thinking, but she worked mainly in the German Social Democratic Party, and she even went through a false marriage to acquire German nationality, because at this time the German Social Democratic Party was supposed to be the most important one. They had the most members, and there was always the idea that the first place of revolution would be in Germany – it was a surprise that it came in Russia – and therefore Rosa wanted to work there. It wasn't because she loved the Germans; she wrote terrible things about Germans!

Aud What is it like to be a woman directing films of that size – and particularly such political films – in Europe today?

MVT I think I have more difficulties in making them, perhaps, than my male colleagues, but I knew from the beginning it would be like that. I mean, Rosa is attacked not only because she is so radical and so intelligent, but also because she is a woman. She had a lot of trouble in her Party, and her work was even called 'hysterical Marxism'. You know what that means! The word 'hysterical' is never used for a man; It's always the women who are hysterical if they are radical. So I think that I am aware of the difficulties, but I don't care!

Aud Do you think things are changing?

MVT I hope so. In Germany there are many, many woman film directors now and we try to do our work, though it's still difficult. But also, you know, I'm a little bit tired of all the lamentations: 'Oh, we poor women!' Just do your work and then you will see, and you must try to give the courage to other women to do it also, but be beyond all these lamentations!

Aud Do you ever work together with other German woman directors?

MVT We have a sort of club or society for women working in the cinema. We organized ourselves so that we could have more power with the television stations and the people giving the money, and we said, 'We are half the population, we want to have half the subsidies.' We didn't get it! But we meet each other very often and we try to help each other. It doesn't always work out, but we try.

Aud Have any of your films gone on general release in Germany?

MVT Not wide distribution, no, just local. German films are not on the level of American films, you know. In our country, 80 to 85 per cent of the public goes to American productions, so our films just have the small part of 10 per cent. What can we do? I can just get by. *The German Sisters*, for instance, was a success, and *Rosa* too, but always on our own small scale; we can't compare ourselves with the income of American films. But we don't want to *do* American films, so we are satisfied.

Aud What I find very striking and very moving in your films are the great moments of tenderness between women, like the exchange of sweaters in *The German Sisters* and another film – I can't remember the name – where the woman caresses the young girl's hair and she doesn't even know. You seem to feel very strongly that women have this secret, intimate bond with each other.

MVT Yes, and even in *Rosa*, when she is very unhappy she goes and lies in the lap of her friend. I found in a letter of hers that with Luise, who really was her closest woman friend, she did that when she felt very weak, like a child. For me these moments are very important, yes.

Aud I read in an interview somewhere that you felt very drawn to the subject of sisters although you didn't have one yourself. Why is this?

MVT Yes, I did two films about sisters, and I did them before I knew that I *have* a sister in reality. My mother gave away the first child she had for adoption, and I always thought I was the only child. Then, after I made *Sisters, or the Balance of Happiness*, I did an interview on television and I spoke for the first time about my mother – that she was not married, so I have my mother's name, and that she was already 42 when I was born. My sister saw this television interview, but because my mother's name is also written on her birth certificate and she had always thought it was the name of my *father*, she didn't make the connection. Then she wrote to me and asked me if my mother was called so-and-so and was born in Moscow in such-and-such a year. At this time my mother was already dead, so I wrote back and said that if she knew something about her she should tell me, because I was very, very fond of my mother, we were very close, and afterwards it was a shock for me that she never told me that she had had this child. Then I met my sister, and she looks much more like my mother than I do, so that was a strange moment! And perhaps that was why I had to do two films about sisters, because unconsciously I knew that I had a sister. It is very odd. In *Sisters, or the Balance of Happiness*, one of the sisters is called Maria and the other is called Anna, and during the writing I always thought, 'I must change those names, they are so Biblical!' – but I couldn't. My second name is Maria, and it turned out that her second name is Anna!

Aud I read somewhere recently how you found it very, very hard to make *Rosa*, and sometimes you felt like giving up and abandoning it. Did you learn anything about yourself from making it?

MVT I don't know if I learned something about myself, but I learned a lot about her. I'm not as patient as she is, and I'm much more self-pitying. I learned from her that you have to be not self-pitying.

Aud Are you optimistic politically?

MVT No, I am rather pessimistic about our history and about the future, and perhaps this feeling is in *Rosa*, too. *She* was not pessimistic, *I'm* pessimistic, and that goes into the film a little bit. But we are living in another time. *She* had this programme and these ideas, and we are living now so many years after her, yet you can't find the realization of her ideas anywhere. That's why, in *Rosa*, I included this speech by Bebel[5] at the beginning of the century, where he says that the nineteenth century was a century of hope and the twentieth century will be the century of fulfilment – and of course, this century was not the century of fulfilment at all. They had so much hope, and *she* had, but I do not have as much hope anymore.

Aud Did you once have that hope?

MVT Yes, but you know, with German history it is not so easy, and now, with nuclear weapons . . . You *have* to do *something* against it, but the people who are trying are very few.

Aud Do you think there is any chance of the German Peace Movement?

MVT Yes, perhaps I put it too strongly. Everything that Rosa said against militarism is very real in our country now for the Peace Movement.

Notes

1 Eric von Ludendorff (1865–1937). From 1916 until the Armistice, Ludendorff was virtually the co-ruler of Germany with his fellow-general, Paul von Hindenburg. He escaped to Sweden in disguise in 1918 after the German surrender. He supported the Kapp putsch (1920) and Hitler's abortive putsch in Bavaria in 1923, but while he remained an extreme reactionary and a vocal anti-semite throughout his life, he turned against the Nazis in the 1930s and refused the title of Field-Marshall when Hitler offered it to him.

2 On 9 November 1918, Kaiser Wilhelm II abdicated and fled to

Holland. Philipp Scheidemann (1865–1939) immediately proclaimed a new German republic, with himself as Chancellor, in order to forestall the declaration of a socialist republic by Karl Liebknecht. Friedrich Ebert (1871–1925) then formed a government, and on 10 November he reached an agreement with Wilhelm Groener, Ludendorff's successor, according to which Groener guaranteed the army's support for the new régime in return for Ebert's promise to use all necessary means to suppress the German Communist Party. The Spartacist uprising in January 1919 was quickly crushed, and both Ebert and Scheidemann colluded with the ensuing reprisals against the German left conducted by the Freikorps, in the course of which Liebknecht and Luxemburg were murdered. Scheidemann resigned as Chancellor later in the year because he refused to accept the terms of the Treaty of Versailles. Ebert remained President of Germany until his death in February 1925.

3 Stammheim is the maximum-security prison in which Gudrun Ensslin, Andreas Baader, Ulrike Meinhof and Jan-Carl Raspe were confined for life in 1972 for terrorist offences. All four were found dead in their cells – Meinhof in 1976, and the other three in the following year. The Baden-Württemberg *Land* authorities announced that the prisoners had committed suicide, and this verdict was subsequently confirmed by a parliamentary commission of inquiry, but it is very generally assumed that they were murdered. Helmut Schmidt was the Chancellor of West Germany at the time of their death.

4 Clara Zetkin (1857–1933) was a co-founder of the Spartacus League in 1916. In 1919 she was elected to the Central Committee of the German Communist Party, and she became a member of the Presidium of the Third International in 1921. She spent most of the last twelve years of her life in the Soviet Union.

5 August Bebel (1840–1913) co-founded the League of Workers' Groups with Karl Liebknecht. The League was later incorporated in the German Social Democratic Party.

8 Gene Kelly

Gene Kelly was born in Pittsburgh in 1912, and after studying at the university there, he began his career as an actor and dancer on Broadway in such shows as *Leave It to Me* (1938), *One for the Money* (1939) and *The Time of Your Life* (1940). He also choreographed *Billy Rose's Diamond Horseshoe* (1940) and *Best Foot Forward* (1941). He became a star in 1941 when he created the title role in Rodgers and Hart's *Pal Joey*, and the following year he made his film debut in Busby Berkeley's *For Me and My Gal*. Thereafter he worked almost exclusively in movies, though he returned to Broadway in 1958 to direct Rodgers and Hammerstein's *Flower Drum Song*. He made four more films in 1943, but it was his sixth movie, *Cover Girl* (1944, Charles Vidor), made not at MGM but at Columbia, which established him as the most important male dancer since Astaire. He returned to MGM in 1945 for *Anchors Aweigh* (George Sidney), the first film in which he collaborated on the choreography with Stanley Donen, and during the next twelve years he became – in his capacity as singer, dancer, choreographer and director – one of the principal creative forces behind the Golden Age of the MGM musical. His films include The Pirate (1948, Vincente Minnelli), *Words and Music* (1948, Norman Taurog), *Take Me Out to the Ball Game* (1949, Busby Berkeley), *On the Town* (1949, Kelly/Donen), *Summer Stock* (1950, Charles Walters), *An American in Paris* (1951, Minnelli), *Singin' in the Rain* (1952, Kelly/Donen), *Brigadoon* (1954, Minnelli), *It's Always Fair Weather* (1955, Kelly/Donen), *Invitation to the Dance* (1956, Kelly) and *Les Girls* (1957, George Cukor). Gene Kelly has also given a number of remarkable dramatic performances, most notably in *Christmas Holiday* (1944, Robert Siodmak), *Marjorie Morningstar* (1958, Irving Rapper) and *Inherit the Wind* (1960, Stanley Kramer). He appeared in the second of Jacques Demy's *hommages* to the Hollywood musical, *Les Demoiselles de Rochefort* (1968) and directed and choreographed *That's Entertainment II* (1976). His most recent film is *Xanadu* (1980, Robert Greenwald). During the 1960s he directed four films in which he did not appear, including *Gigot* (1962) and one of the last great musicals,

Hello Dolly! (1969). Gene Kelly was awarded a special Oscar in 1951 for his versatility as an actor, dancer and singer, and for his contribution to the art of film choreography. He was honoured by the Kennedy Center in 1982, and in 1984 he received the American Film Institute Life Achievement Award.

The following lecture took place on 20 May 1980. Gene Kelly was interviewed by the writer and critic, John Russell Taylor.

Gene Kelly

John Russell Taylor Obviously, throughout your life it has been a complete necessity to do what you say in *Singin' in the Rain* – 'Gotta dance!' Now, why do you think that was, and how did all this happen?

Gene Kelly Well, if you have all got about eight hours I can get on with it! I was sent to dancing school as a little boy and I revolted against it because, at that time, it was considered very effeminate. I took it up again in high school because the girls liked the fellows who could dance well, and I was an athlete, so I wasn't worried about getting punched in the nose; gradually I took it up seriously to make some money to go through college. When I did get through college I decided to stay in the theatre. It's that simple.

JRT Did you always feel the necessity to do it all, or did it gradually come to you that you had to choreograph and direct as well in order to get your vision of the dance on the stage and screen?

GK I started as a teacher; I never thought that I'd be a performer. Then, when I went to Broadway and entered the theatre, I wanted to be a choreographer, but frankly I couldn't get a job. So I went on the stage as a dancer, and I could do and play a few things. As I got into my second show, somebody gave me a line to say, and I thought, 'Well, this is easy, you get paid more!' It's Western Union rates, or something like that – you get paid more than dancers. Dancers never get paid very much money just dancing! Gradually I learned to be an actor by working in summer stock and, as you said, maybe I learned to do it all – some of it not so well, but . . .

JRT Did you have any desire at this stage to go into the movies, or were you one of those superior New York people who thought, 'Well, I might dabble if they really force me . . . '?

GK I was an effete eastern snob, yes. I was only interested in the theatre. I went out to do one movie to make some money, but after I got there I found it was quite interesting! Then I had to go into the Navy during the war. Frankly, I got very excited about the problems of dancing for films. It seemed that nobody cared much about it, and the more I asked about it, the less information I seemed to get. So I stayed in California, apart from a few trips back to New York. I directed *Flower Drum Song* for Rodgers and Hammerstein, a few jobs like that, but mostly I've stayed with films. That's been my life ever since.

JRT I think you're much too modest about your work purely as an actor. One of your performances that I still cherish is in *Inherit the Wind*, where heaven knows you've got the most extraordinary competition from Spencer Tracy and Fredric March, and I think that's a wonderful performance. But didn't you originally go out to Hollywood under contract to Selznick? That must have been as an actor, surely?

GK Yes, I was to be in a picture for Alfred Hitchcock. I still have the contract: it says, 'Kelly to do the Hitchcock picture.' I asked Hitch about that later, just a few years ago, and I said, 'Sir Alfred, what picture was that?' and he said, 'I never wanted you in a picture. During that year I was making a film with Jimmy Stewart and I didn't even know you were coming to Hollywood.' I'd wondered about it for years, and in my mind I thought that Hitch had wanted me for *Strangers on a Train*. I was just positive it was that picture, but he said, 'No, I never had you in mind at all.' He never saw me on the stage, nothing.

JRT Though you did many other things while you were at MGM, we associate you particularly with the Arthur Freed Unit. You were there from very early on in the development of that extraordinary group, so could you tell us something about how that started and how you fitted in with it all?

GK I started in an Arthur Freed movie with Judy Garland called *For Me and My Gal*, and by a stroke of Irish luck it was a hit, though if you look at it today it's a bit on the old-fashioned side. There was really no one in the Freed Unit, so-called, at that time, but the group evolved gradually, and I think it came to fruition with *Meet Me in St Louis*, which is my favourite musical of all time. Charles Walters did the choreography. I had asked Chuck to come to MGM to do *Du Barry Was a Lady*, which was a pretty bad picture, and it was also an Arthur Freed picture. I said to Arthur, 'Why are you *doing* this?' and he said, 'Well, the studio bought it and assigned it to me.' There were a lot of pictures done in that way before Arthur began to acquire people from New York. The first time I remember him having a whole bunch of easterners from the theatre was *Meet Me in St Louis*, and after that we sort of took off, and we would say, 'Let's get Mike Kidd! Let's get Gene Loring!'[1] They were ballet people, and as dancers we liked to have them around, but they were also very interested in cinema. We all felt that musicals were an art form, although before we started this little repertory company and it began to grow, everyone said, 'Oh, they're doing a little musical over there!' and treated us like second-class citizens. But we believed in it, and I think our musicals got better and better. Arthur would always say, 'Look, you guys go ahead and do it. When I see it in the rushes I'll know whether it fits or not.' And he was very hard to fool! You could fool some of the executives about musicals, but not Arthur.

JRT When you were working in the theatre, you worked with a number of people who were then at the outset of their careers and who became very important in the MGM musical: people like Martin and Blane,[2] Betty Comden and Adolph Green . . . Were you in any way instrumental in bringing these people out to California?

GK Yes. Comden and Green and Judy Holliday were part of an act called 'The Revuers', and we met in summer stock when we were all learning our trade in the 1930s, and we just loved each other right away. They were so bright and quick, and they could do so many things. They all came out to do a picture called *Greenwich Village*, which was atrocious, and they had one of their bits in it which they wrote and performed themselves, but it was cut out of the movie and so they were quite disenchanted with Hollywood. I got them back to do *Take Me Out to the Ball Game*, which I wrote in self-defence when I got out of the Navy, because they had a picture ready for me where Frank Sinatra and I were supposed to take over an aircraft-carrier and turn it into a nightclub. I couldn't do *that*, but what *could* I do? – I had to work. So I said, 'I've got a better idea.' I remembered an old baseball pair called Nick Altrock and Al Schacht who would go into vaudeville every winter and make a living; they were quite funny, and they were good ball-players, too. So I said, 'Altrock and Schacht! "Take Me Out to the Ball Game"! Big hit, big hit! Song'll be around for years!' They said, 'That's good, how would it go?' So that night I wrote all night, and in the morning I got my protégé and friend, Stanley Donen, and said, 'Read this and tell me if it's any good', and he said, 'Gee, I like it! So we got it made into a screenplay with a professional screen-writer. I got Comden and Green called in to do all the songs, all the special material. From then on they became a big part of the Freed Unit, and I think a very important part.

JRT *Take Me Out to the Ball Game* is an interesting film in a number of ways. When you see it now, it looks like a sketch for *On the Town* – the same pattern, the same sort of ideas, the same three male stars – and yet it's oddly backward-looking in that it was directed, after all, by Busby Berkeley, the great figure of the Warner Bros. musicals in the 1930s. How did you get on with Berkeley?

GK Well, by that time I got on very well with him, but Buzz always let us overplay, he always liked to let us ham it up, and it was very easy for me to do that! I looked like a 35-year-old Mickey Rooney! When I was in the theatre on Broadway, there were no microphones. For example, if it was 'I LOVE YOU!!' you had to hit the back row, and at the same time you had to make sure the people in the front row didn't feel uncomfortable. So it was very easy for us to come out in motion pictures and overact, which I *did* all my life. I was good in the long shots, but when they made a close-up I was really awful, though on the stage I was considered a very good actor. On the screen I still can't do a close-up, I still haven't mastered it, and it's the finest part of screen acting, conveying something hard and real. The only excuse I have is that I was paying so much attention to dancing, which I was. I was exploring new techniques and new things to do, and I really wanted to change the dance and style of the American male; I wanted to change his wardrobe, I wanted to do all that . . . and I knew the cinema was the way to go. So I stayed with it and luckily, in the end, we had all these great people. While we're on this subject, may I say something? There is a lot of misinformation which movie buffs seem to take in about 'auteurs'. Let me tell you that there is no such thing as an 'auteur' in the musical film. You need songwriters, you need choreographers, you need screenwriters, you need set designers and costume designers, you need somebody between their fights to co-ordinate the colour – one says, 'This would look good in green,' and the other says, 'Well, I would like the set to be puce,' so there has to be a compromise. You need all kinds of people to make a musical, so though some of us can actually pronounce 'auteur', we know that it doesn't exist. For instance, if it hadn't been for Comden and Green you wouldn't have seen that last number we just screened, 'Singin' in the Rain', because they thought up the whole idea for the film, but they didn't see this particular piece of song and dance until the film was finished, they were back in New York. So they are not 'auteurs', I am not an 'auteur', and nobody else is an 'auteur' that makes a film. It takes a lot of people, a lot of co-operation. There are very few people I can think of as 'auteurs'.

JRT I'd like to follow up something you were just saying about this specific number, something which has always fascinated me and which it's very difficult to understand from the outside. Exactly how is a number like this evolved? How does the dancer work with the choreographer (in your case it happens to be the same), how do they both work with the director (who in your case is also the same) . . . ?

GK I fought with myself a lot!

JRT How do these things start?

GK Actually, a dance starts the same way a writer starts writing a script, a poem, or a novel. It starts in the choreographer's head, and he sits down – usually in a chair. He doesn't get up and shake his hips and the dance flows out, any more than a writer sits down and starts to move his pencil and, lo and behold! – it's *A Doll's House*! 'Singin' in the Rain' seems to be an easy idea. I remember that Arthur Freed, who wrote the lyrics, wanted this song in the film very much, but he had no idea how to put it in and neither did Comden and Green, so he said, 'Gene, what will you do with this?' I said, 'I have to have an excuse, because I have an idea for this number, but to go out and sing in the rain without looking like an idiot, one must have quite an impulse! That's the scene after I fall in love, so when I'm sure I'm head-over-heels with Debbie Reynolds, I go out in the streets and I act like an idiot; I revert to what we do as children and splash in the puddles.' It's not a difficult dance technically, it could be done by any dancer: it's a dance which has to be *played* more than it's danced. What *was* rather hard to do was the lighting of the rain – nothing like it had been done before in that big an area – and that problem was solved by Harold Rossen, the cinematographer. Without him we could never have done that number. Stanley Donen and I were very worried about how I could go down the street and not get my reflection in the windows, because if you don't light the rain from the back you don't see the rain. For example, if you're watching a football game on television and the camera is at a certain angle, they look like they're playing in sunshine, but when the angle changes you see the rain. So the back-lighting was very tough, and the technicians had a much more difficult problem than I did. I think I composed the number in three days. I didn't have a way to make a transition from the love scene into the number, but Roger Edens, a musical genius at the studio, who was really the back-bone of the Freed Unit and who wrote a lot of songs on his own, came up with a little tune which he played for me, and I said, 'I could hum it or whistle it like a guy would walking down the street or in the shower, just feeling good.' So the number came about with the co-operation of quite a few people. As I said, the dance is not a difficult dance, I could teach it to quite a lot of the kids I've taught in the past . . . so that's the involved story of a very easy number!

JRT How about some of the numbers which are obviously much more involved, like the ballet at the end of *An American in Paris* or the Broadway ballet in *Singin' in the Rain*? They must have been terribly complicated to organize.

GK They were, and they took time to work out and also a lot of strategy. After we got the studio to give us the money, we had to use the same dancers in a lot of the scenes, so we had to say, 'If this dancer is in this scene, we can't show her face in the next scene which takes place somewhere else,' so I would have to have her back to the camera and do it that way. We took a month to rehearse that ballet in *An American in Paris*, and we took roughly the same time to rehearse the big number in *Singin' in the Rain*. For the Broadway ballet, I had to get a partner who was a fine dancer, and because Cyd Charisse had just had a baby and wasn't in shape, we had to give her about two weeks to work out. That was good for me because I kept thinking about the number, and we made up this whole story about a kid coming to New York. There was a very elaborate fantasy sequence in which Cyd wore a long, long veil which I wanted to billow around us as we were dancing, and I experimented with aeroplane motors, and yards and yards of light material. We'd tilt one of the motors down and the air would bounce off the ground and throw the veil up high, but the fellow who was handling the motor had to be a big, strong man to do that, and sometimes we needed two of them. We also had to have an assistant there to time it, saying, 'One, two, three, four – push!' and then they'd tilt it down, or they might push too hard and we'd have to do it again. When the air from the aeroplane motors blew directly at us, I had to lift Cyd Charisse up and at the same time wrap the veil around me. Well, I don't know what the wind resistance was in scientific terms, but it took all my strength to do it because the force from those motors was tremendous. My stomach muscles were tightening, my arms were like steel bands, it was like lifting this room. Of course, you can't let that be seen on screen. The *An American in Paris* number was really a tribute to the great impressionist artists, so we tried to keep the dancing secondary. A couple of times we burst through with something nice, but really it was the decor and the colour which were important. We brought out a lady called Irene Sharaff, who did *Meet Me in St Louis* as well, and she was a great costume designer: she would mix these colours in the style of Dufy and Lautrec, and so on. It was hard not to let the dancing go overboard, not to make it too much, but we tried. If you see a Dufy painting it's so light and delicate, and we wanted the choreography to be the same.

JRT You have never been involved, as Fred Astaire *was*, in a regular partnership, though you have danced with most of the greatest female dancers on the screen. How much choice did you have about who your partners would be; and how conscious were you of adapting your style to their styles?

GK I was completely free in choosing them, and I chose them for the role. I discovered a few of them and put them in pictures – Debbie Reynolds, Leslie Caron, Vera Ellen . . . Vera had not done a successful picture, although she had been out there for Fox. She was on her way back to New York to the theatre, but I wanted to use her in the 'Slaughter on 10th Avenue' ballet in *Words and Music*. We were doing a whole new thing there, but we had total freedom . . . So no, I was never part of a team like Astaire and Rogers. I think it was good for me to dance with different girls.

JRT One more inevitable question about team-work. I think people are fascinated by this two-headed monster of Gene-Kelly-and-Stanley-Donen as choreographer and director of films, and want to know how that worked out. Surely every ship has to have a captain: which one of you was captain?

GK I was captain, I was the senior. Stanley was never a choreographer in the inventive sense, but he had a great critical faculty and a great understanding of mood. I would call

Stanley down and say, 'Look at this, do you feel anything is wrong with it?' and he would say yes or no. Then we would talk about how we would shoot it and how to move the camera. It's not only good to have another opinion, it's also good to have an opinion from a dear friend and trusted colleague who is not a yes-man. They exist in every business in the world. If you call somebody down, they usually say, 'That's grand! That's marvellous!' If Stanley thought even one measure was not up to standard, he would say, 'I don't like that measure,' and he *knew* dancing. He never was a big dancer himself, but he recognized when a dance was right, and his aid was invaluable. This kind of partnership exists with every film dancer. Astaire had Hermes Pan and I had Stanley, and if I didn't have Stanley I would have Carol Haney or Jeanne Coyne.[3] It's very important to have someone whose criticism you can rely on, because once you put it on film it's up there for ever. There's nothing you can do about it unless you sneak out and burn it.

JRT Shall we move on to some questions from the audience?

Audience What is your favourite of all your numbers?

GK I think my favourite number is the dance with the squeaky board in *Summer Stock*. It was certainly the hardest one to rehearse. That was not my idea in the first place. There was a fellow named Nick Castle, who was a choreographer who did tap-dancing, and we were working with Judy Garland. Judy was very ill and wouldn't show up some days, so at noon they would call the company and say, 'You're free.' So around three o'clock one afternoon we went round to Nick's house and his wife brought out the Scotch, and he sat there – he stuttered a bit – and he said, 'G-G-G-Gene, l-l-l-listen to this sound,' and he started tearing this newspaper – tch, tch, tch. I said, 'Nick, that's a number! Why haven't you ever used it?' and he said, 'W-W-W-What can *you* do?' So we came in the next morning with piles of newspaper, and actually Nick was right, because there wasn't enough to build the number with just this paper. Then I said, 'Nick, we've got to go around and around town to find another sound and tie them up!' So we went out, we were scraping grates and people were staring at us, and we tried – everything! – but we couldn't find a sound. I walked in the rehearsal hall one day and I said, 'I've had it!' and I said goodbye to Nick and I passed the empty stage – and there it was! I looked at the boards and I said, 'My God! A squeaky board!' It was sitting in front of us all the time. Of course, the board didn't really squeak, we dubbed all that in. So between the board and the paper I had worked out several bars of the dance, and the next day I called Nick in and he said, 'M-M-M-Man, that's great!' and we knew we had a number. But then we found that some newspaper would tear and some wouldn't tear, so we d-d-d-didn't have a number. We tried the old trick of scoring the paper with a razor blade, but then the minute I jumped on it, it would just fall apart. Eventually, we got down to a copy of the *Los Angeles Times* from 1932 – this was after a couple of weeks of sweating it out! – and we found that for some reason we could get the 1932 *Times* to tear properly. After all that it was easy to photograph, because the number was right up there on an empty stage. It may not be my best number, but it's my favourite . . . and my favourite pictures are not always the best, either. My favourite picture is *On the Town*, because it was a breakthrough, but I happened to see it again last year and I thought, 'My God, this is terribly dated!'

Aud With reference to the sound of the squeaky board being dubbed, I've often wondered, when we see your tap-dancing feet, what exactly are we hearing?

GK You are hearing a post-dub of the taps. The reason for that is that when you have the play-back on set you take a record, because you can't have a forty-piece orchestra there playing with you – they get in the way. Nowadays it's taped: tape is more efficient and more noiseless, but it's not a perfect sound. But whether it's tape or an acetate disc (which is what we used all the time because it was the best sound we had then), there is enough distortion in it, and you can't get a homogeneous sound for the music and the dancing. So we take the pristine record or tape, and we have to dub the sounds in later. It's the most difficult thing in pictures and it galls all of us, because you have to watch yourself do this and that, and then copy yourself. It's pre-dubbed occasionally, but if you pre-dub and then you get an inspiration on set, you're stuck, and if you're dancing alone you often start improvising. I know I do, and I know other dancers who do. You get a little more freedom, call it inspiration or just a stronger urge to go further and add something . . . so we usually post-dub the tapes. Songs, by the way, are pre-dubbed, very seldom post-dubbed, unless you have some pretty bad clinkers that you want to clean up.

Aud Can you tell us something about the number in *Anchors Aweigh* where you dance with Jerry the cartoon mouse?

GK That was very difficult to do technically. It had never been done before and, of course, everyone said it couldn't be done, and the studio wouldn't give us the money for it. So I called Walt Disney, and I also asked to speak to one of our executives, Eddie Mannix, who was a friend of his, and he said, 'Have Gene come over.' It turned out that Walt was doing the same kind of thing – he even had sketches on the board – but he said, 'Your idea is better because yours has a form.' Walt would shoot the film and then superimpose the animated figures running around, but it had no compositional form, it had no choreography. Technically, that number was most difficult for the cameraman. The viewfinder in the camera has a little cross on it, and they had to keep me on *this* side of the cross and the mouse on *that* side, but the problem for the poor operator was that there was no mouse! So I had to have Stanley Donen count us through it. He'd say, 'One, two, three – pan! Four, five, six – pan!' so that I'd be on this side of the field and the mouse on the other. The operator claims he got an ulcer from that number, but he was always complaining anyway.

JRT This is obviously something that's continued to fascinate you, because you dance again with animated figures in *Invitation to the Dance* and in your television film, *Jack and the Beanstalk*.

GK It's a lot of fun. Now that the cartoonists and the photographers have learned the technique, there's not that kind of mystery about it, and they even use it in television commercials now. That just happened to be the first time it was used. I used it in *Invitation to the Dance* because the studio wanted to cut out the ballet I'd already done, and so the quickest thing we could think up that would be completely different was to do a fairy-tale, which I thought would appeal to children. Of course, it turned out to be a very difficult, very long piece of work. *Jack and the Beanstalk* was another fairy-tale, and animation is fine for that kind of thing. When I did the dance with Jerry, the character I was playing was talking to a group of kindergarten children and telling them a big lie about a sailor's adventures, so that was a fairy-tale too. I wouldn't recommend it for serious subjects.

JRT Can you tell us who is the dancer you admire the most?

GK It's a very difficult question to answer and I'd rather dodge it, because there are classical dancers, ethnic dancers, tap-dancers, flamenco dancers . . . you can go on and on, and so many of them are so skilled and so exciting in their own fields. Years ago I would probably have answered Martha Graham in her youth, because she had a great influence on me . . . It's not a fair question, but I *will* say that I think there are more exciting dancers today, and greater dancers in every field than, I believe, have ever lived.

JRT You told me that you had a particular favourite among film dance numbers which rather surprised me. Would you care to tell people what that is?

GK Yes, my favourite dance number is one Fred Astaire did with Cyd Charisse in *The Band Wagon* called 'Dancing in the Dark'. It's so beautiful, I've seen it many, many times, and I would always like to see it. To me it's the perfect courtship number, and I'm jealous I didn't do it.

Aud How would you describe the difference between yourself and Astaire?

GK Well, the difference between myself and Fred is vast. There is no similarity in our styles except that we both wear trousers; even our clothes are quite different. In a top hat, white tie and tails I look like I'm an iceman going to his annual dance, and if there is one thing I *did* do for American dance, it was to change the male costume. I would often have to go to premières of *That's Entertainment!* with Fred. We were the show-off males, the old movie people, and we would trudge up there, take a bow and then go out and have a drink.

Aud Tommy Steele tells a story that when he started rehearsing with Astaire on *Finian's Rainbow*, he did a step or something, and Astaire stopped him and said, 'Where did you learn that? Did the Irishman teach you that?'

GK Tommy might have been indulging in a bit of hyperbole, he might have made up that story, though I did teach Tommy a couple of numbers which we did together for one of those television specials. Anyway, it's a nice story, thank you.

Aud Can you tell us what it was like working with Judy Garland?

GK I've always thought that Judy was the finest performer we've ever had in America. She wasn't a trained dancer, but when you taught her a series of steps, she would work on it very hard to get it as well as she could. You had to watch that you didn't stretch her limits. She couldn't do things that a trained classical dancer like, say, Cyd Charisse could do, so you kept it on a certain level, but her brain was amazing. She'd hear a song and know it, and *you'd* feel like a fool because you'd still be practising it, and she read a page of dialogue and then she could play it back with you, and you still had to look at the script. She was the quickest, brightest person I've ever worked with, and she also had a great sense of humour. In the days that I knew her, up until she began to get ill, she laughed all the time, she seemed to enjoy her work, we had great fun together. To me, she was the best all-round performer. You couldn't say she could dance as well as a certain dancer, of course not, and maybe you prefer a certain singer to Judy, though I didn't and still don't, but all round, when you put them all together – acting, singing, dancing – she just was superb.

Aud Mr Kelly, what do you think of discos and disco dancing?

GK There's nothing startling about that; it's just the rebirth of jitterbugging, as we used to call it. I guess it's fun, but I'd sooner listen to good rock than most of the disco music I hear. The dancing that's done to rock-and-roll is based on fertility rites, it's an atavistic form. Everybody is by himself: the girl may be doing this, the guy may be doing that, there's not much form to it. When it *is* formalized by a choreographer, my objection usually is that it's completely unisex. The man does the same steps as the woman, and to me that's like having a male opera singer singing soprano and the female singing bass; there's something wrong with that. I think that when a man dances he should dance like a man and a girl should dance like a girl, and while you may often want them to dance in unison, it's usually better choreography where you divide the sexes into different branches.

Aud Do you ever wish you had gone into any other profession?

GK No, not really. I worked my way through university by dancing and teaching dancing, mostly working with my brother. I got my degree and entered law school, and I was there two months when I said, 'What am I doing?' We had a class on torts! I had majored in economics, but I'd be in a terrible mess now if anybody asked me about that; even the economists don't know. I just said, 'Well, I *know* I'm a good dancer,' and since then that's the only thing I've wanted to do. I like all aspects of show business, I just like the dancing part best. Obviously when you get to be in your forties, and then hit your fifties, you know that your not going to dance much more and you reach out in other directions, but if I had my druthers I'd sooner do that, if that's what you mean.

Notes

1 The dance director Eugene Loring. His credits include *Ziegfeld Follies* (1944), *Yolanda and the Thief* (1945), *Funny Face* (1956) and *Silk Stockings* (1957).

2 Hugh Martin and Ralph Blane, composers and lyricists who worked together on such films as *Thousands Cheer* (1943), *Meet Me in St Louis* (1944) and *Ziegfeld Follies* (1944).

3 Carol Haney and Jeanne Coyne were dancers and choreographers with the Freed Unit at MGM. Jeanne Coyne was married to Gene Kelly from 1960 until her death in 1973.

9

Dirk Bogarde

Dirk Bogarde was born Derek van den Bogaerde in London in 1921, the son of a Dutchman who was the art correspondent of *The Times*. In 1939 he joined a small suburban theatre, the Q, as a stage manager, and went on to make his acting debut with the Amersham Repertory Company. Between 1940 and 1945 he served with the Photographic Interpretation Unit of British Army Intelligence, mainly in the Far East, and rose to the rank of Lieutenant. After the war he returned to acting, playing one of the killers in a television version of *Rope* (1946), making his first film appearance in *Dancing with Crime* (1947, John Paddy Carstairs) and co-starring in a highly successful play, *Power Without Glory*, which transferred to the West End and was also televised. His notices in the play led to a seven-year contract with the Rank Organization, and he went on to become one of the biggest and most popular stars of 1950s British cinema, appearing in at least two, and sometimes as many as five, movies a year. The titles include *The Blue Lamp* (1950, Basil Dearden), *Hunted* (1952, Charles Crichton), *The Sleeping Tiger* (1954, Bogarde's first film with Joseph Losey), *Cast a Dark Shadow* (1955, Lewis Gilbert), *The Spanish Gardener* (1956, Philip Leacock), *Ill Met By Moonlight* (1956, Michael Powell/ Emeric Pressburger). *A Tale of Two Cities* (1958, Ralph Thomas), *The Doctor's Dilemma* (1959, Anthony Asquith) and *The Singer Not the Song* (1961, Roy Ward Baker). He also starred in the four hugely successful *Doctor* comedies, all directed by Ralph Thomas. *Victim* (1961, Basil Dearden), in which he played a gay barrister and which alienated a large proportion of his public, marked a decisive turning-point in Dirk Bogarde's career, and over the next decade he made a series of remarkable films which established him as one of the contemporary cinema's most powerful actors. The period is dominated by his collaboration with two directors: Joseph Losey, for whom he made four films – *The Servant* (1963), *King and Country* (1964), *Modesty Blaise* (1966) and *Accident* (1967); and Luchino Visconti, who directed him in *The Damned* (1969) and *Death in Venice* (1971). His other 1960s films include *Darling* (1965, John Schlesinger), *Our Mother's House* (1967,

Jack Clayton) and *Justine* (1969, George Cukor), and he has since appeared in, amongst other works, *The Night Porter* (1973, Liliana Cavani), *Providence* (1976, Alain Resnais) and *Despair* (1978, Rainer Werner Fassbinder). In the 1970s Dirk Bogarde began a second career as a writer, and he has now published three volumes of autobiography and several novels. During the 1980s he appeared in a number of television movies, including *The Patricia Neal Story* (1982), in which he played Roald Dahl, *May We Borrow Your Husband?* (1986), which he also wrote, after a story by Graham Greene, and *The Vision* (1987). His most recent film is *Daddy Nostalgie* (*These Foolish Things*) (1990, Bertrand Tavernier).

The following lecture took place on 14 February 1983. Dirk Bogarde was interviewed by Tony Bilbow, the writer, critic and broadcaster.

Dirk Bogarde

Tony Bilbow Dirk, I think it's a very courageous thing for any actor to actually pull up his roots and leave the country, which is precisely what you did in the late 1960s. What brought you to that decision?

Dirk Bogarde Unemployment! I hadn't got any work.

TB Do you mean not the sort of work you wanted?

DB Oh, I mean that, yes. I never do the work I don't want to do, but there really wasn't *any* work for me to do. The last thing I did in England was in 1966, and that was a voice-over for the Ministry of whatever-they-call-it – the people who cut down trees. And I thought, 'Well really, if I've got to do voice-overs for the Timber Commission for the rest of my life! . . . '

TB But when you actually arrived in Rome you had cut yourself off from this country. You'd burnt your bridges . . . and you'd literally burnt all your newspaper cuttings, for example. Was that a symbolic thing?

DB No, it wasn't symbolic at all. It was just an awful lot of newspaper which had to be got rid of! I went abroad with a couple of suitcases and a rather bad script which a man called Visconti had seen fit to send me. It was *The Damned*, and it was very bad.

TB Do you remember how you felt at that time in Rome? Were you full of hope?

DB Not really. I was actually in more trouble than you know because I hadn't got any money, and I did a commercial for an American company which entailed my running up and down the Spanish Steps all morning in a pair of somebody's sunglasses. I didn't have to speak, and nobody could see me because of the dark glasses, which was smashing. At the very top of the Spanish Steps a lady would turn, and the catchphrase of the commercial was, 'Was that not Dirk Bogarde in XYZs?' And I thought, 'My God, this is life! Here I am in Rome,

I've got somebody's sun-glasses on, and I was paid $25,000!' Well, I didn't get that for a movie!

TB You'd just come away from that concentrated period of work with Joseph Losey, hadn't you? What was the relationship between you?

DB Oh, grumpy – he's a very grumpy man, Joe – but very close. He first of all found me (or rather I found him, I suppose) in 1951, when I was called the Idol of the Odeons. [*Laughter*] You can laugh, but I jolly well was! And I know 1951 was a long time ago! Joe wanted help to make a movie because he'd been turned out of America by McCarthy; I was bankable, and they sent the script to me. It was a bad script, and Joe *knew* it was a bad script, but we made it together and we had a funny kind of rapport. We made the film in a studio called Nettlefold, which I think has now been taken over as a housing estate, and it was so lousy that we used to go and shoot a gun through the roof to keep the sparrows off during sound-takes. That's how we made *The Sleeping Tiger*. So the years went by, and I said, 'It would be nice to work together again some day,' but we never did for ten years, and then he found *The Servant*. We'd had it floating around for quite a long time, but in those days I was very much younger and I was going to play the boy. By the time we got around to making it in 1961 I was too old, so I said I'd produce it with him. He said, 'We've got to have somebody to play the servant,' so I said, 'Let's have Ralph Richardson, he'd be super!' and he said, 'No, we've got to have a film-name because there's no one in the movie.' We hadn't got any money, and we had an unknown boy called James Fox whom I'd found on television. The only bankable things we had were Sarah Miles and a very good script by Harold Pinter. So we went on that, and I grudgingly agreed to play the servant, which was very fortunate for me.

TB When you'd finished the five films with Losey, did you feel that that vein had been worked out?

DB Yes, it had been. I think we knew too much about each other.

He knew too much about my work – the *way* I would work – and I think we both felt stuck, and we'd both got so tremendously disillusioned by trying – I'm saying this in all truth – by trying desperately to make a new kind of film in Britain. And it didn't work . . . Well, it worked extravagantly for the critics, but not for mass audiences. So I think we both took our own route. He went his way, I went mine.

TB You went your way to Visconti and *The Damned*. I was very interested to learn that the very first scene you shot with Visconti, he made you do it six times and he printed all six takes.

DB That's right.

TB Why was that?

DB I don't know! I've called Visconti the Emperor of the Cinema, and he *was* very imperious: very authoritative, very tough. I was dragged up from Rome to do this damned location shot because they had to get rid of the location, so they had to get rid of me too, because I was in it. He simply said, 'It's going to be lunchtime, you know. In two minutes we have lunch, so you do this very quick: it's nothing! You open the door, you see the man there and you see the boy in bed, you're very shocked. Oh là là, you say! Is awful! This dreadful thing is happening!' And I said, 'Well, where *are* these two?' and he said, 'Oh, they go to lunch, they have lunch!' (It was in Austria, and I'd driven through the night from Rome for this shot!) So he gave me an apple-box for one character and another apple-box for the other, and he was looking at his watch because lunch was coming up, the crew were going to break and he was hungry. So I opened the bloody door and I went in, just looked at the two boxes, and came out and shut the door. That's all I had to do . . . I mean, I had to register some kind of shock, or whatever it was. There was a little pause, I was waiting, I didn't hear anybody say, 'Cut!' Then Visconti came to the door stroking his nose and he said, 'You think you would do this another way? Maybe you do this smiling?' So I did it smiling. He came back and he said, 'You do it angry?' and I thought, 'Oh God, I'm in *Coronation Street*!' So I did it six different ways, and it was now well after one o'clock and the troop hadn't broken for lunch, and he'd forgotten his. He printed all six because he was so surprised that an actor was able to do six different versions of one look. It wasn't very difficult for me because I'd have very good training in Britain, but it rather surprised him.

TB How did *Death in Venice* come about?

DB Well, as I said, I thought *The Damned* was awful. Visconti made me do it, and I did it, and he cut me out of it, so that was all right! But in return he gave me *Death in Venice* as a gift because he'd seen me open the door six different ways. [*Laughter*] It's true! He said, 'If you can do that with your face without saying any words at all, you can play *Death in Venice*.' There was no sentiment about it. My only worry was that I wasn't at that time quite old enough, but in fact I was. I was 49 when I did it, just on the verge of 50, and if I'd been older it would have been too much.

TB When he gave you the script . . .

DB I never got a script. I was given a paperback!

TB The rapport between you and Visconti was obviously extraordinary. For example, there's a scene by a marble wellhead where you have to slump down into the muck in the street . . . Could you tell us about that?

DB Yes. Visconti was so strange. We never discussed *Death in Venice*. The night before we left for Venice to start shooting I telephoned him at his house in Rome (by this time I was able to call him Luchino, which was a great moment) and I said, 'Can I come and talk to you just for half an hour about *Morte a Venezia*?' He said, 'What do you want to talk about?' and I said, 'About *it*, and for only half an hour.' So he said, 'Only half an hour, because I'm very busy and we have a big dinner! Come!' So I went to his house – a beautiful house – and there he was with all his toys and his paintings, sitting rather moodily waiting for me. And I said, 'I don't know how to play this man, I don't know anything about him.' He said, 'Bogarde, how many times have you read the book?' 'About thirty.' 'Well, you go and read about another thirty, and white wine is there if you want. Be quick! Now I have my dinner.' And that is all we ever did, so the point that you're mentioning . . . I've now deflected myself! What the hell were you saying?

TB By the well-head . . .

DB He gave me only two pieces of instruction in the whole film. One was under the Rialto Bridge when he shouted through a megaphone and said, 'Stand when you feel the sun hit your face!' I didn't know why, but I felt the sun and I did stand. The other one was one night when we had to go to shoot in a tiny little dirty square in the centre of Venice in the slum area, near the docks. I had one white suit – we were very poor! – it was pouring with rain, they'd filled the square with garbage cans and rubbish to make it look like the plague in 1910, and we had real rats running around. There was one of those very beautiful Renaissance well-heads in the middle of the square, and I had to go and lean against it and think of Fate and life's futility and hopelessness, and laugh to myself at my own idiocy. In doing so I had to slide down the side of the well and lie prone on the ground in a white suit in pouring rain with the whole of Venice's garbage around me, and I knew that if I didn't do it properly in one take we were done, because that white suit would never survive. And it *didn't* survive! I was so worried that I was nervous, and I did the take wrongly. I heard Luchino's voice saying wretchedly through the rain, 'No, no, Bogarde! Too young! You're too young!' So, disaster! At the same moment, the entire unit came rushing around with great handfuls of white chalk, saying 'Bravo! Bravo!' I was smothered in white chalk from head to foot, and we did another shot and I did it right. But he'd seen and he knew exactly what he demanded of me: he knew what it would take. He also knew that to go again was humiliating, because that was the only time in five months that I ever had to do more than one take, which is not bad! Then he did something he used to do so incredibly; he'd give you a reward, a thank-you, but it never came the way you thought it would. He suddenly said, 'Bogarde!' – I was filthy, I was covered in chalk, muck, what have you – and he took me away, put his arm around me and said, 'I have one little *cadeau* for you.' And in the corner of the square there was a very old, tumbled, narrow house with washing all around it, and kids leaning out and staring down, which I would never have noticed, and he said, 'There is my present! This is for you. It is the house of Marco Polo.' I was his friend; it was very moving. No one knows it's Marco Polo's house – they haven't got it in the guidebooks – but *he* knew it was, and he wanted simply to show that to me. That was a thank-you for getting it right, or for laughing right.

TB May I ask you a rather philistine question about money? Did you actually make a lot of money out of *Death in Venice*?

DB No. I haven't been paid yet.

TB Why?

DB Well, I don't know. I keep on trying to find out, but they keep on saying, 'We're not in profit, we're two million in debt!' I don't know how we *can* be.

TB Were there any reasons why it should not make money?

DB Well, the American Money said, 'This is not a normal picture . . . We would be happier if you could change the sex of the younger protagonist.' Luchino said, 'But I can't change Thomas Mann! It *has* to be a little boy!' and they said, 'No, we think it would be a great deal better if you go with a little girl.' Then Luchino lost his temper and said, 'Do you really mean to tell me that they prefer a little girl in America?' and the gentleman said, 'Yeah, morally we would approve of that.' To his honour, Luchino replied, 'You really mean that child molestation is allowable in America?' There was nothing he could say. When the film was finished, we ran it in Los Angeles for the American Money, and they sat in a projection room in their blue plastic suits, and there wasn't a sound at the end of it, and Visconti was extremely pleased because he thought that the film had perhaps knocked them silly. And of course, it hadn't. They didn't know what to do with themselves, they didn't know where to look, and we realized that we had a disaster on our hands because nobody turned around and looked at us at all; we just saw all the backs of their heads. Suddenly, a little man, whose name I know but mustn't say, got up in anguish and agony and said, 'Mr Visconti, can I ask you just one question? Who wrote the theme music for your movie?' He was the domestic distributor, and he felt that he'd better say something, but Visconti was so grateful that somebody had spoken to him that he said with great politeness, 'Gustav Mahler wrote the music.' And Mr XYZ turned around – this is true! – and said, 'I think it was just great! I think we should sign him!' If you think that's not true, I promise you it is . . . Anyway, they *did* find out who Gustav Mahler was.

TB Of course, with your great respect and regard for Visconti, you did actually have the temerity to turn down the part that he offered you in *Conversation Piece*.

DB Yes, I did.

TB How did you find that temerity?

DB Well, it was a bloody awful part, but the main thing was that I was supposed to be playing *him*, and I found that an invidious thing to do: I couldn't have presumed to do that. We hardly knew each other socially, but I could never have played him.

TB In your book you quote him as saying to you, 'Are you still feeling distaste for my work?'

DB Oh, he was furious! And I said, 'I don't feel distaste for your work at all, Luchino. I love your work. I just didn't like the film, I didn't like the scenario, and I didn't want to play you.' And he said, 'No, you're perfectly right, you could not play me! Burt Lancaster was much, much better, because Burt Lancaster has *brio*. You lack brio.' So I gave up . . . but it wasn't a good film and I don't think it worked, even with brio.

TB There was a short time – I think about two years – when a lot of people say you retired . . .

DB I've never retired! I retreated. It's a different thing.

TB What sort of scripts did you get sent during those two years?

DB Oh, kinky schoolteachers, neurotic priests walking through corridors towards confession, one or two mad bishops, a couple of bent coppers . . . You name it, I got it!

TB What brought you back? Was it the need for money?

DB Yes, but I also knew that I had to get down to work again. Halcyon days don't last for ever.

TB And you went to work with Alain Resnais. You had in fact been talking to him as long ago as 1966, hadn't you?

DB Yes, we did try to make movies here in Britain about eighteen years ago, but we neither of us were bankable enough. We wanted to make *The Adventures of Harry Dixon* and a life of the Marquis de Sade, which was going to be the *true* story of Sade, but nobody wanted it because it was not about lashing girls around with whips and being locked up in turrets and dungeons, and all that kind of stuff. So we never got off the ground, and as we had no money to make the films they got chucked aside, but eventually, about five years ago, we did *Providence*.

TB And he was another director who never actually told you what to do?

DB No great director ever, ever, ever tells you what to do, or how to do it. A great director will only ever tell you what *not* to do.

TB He's trying to help you find what you are looking for . . . ?

DB He's waiting for you to find your own level of concentration, or emotion, or whatever it is you've got inside, so that he can take it from you and mould it and use it to his own end. That's the truth of a real director. But the director who says, 'Now you come over here and you pick up the tea-cup and start . . . ' – that's not a director! I don't know *what* that is.

TB You've said that because you were playing John Gielgud's son in *Providence*, you quite deliberately tried to pick up mannerisms of his.

DB But of course! I mean, if you're playing somebody's son, part of your body has to have the same mannerisms as the parent – a way of saying something, a move of the head, the way you move an arm, or a hand, or a finger. These are the things you very often don't know about when you're doing them yourself, but a stranger will say, 'My God, aren't you like your father?' So in preparing for *Providence* I had to study John Gielgud without him knowing, like when he was talking to me or eating a meal, so I could pick up his mannerisms.

TB Did you ever discuss that with Resnais?

DB No.

TB Was he aware of what you were doing?

DB Yes, I'm sure he was, but we never talked about it. Those are the things that are supposed to be part of your safety-kit as an actor. Perhaps I'm wrong, but I never discuss those things with a director and they don't choose to do so with me, though I think they know what I'm doing. Resnais was peculiar inasmuch as he learned to speak English so perfectly, but he still didn't have the innate knowledge of the language that anyone born in this country has, and for that reason it was very difficult to try and convince him how I should play the part. He kept on saying, 'It is all in *nightmare*, the role! So I said, 'Well, I think I'd better do it three times,' not six times, as with Visconti! So we did three takes of nearly every scene at the beginning, until Resnais was perfectly satisfied that he had got 'nightmare'. Then it was OK, and I found a way to play it.

TB You've said several times in the past that the camera can photograph thought. Can you expand on that a little?

DB No. [*Laughter*] I can only tell you that I have spoken to some of the greatest cameramen in the world and they all agree. If there is no thought behind the eye, then there's no one at home: the camera's photographing an empty room. You can go through all the actions and you can say all the words, but you have to be possessed, you have to be taken over, and the camera will photograph that.

TB Is that another way of describing total concentration?

DB Absolutely! To the point, honestly, of death: it becomes almost deathly. After *Death in Venice* I really didn't want to look at a camera, or be near a cinema ever again. I think it was my moment to say, 'Come on, you've done enough! It takes too much from you.' I went down to seven stone; I've never been fat, but seven stone is very little. I couldn't eat, I couldn't think, I only thought as this bloody man. I was totally possessed by someone I had invented for myself, whom Thomas Mann had, indeed, created, but whom I fleshed out. And it's not worth it, especially if you don't get paid!

TB Visconti actually got rather cross with you, didn't he, because in his eyes you broke that concentration for two days?

DB We had a two-day break because there was some big Catholic holiday in Italy, and I needed to go down to my house in France for the first time. I asked his permission, and he was so enraged! You can't imagine his rage, which was very, very quiet. He couldn't believe that I had broken my bond with him, or with the character, and simply to leave him for forty-eight hours! – he couldn't believe it was possible. I said, 'Please understand, I *have* to do this. I don't wish to go 300 miles through the night to see a house, but I have to be there to sign the deeds. I must do it, and we're five weeks late on the picture, so it's not my fault.' And he said, '*Via, via, via!*' So I *via*-ed, and I also *via*-ed out of Visconti's life for a whole week. I was completely banished. I wasn't allowed to sit at his table, and if he needed to address me (which was very seldom anyway) he did it through a servant.

TB Did you find it difficult to get back into that concentrated effort, or not?

DB No. I drove down to the house as the character and I came back as the character.

TB Now, at about the time of *Providence* your first book, *A Postillion Struck by Lightning*, came out, but in fact your writing goes back a lot further than that. Could you tell us about how you started?

DB Well, one gets fan letters: and one day I got a letter from a woman in America who had been sitting under a hair-dryer at her hairdresser's, and to pass the time she had read a magazine which she found rather distasteful. It was a cheap English woman's magazine, but in it, to her astonishment, she saw a picture of a house that once belonged to her and in front of the house, grinning like an idiot, was myself. She didn't know who I was because she never went to the movies, but she read the rather sorry little article about me and realized I was an actor of some description who now lived in this house which she'd found with her husband in 1929, and lived in until 1939, when the war broke out and they had to go back to America. So she wrote me a letter – very pathetic, very polite, very tiny, very neat – and sent inside a sepia picture of the house as it had been in 1929, covered in brambles and nettles. And she simply said, 'It's a great impertinence to write to you, as I don't know who you are or what you do, but I *do* know the house. Has it changed very much?' And that was all. Now, I don't know why – I never reply to letters, because there isn't time and I can't deal with so much – but I *did* write to her, and we wrote to each other for the next five years. In the end, she wrote a letter to me every single day of her life, on onion-skin – that very light airmail paper. I wrote three or four times a week, but when I began to put it all together and realized that she was dying, I wrote at least a postcard every day until 1975, when she died. I never saw her, we never spoke, and I've no idea what age she was, but she was determined I should write. All I *did* glean was that she was the head librarian at a very important university in America, and that she knew a great deal about literature and writing, and she'd seen something in all the junk I sent her that made her think I could write, or should be forced to.

TB So would it be fair to say that if it hadn't been for her you would never have written professionally?

DB In the final analysis, that is true.

TB Do you find you have to keep proper daily hours?

DB Yes, because I'm terribly lazy, and if I didn't do that I wouldn't do anything at all. I had to make myself write from eight o'clock in the morning until one, and then again from five to seven in the evening.

TB Was she responsible for that mode of working, too?

DB Yes.

TB The dialogue in your books is unfailingly real, which one would expect, in a sense, from an actor. How do you do that? Do you actually declaim it?

DB Yes, I act it: I sit in a tiny little room and I play all the scenes. I scream and yell, and if anyone passed they'd really think I was barking mad. I think very often in novels, and in some films, the dialogue doesn't work because it's not been written for people to say. It's been written for people to read, which is a mistake, because people don't always speak in pure literature.

TB Do you feel a bit like a director directing actors when you're writing?

DB No, I would never know how to be a director! I simply feel I'm doing it all by myself, which is a fearful thing. You're your own director, your own writer, your own producer . . . you take the can.

TB You say you can't direct, but you did in fact take over from Losey for ten days on *The Servant*.

DB Well, he was sick, he had pneumonia, and I took over for ten days until he was better.

TB Was it not an experience you enjoyed?

DB Oh no, it was horrible! I didn't know what to do with the actors and they didn't know what to do with me, and that was the end of that.

TB Could I talk to you a little about *The Night Porter*? You were in fact one of the first British officers to go into Belsen at the end of the war. What kind of experience was that?

DB Well, not very nice. What do you want me to say?

TB I wanted to know how you felt when you . . .

DB Oh dear, how do I explain this? I'm 63: how do I explain what I felt when I was 24? Think of a young man at 24 walking into Hell completely unexpectedly. I can't describe it to you. I tried not to remember it for very many years, and it's sort of gone now. You can't comprehend it . . . Of course, it's gone on again, you see, through my lifetime: in Vietnam, in Beirut . . .

TB Obviously your performance in *The Night Porter* must have been influenced not a little by what you yourself had seen, but Charlotte Rampling had no experience of that . . .

DB She wasn't even born.

TB But the performance was so truthful. Where did that come from?

DB I think it came from the truth of the film itself. We were shooting in an old tuberculosis sanatorium with filthy tiled floors – a dreadful, gloomy, bitter place. Everybody was stark naked – men, women, children – and Charlotte was equally naked, and in front of them was a long table with the SS behind it. There was a crying child sitting on his mother's hip, and Charlotte suddenly noticed that the actress who was playing the mother was wearing a hat with four bows. The bows on the hat of this naked woman broke Charlotte completely, and she fled and sobbed and finally said, 'Why the bloody hat? Why is she wearing the hat?' She thought it was a little directorial trick by Liliana Cavani, but I said, 'No, it's true,' and we showed her a photograph of a camp in Poland which we had got from the archives. The SS were very clever about that, because they stripped you first to remove any trace of your individuality, but this woman had insisted that she had her hat; as the last essence of her dignity, she'd kept her hat on. From that piece of bravery I think Charlotte really got it and realized just what it was all about.

TB When you were filming in Vienna an extraordinary thing happened, didn't it?

DB Well, I was very nervous filming in Vienna wearing an SS uniform, because Vienna was the crucible of Nazism, and if you were a Jew you would have been safer living in Berlin in 1942 than living in Vienna. But as an ordinary, timid actor, and rather skinny to boot, I was very scared and I didn't want to walk around in my uniform while we were doing location shots, so I wore a coat and hid my hat and pretended I wasn't me. They hid me one night in the flat of this sweet old lady, and she showed me photographs of some singularly unattractive children, she showed me her canary birds, she made some coffee, she said television was boring, she said it was very cold, and so on. Then the time came to go to shoot, and because I'd just forgotten what I was wearing by this point, I took my coat off, and she screamed! I thought, 'Oh God, I've upset her! Why did I do such a stupid thing?' Then I turned, and it had been a scream of joy! I saw two startled, pale-blue eyes of sheer pleasure. The interpreter whom I had with me was telling me to get down the stairs quickly, and he came up later and said, 'I'm sorry, but will you shake her hand?' So I shook her hand,

and he said, 'She is very happy because it reminds her of the good old days.'

TB I think we'll move on!

DB I think we should.

TB Fassbinder, Nabokov and Tom Stoppard . . .

DB Yes, what a mixture! Mr Stoppard telephoned me one day from London airport (he must forgive me for this, though I suppose he won't!), and he said, 'Hello, hello, hello, it's Tom Stoppard! I'm at London airport.' I said, 'Oh, congratulations!' and he said, 'I've just got in from Munich,' so I said, 'Absolutely splendid! I am pleased!' 'I understand you're not making any more films, is that right?' 'No, I'm not making any crap!' There was a dreadful silence, and then Tom said, 'I don't write crap!' Anyway, then he told me that he was doing a Nabokov story with Fassbinder, that they thought of me to play the role, and would it excite me or interest me? and I said it would indeed. So Tom, Fassbinder and all the German entourage arrived in the south of France to see me, and I waited in this restaurant for Fassbinder to come down to dine. I'd never met him, but I was terrified of him. I'd heard all these extraordinary stories, I knew the magical stuff that he did, I wanted very much to work with him, and I didn't want him to think that I was an absolute wet stick. He was ages, so I said, 'Where is he?' and they said, 'He's having a bath, and it's rather a long bath, because he hasn't had one for four years.' And he really didn't care much about bathing or anything! . . . He was, next to Visconti, the greatest director I've ever worked with, and he was the antithesis of what he seems to be. He did behave very badly to the press in England and France, like a spoilt boy, but he's actually a man of the most illuminating sensitivity, gentleness and sweetness. I can't speak German, and I remember saying, 'If you go on like this with an interpreter I'm going to lose my mind! I can't work with you through an interpreter who was born in Egypt. Talk to me! I know you can speak English.' And he did. He said, 'I'm frightened to speak to you in English because the crew will laugh at me – my German crew,' and I said, '*They* all speak English to me, you won't be losing face!' So we spoke in English, and it was very good that we did because we made *Despair*, which was a mess in the end, as it happens, but nevertheless a bloody good film.

TB I know you feel it's your best performance. Why do you say that?

DB Difficult to say, because it's a technical thing: I think it's the best *technical* performance I've given on the screen. I think it's the culmination of all the work I've ever tried to do, and if you take it layer by layer, inch by inch, step by step, it is a perfect example of a developing madness which becomes paranoia. Now, I don't know anything about that and I'm not really very mad myself, but the lengths I found I could go to in that satisfied me enormously. I did a lot of research for that.

TB Did you feel that you were possessed, as you did with *Death in Venice*?

DB Yes, completely possessed. I asked Fassbinder only one question before we started shooting – I always do ask them *one* question! – and that was, 'Is there a precise moment when Herman Herman goes mad, or has he gone mad before we start?' and Fassbinder said, 'He's been mad like you and me – always!' That's all he said, so I had to work it out for myself, pussy-footing through. And you know what we did? We always do it, don't we? We shot the end scene of the film on the first day, so I was well and truly stinking mad by that point, and then had to work right through the movie backwards to sanity.

TB One aspect of your career that is not very often touched on is your work in the theatre. You were in the theatre for some time as a young man, and you went back briefly in the 1950s and the critics jumped on you, several of them assuming that it was your first shot at the stage.

DB I remember all of them very clearly! I didn't love the critics very much, though I can't blame . . .

TB Yes, you can!

DB I can't, really, because I was a film star, you see. I tried to go back to the theatre to do my true work, which was serious acting, which I have now achieved in the cinema. But of course, *they* couldn't understand that, and neither, indeed, could my audience, who were teenagers and who used to scream, 'I love you! I love you!' They were very sweet, but if they didn't like you they used to throw meat pies at you; they literally did in Cardiff. All the plays I was in were rather serious, and I was distressed for the other players, who were really suffering a lot.

TB My point is, you see, that you were in fact deterred . . .

DB I was *stopped* – don't worry about 'deterred'! When I got my last set of reviews saying, 'Dirk Bogarde unwisely attempts the stage', I thought, 'Well, that's it! I've been acting since I was 14, and if he hasn't twigged that . . . ' He's still writing notices, that man. I could shoot him.

TB It's a pity you didn't, because you didn't play Hamlet when Olivier wanted you to.

DB Olivier *did* ask me to do Hamlet in Chichester. Well, I thought that was putting your head into a can of worms!

TB But was the main reason that you didn't do it because of what the critics had said?

DB Yes, I wasn't going to risk it. It wasn't worth it. I would have been torn to shreds, and I don't think I would then have gone on to be a film actor. In any case, I don't think I would have been very good. I mean, everybody has a bash at Hamlet. It *is* a bit boring.

TB Is there now any play you would consider doing?

DB No, I've lost my nerve now: I couldn't go on the stage again. I loved it, but if you get clobbered too many times it's wiser just to pack up and go. I found my own route, right? – but it's not

in the theatre. There's another thing, which is very typical of me
... I'm very quickly bored, and a run of a year, night after
night after night, I think, would kill me.

TB Your latest film is . . . I'm not sure if it's called *Act of Love* or
The Patricia Neal Story?

DB I don't know what it's called, and I haven't been paid for that
one, either! . . . Why do I do this? Why do I bring this myth
upon myself that I never get money? We made it as a movie
called *Act of Love*, which is about Patricia Neal and Roald Dahl,
and it was slammed on on New Year's Eve at nine o'clock in
Britain, and then it was called *The Patricia Neal Story*. I think it's
very good, and I think Glenda Jackson and I are very good, but
nobody would buy it because it's downbeat. Well, it happens
to be about the most hopeful movie I've ever seen in my life,
because Miss Neal did indeed have a brain tumour, and she
was paralysed, and her husband did bring her back to life.
What *is* hope? . . . And the film, without preaching, or being
boring (which it isn't), does at least show that by will-power and
with help, you can make something work. I thought it was very
well worth doing. But no, it's not commercial, we're too old,
we're not bankable . . . They use any excuse. So why do they
shove it on on New Year's Eve at nine o'clock? Even my
beloved sister said, 'I can't watch, darling. I said we'd go out to
dinner.' It was a kind of mischief, I think.

TB Are there any roles you wanted to play, but didn't get the
chance?

DB This may surprise you, but the only part I think I would have
liked to have played is Isherwood in *I Am a Camera*. I was
going to do it once with Glynis Johns as Sally Bowles, and in fact
I got that part twice, but I didn't like the director on either
occasion, so I left. The other part I would like to have played
(though I think I might have made a terrible mess of it) is the
Louis Jourdan part in *Gigi*. They wrote it for me, but I
chickened out at the last moment because I thought that if I
didn't pull *that* off, it would really have been the chopper! They

don't give you a second chance. If you can believe this, I did 'This is a far, far better thing I do' instead. That'll teach you! . . . Except that they seem to love it in Japan.

10 Yves Montand

Yves Montand was born Ivo Livi in the village of Monsummano near Florence in 1921. Two years later his family was forced to flee to France when Mussolini came to power, and they settled in Marseilles. He left school when he was 11 and worked in various jobs in order to supplement the family income. He made his début as a singer in a local club when he was 18, moving to Paris towards the end of the war to continue his career. He gained a contract at the Moulin Rouge, where he met Edith Piaf, who helped to promote him as a singer and introduced him to the screen in one of her films, *Etoile sans lumière* (1945, Marcel Blistene). In the following years he appeared in several more films, including *Les portes de la nuit* (1946, Marcel Carné), while also growing in popularity as a singer. His performance in *Le salaire de la peur* (*The Wages of Fear*) (1952, Henri-Georges Clouzot) established him as a major film actor, and it was followed by roles in such works as *Tempi Nostri* (1953, Alessandro Blasetti), *Marguerite de la nuit* (1955, Claude Autant-Lara), *Uomini e Lupi* (1956, Giuseppe de Santis), *Les sorcières de Salem* (1957, Raymond Rouleau), *La lunga strada azzura* (1957, Gille Pontecorvo) and *La loi* (*Where the Hot Wind Blows*) (1959, Jules Dassin). After a highly successful one-man show on Broadway in 1959, he made his American film début in *Let's Make Love* (1960, George Cukor), and during the 1960s he made several more English-language films, including *Goodbye Again* (1961, Anatole Litvak) and *On A Clear Day You Can See Forever* (1968, Vincente Minnelli). His international reputation was further consolidated by his performances in *La guerre est finie* (1966, Alain Resnais), *Vivre pour vivre* (1967, Claude Lelouch) and a trilogy of films with Costa-Gavras, *Z* (1968), *L'aveu* (*The Confession*) (1969) and *Etat de siège* (*State of Siege*) (1972), and during the last two decades he has starred in a succession of European films encompassing many different genres. They include *Le cercle rouge* (1970, Jean-Pierre Melville), *Tout Va Bien* (1972, Jean-Luc Godard/Jean-Pierre Gorin), *César et Rosalie* (1972, Claude Sautet), *Vincent, Francois, Paul . . . et les autres* (1973, Sautet), *Le sauvage* (1975, Jean-Paul Rappeneau), *Les routes du sud*

(1977, Joseph Losey), *Clair de femme* (1979, Costa-Gavras), *Garçon* (1983, Sautet), *Jean de Florette* (1986, Berri) and *Manon des sources* (1986, Berri). Yves Montand's most recent film is *Trois places pour le 26* (1988, Jacques Demy), a musical comedy based on his own early life in Marseilles. He is currently writing his memoirs.

The following lecture took place on 25 July 1989. Yves Montand was interviewed by Don Allen, a critic, writer and broadcaster and Director of External Affairs at the West London Institute.

Yves Montand

Don Allen Can I begin in the time-honoured way by asking you about your beginnings? You come from a very poor peasant family, don't you, and you were the youngest of three children?

Yves Montand Oh yes, we lived together very, very happily. We had nothing to eat – I mean, we had difficulty eating – so my mother and father had to work a lot. We had fights sometimes, but we were a very tender and very warm family, a very strong family, and when I heard that friends of mine wanted to leave home because they fought with their father or their mother, this surprised me very much. My father was a very fantastic man, a good peasant from Tuscany.

DA And he brought you to France when you were 2 years old because of the rise of Fascism in Italy. How much did you feel you were an immigrant, because you were there from a very early age? You must have spoken French as your first language?

YM I didn't feel I was an immigrant at all, because at home we immediately spoke French, and my father and mother answered me in Italian. Of course, I realized what racism was at that time when they called us 'Baby Macaroni!' or something like that. It's the same in every country, probably, because instinctively we are racist. Our conscience tells us, 'Don't do that, it's not good! You're a bad man if you talk like this!' but probably, like animals, we want to stay in the same group. We must always fight against that, of course. But I didn't realize that they were talking to me when they said, 'Macaroni!' especially in Marseilles as there were plenty of different people who came to live there – Italian, Greek, Spanish, North African, Polish . . . We were already a small Europe.

DA We always see you as a Frenchman. How Italian do you see yourself as being?

YM You're right, but I never deny my origins, never! I'm not ashamed to have been born in Tuscany; but the journalists considered it wasn't necessary to put that I was born in Italy. When I was in New York, some said, 'He's Jewish,' because my name is Livi. Some said, 'He was born in Canada,' some said, 'Born in Venice.' So I was born in Tuscany Italy, but I came to France when I was 2 years old and I consider myself completely French . . . let's say European. But I want to say thank you to France for accepting us into your country and giving us the chance to live in freedom. It was not very easy at the beginning, but thank you, my country, thank you, France!

DA There's a nice story about how you came to be called Yves Montand, isn't there?

YM *Oui*. My real name is Ivo Livi, but when my mother called me at the window at night she spoke in Italian–French, a mixture of both, and she called me, 'Ivo, *monta*!' – 'Come on, come up here!' Not Italian, not French, but I understood what she said.

DA You actually started work very early, when you were about 11½ years old.

YM We had to, especially because Papa wanted to do something by himself – he was an artisan, a craftsman – and he failed, so everyone had to work. It was very young for a kid, but no drama, we're not going to cry! That's life, it's OK. When I came home the first week with my money inside the envelope, and I gave it to my mother, I was very proud. She took the money and she gave me five francs. I said to her, 'Don't spend everything!'

DA And the jobs that you did were incredibly tough manual jobs. You worked in a spaghetti factory . . .

YM Yes, I was a delivery boy. Then I went to work on the waterfront, in the beginning not as a docker, but taking merchandise and loading it on trucks to go to Marseilles. No drama! I think it was a very good school, and I learned a lot. Sometimes I think it was better to learn there than from books. What we learn in the street is very, very important.

DA And then you decided you didn't want to spend the rest of your life using your muscles to earn a living?

YM Well, first of all I wanted to go and sing in the suburbs of Marseilles, to buy a packet of cigarettes without spending anything, because if I went on stage and sang they would give me money, and this, I thought, would pay my expenses. This was my first reason. The second was that I liked jazz a lot, I liked Fred Astaire, and I liked American actors very much. My generation grew up with the spirit of American democracy. It was very peculiar: on the one hand we were left wing, and at the same time we wanted to live under American democracy. I don't want you to make a mistake! – I think probably American democracy doesn't always work very well, but I hope that it will stay there for a long time.

DA So how *did* you begin to get into show business?

YM Well, we lived in the suburbs in the north of Marseilles, as I told you, and every Saturday night they gave a little concert and the workers would come with babies in their arms, and they drank beer, they ate peanuts, they were yelling, the babies were crying, etc. etc. We would go on the stage, which was made of boards used by builders, so when you danced all the cement came out.

DA And you were tap-dancing then?

YM No, no, I just moved. It was very sympathetic and warm, and they applauded very well. When they didn't like you they still applauded, but not so intensely. That was also a very good school. We didn't sing with a microphone, and we always considered that real artists didn't use a microphone at all, like Piaf. Piaf could fill the Moulin Rouge – 3,000 seats! – without a microphone.

DA Then you were discovered, in a sense. How did that happen?

YM I discovered myself!

DA You must have been discovered, because you didn't stay there in Marseilles, or you wouldn't be here today.

YM Ah, I'm sorry. I started to sing in a small theatre in Paris called the ABC on 18 February 1944. The Nazis were still there, and they wanted to take me to work in Germany, so I escaped from Marseilles.

DA You just escaped by the skin of your teeth from a compulsory work camp?

YM Yes, and I went to Paris, because at that time the Nazis occupied France completely and my friend Aubiffred, the manager, told me, 'I think the best thing you can do is go right out in the open in front of everybody, under the light.' It was a big risk, I think, but it worked, believe it or not.

DA And the songs you were singing were the same ones you had been singing in Marseilles?

YM Yes, the imitations of Chevalier, of Astaire, and a French cowboy song, 'Oui, Monsieur', and also the scat singing of Louis Armstrong . . . Well, I *thought* it was scat!

DA I was supposed to ask you before, but do you think you might actually sing something for us later this evening? This is not at all prepared; he may say no!

YM They never *believe* it if you say that! It happened in the Festival at Cannes with Barbara Andridge. It was a very nice evening, and she went on stage and she wanted to sing 'Autumn Leaves', and she said, 'Unfortunately I don't have the words and I would like to ask Monsieur Montand to help me.' She sang marvellously, but very high – not my tessitura . . . but it worked very well. A miracle, anyway, we'll see later.

DA So you've begun your stage career in Paris, and Piaf came along fairly soon after?

YM No, not as quickly. I sang in the ABC Theatre and then in a nightclub. And then Piaf was going to sing at the Moulin

Rouge, and the guy who was supposed to sing with her got flu and couldn't sing, so she said, 'Tell me, I heard that you have one man who came from Marseilles. You told me that he is wonderful, etc. etc. You told me that I'm afraid to sing with him. Send him back, send him to me!' So I came to her! I couldn't believe it! And I was afraid, of course. She was beautiful; she was in a blue dress with flowers, and she was very charming. We had the rehearsal, and then in the afternoon we sang. Of course, there was no microphone and there was no light, no spot – they opened the roof – and believe me, it was not very easy in front of 3,000 people! When I came on stage I was wearing a white cowboy hat made of cardboard, and walking like this, and I sang a French cowboy song and another song called 'Je vends des hot dogs à Madison et à Great Central Park', and the reaction of the people was fantastic because, of course, at that time we were waiting for the American and English people to come and liberate Europe. Then Piaf came backstage and she was very happy, very proud – then, she was with somebody else, not with me – and she said, 'You sing very well, but don't forget you are a success because you are singing American-style songs, and we are waiting for them at this moment. Later you must learn very good French songs.' I was very pretentious, and I thought she was a little bit jealous! Then she went on stage – I had never seen her sing live before – and when she came on she was very, very small, and she took a long time to get to the middle of the stage. Then she opened her mouth, and after three songs I was crying. I hadn't realized. And then, of course . . . *voilà*!

DA And then, of course, you had a very intimate and close relationship with Edith Piaf?

YM And I want to say thank you to Edith, thank you very much, because she taught me a lot . . . I would say almost everything, but that's not completely true. A lot, yes.

DA You actually made a film with her, didn't you?

YM Yes, *Etoile sans lumière*, but it was her film, really; I had a very

short part. The second film was *Les portes de la nuit* with
Jacques Prévert and Marcel Carné, and I was suffering a lot
because, first of all, it was written for Jean Gabin, whom
nobody can replace and he had his special Parisian accent. I
came from Marseilles, living with a Tuscan family – can you
imagine my accent?! Also, I had to play the part of an old man,
55 years old, when I was 24 years old. I think it was a bit too
tough and I didn't feel right, and the film wasn't a success
when it came out. Today, of course, it is a classic of the period
of the liberation of Paris.

DA So you made those films and you made others as well, but you
then had a period when you were concentrating on your
singing career. I don't know if you think of yourself primarily
as a singer, or primarily as an actor, or whether you don't make
the distinction.

YM Well, when you go on stage it's something different because
you have contact with the people right away, and the contact is
a good. What you call it? – a compass: they don't say anything,
but you have a feeling when you're going over, or when
you're in the right place. In a movie you shoot the scene, you
act, you smell that it's OK, but only for one minute; and every
day it is one-and-a-half minutes, two minutes, three minutes,
for a long, long week. When people go and see a movie and
they say, 'I saw you in the film last night,' that's not correct. We
did act, but not *now*, and so you cannot rectify anything. When
I see my pictures on the TV or something, I want to reshoot
almost everything! Almost, almost . . .

DA But if you only had one choice, to be remembered either as a
great singer or a great actor, which would you choose?

YM I would prefer not to choose. When I'm singing I'm very happy,
and I like it when I'm making a good movie. I don't want to have
a career, because if you think about a career, sometimes you
kill everything, you kill many things. I would like to be a good
man . . . I mean, I *try* to be.

DA So then we come to the watershed year of 1952 when you were persuaded by Simone Signoret, whom you had married in 1951, to accept the part in Clouzot's *Wages of Fear*. I gather that when he first approached you, you were hesitant?

YM We married in 1951, but we met in 1949. Yes, I was not very happy when I was filming and I didn't want to film anymore, and Clouzot insisted I play the part in the movie with my friend, Charles Vanel. I said, '*Je regrette*, I don't want to, because I don't feel fine, I'm not happy.'

DA Why was that?

YM I couldn't make the translation between what was me and what was the *personnage*, the character. As you know, we are there to give life to somebody else, and sometimes the character is very close to your own personality, like in *Vincent, Francois, Paul . . . et les autres*, which is almost me in life, or in *César et Rosalie*. This is OK. But to play a tough guy without *being* a tough guy, because this character makes trouble, you know? . . . that's very different, and I didn't feel like it. Then Simone told me, 'Listen, when you are singing a song called 'Battling Joe' with a story about a fighter, you believe that you *are* a fighter, and if *you* believe, *they* believe. They believe because you are involved with this Battling Joe. So in movies it is the same.' I said, 'Yes, but I tried to work with a play by Anouilh. You are Albert! Go ahead!' And I tried and tried and it didn't come, it didn't work, and suddenly one day it came and then I felt fine. Then it can also become dangerous, because you can go too far if you want, and the *personnage* can take over. It is very wonderful to be able to do it, but you and the character must be very vigilant, because you can kill yourself otherwise.

DA Were you surprised by the success of *Wages of Fear*?

YM *Oui*, but I must tell you that the story was a wonderful story, and the trucks and the nitro are the big stars in the movie. This kind of movie we can do with any old actors, almost even if they are bad actors.

DA Then in 1957 you did *The Crucible, Les sorcières de Salem*, with Simone Signoret. That was a critical success, but not a great popular success?

YM No, no, it was a big, big hit: we played for one year in a theatre with 2,000 seats. The adaptation was written by Marcel Aimé for the theatre and by Monsieur Jean-Paul Sartre for the movie, and at that time, in 1955, we still believed – even Monsieur Sartre believed – that the good people are here and the bad people are there, and obviously that was very dangerous. We really believed that we were very nice and wonderful people and the others were not nice people, but he wrote in that kind of way: everyone was too obviously good and bad. Of course, we must condemn the trial in Salem and we have to be against Monsieur McCarthy, but not so much black and white, goodies and baddies. Are you clear?

DA Yes, very clear. When *did* you become committed to the far left of politics? Although you weren't a card-carrying member of the Communist Party you were a fellow-traveller, and you certainly suffered because of it. How far can you trace back the dawning of your political . . . ?

YM Listen, I want to be very clear about this. At that time I met women and men who were really fantastic. Sometimes I still meet some of them, and we talk in a very relaxed way; two or three of them still stay in the Marxist–Leninist perspective. First of all, above all, they are friends, and I think it is very important in life to say 'Hello' to you, not because the Party says 'no' or says 'yes', but because you are my friend. Right? This, I think, is very important. I was concerned with politics when I went to work in a factory when I was 11½ years old. I knew nothing about politics. The only thing I knew was that my father was suffering, my family was suffering, because of Fascism. They tortured him, so I couldn't be Fascist, clear? Fine! Now, we were in the suburbs of Marseilles, we had to struggle, we had to fight just for bread, just for survival – you know what this means. So even if you don't want to be concerned with politics, politics concerns *you*, and it became for me just like a logical reaction: sometimes I say that I was born in the street of communism. We didn't know what was happening in Russia, and for a million people it was paradise. Of course, there were some very intelligent people who said to the workers, said to *us*, 'Be careful, it is not paradise! Believe me, it's terrible!' and we would say, 'Come on! You don't know the problems of the Russian people! They are in a besieged fortress, so of course many things don't work, but tomorrow you will see that everything will be fantastic. There will be bread, good living, we will have everything we need, we must change the world all together!' We realized a little bit too late that it's not so simple, but I think the courage consists of saying to yourself, 'I made a mistake, I don't want to cheat any more, I don't want to say something is true when it is untrue just because I'm afraid it might help the conservatives.' This I don't want to hear any more! The Party is like a family, and if you leave the family you are going the wrong way; if you do something they don't like they think you are cheating for some reason, even if you are an honest and generous man. I want to say to you no, I don't accept that! When I see some men and women in the conservative class do something positive, I want to be free to say that what he does or what she does is fine. Maybe they are not my people, but it's still good. Is that clear?

DA Right, you don't want to follow a party line.

YM No, I don't want to. This is why I was so involved in making *The Confession*: I know what I'm talking about, you know. I am also guilty, because I have insisted that people think like me for years – for years! – and what is the result? 'Oh, I'm sorry, I made a mistake, I didn't know.' No! Too easy! So, in this case, don't do the same thing again. If you want to serve your feelings, OK, serve your feelings, but I don't want to be in any kind of party any time. I've felt this way since 1956, in fact, and definitely after the invasion of Czechoslovakia.

DA No labels?

YM No, I don't want it . . . But I prefer to talk about something other than politics. I came to your country and I am very happy and very touched about what happened to me here, and I prefer to talk about something different.

DA Sure. I just wanted to give you the chance to go into the political question . . .

YM No, because you have enough political people here at the talk.

DA OK.

YM It's their business, not my business. I give my opinion because you ask me, or in France because the television journalists ask me, but I prefer to talk about something else.

DA Right, let's talk about Marilyn Monroe, which is something completely different. In 1960 you made *Let's Make Love* with her, and she said you were the most exciting man she had ever met. I don't know if you want to talk about your relationship with Marilyn Monroe?

YM No, I think the person who talks about Marilyn Monroe very well is Simone Signoret. Simone wrote ten pages in the book *Nostalgia Isn't What It Used to Be*, and the way she talks about Marilyn Monroe is just fantastic, so I think it is better to stay with what Simone put in the book than to explain many things, personal things. The only thing that I can talk to you about is professional work. We worked very, very hard at that time, because I was so mad with my sentences. I couldn't speak one word of English, and I played that movie only by learning my words like a song, but I didn't understand what I said. I knew the story, I knew the situation, but the words shouldn't look like a lot of small worms! Imagine if I said to you, 'In eight days you are going to talk in Russian because we need it!' Come on!

DA I'll let you know!

YM They gave me a coach, and it was a very big suffering for me because usually coaches are former actors, and you think, 'Why did *he* become an actor?' But he knocked at the door and said to me, 'So you are Yves Montand,' and I said, 'I think if you say Yves, it's enough,' and he said, 'Oh, like a girl, then?' and I said, '*Oui.*' So I had to listen to him, and I practised my sentences until four o'clock in the morning. Then I went to sleep, then I woke up, and I spoke my words – not with intelligence, but memory.

DA Let's go on to the films you made with Costa-Gavras, two of which were written by the Spanish writer Jorge Semprun, who is a close personal friend of yours. He wrote a biography of you in the early 1980s which is very moving.

YM Now he is the Spanish Minister of Culture, and unfortunately I don't see him any more. I think they are very good films. We didn't say one day, 'We're going to make political movies.' Not at all! Never did that!

DA Did you meet Costa-Gavras through Jorge Semprun?

YM No, I met him just before Semprun and then we all worked together. Sometimes they came to my house in Normandy – a beautiful house, very beautiful. I bought it with my own money. It's French money, but it's good.

DA Nothing wrong with money, as you told me this morning.

YM Believe me, I don't have any complex about that, because I know what it means to earn money! I used to be poor, but now I'm rich. Plus I don't exploit anybody.

DA Semprun also wrote *La guerre est finie*, which you made in 1968, before the Costa-Gavras films, and I imagine that your character, the courier making clandestine trips to Spain back and forth across the Pyrenees, was based on Semprun himself?

YM Yes, of course. I went there too and I saw what was going on, so I know better than those who stayed in Paris. They were very generous people, ready to die if necessary, but they did not have the faintest idea how it was in Spain. They would say to the Spanish people, 'Come on! Why don't you do this and this? Then Franco will collapse tomorrow! The workers on May

1st must do this, and the army is going to do this!' Like in a movie! But, of course, Franco died in his bed, very quietly.

DA It's always easier from the outside.

YM Of course. But the people in Spain said to me, 'No, it's not true! It doesn't work like this! Spain is changing, and you stay in the dream of 1936, the dream of the revolution!'

DA Perhaps there's a sort of reflection in the Costa-Gavras films of your own political movement from the extreme left to what you might call the centre-right . . . even though you might not like the label, and you've explained already that you don't like labels . . .

YM No, you're mistaken. I'm still against intolerance, injustice and for democracy, because things are always changing. We stay blind, of course, we don't want to see anything else, and that's OK, it doesn't bother me. Believe what you want to believe, but don't disturb me! And it's true that things change faster than we can imagine; we are here and already things are there! Sometimes I want to say, stop! Life should not be running all the time! Life is stopping to talk to someone, to say, 'Hello! How are you? How do you feel now, good? You're working well? Can we drink something?' But it's impossible, we run all the time, all the time . . .

DA You've said that one of your favourites amongst your films is *César et Rosalie*, which you made for Claude Sautet, who is also a friend of yours.

YM *Oui, César et Rosalie* is what I call *une rencontre*. It was the right moment, a good script, it worked very well. We didn't sit down and say, 'Well, what kind of movie can we make? Do you have any ideas?' I mean, we sat around and talked, but it should just happen, like that.

DA Was there a lot of improvisation in that film, a lot of spontaneity?

YM Oh yes, but you can be spontaneous and improvise when you have good lines; you can do anything you want then, because the lines always come at the right place, but not the contrary. But actors are lucky in some ways, because the one who is responsible for the movie is really the director. When you're good in the movies, OK, bravo! – but it's the director who is the chief, and if we're not very good, he is responsible, not you. It's true! Critics sometimes say, 'I saw this man or girl in a movie and they were showing off too much.' How *can* they show off too much? A director is there, watching. Why didn't he say to her or him, 'Eh! Easy, easy!' He never said that, so it's his fault. You have to trust the director; it is a love affair between him and the actors. Sometimes it's uncomfortable, but we trust and believe him because we doubt ourselves all the time. After we finish a scene, everybody – Marlon Brando, everybody! – wants to know how it was, if it was OK, and we are anxious until the day after, when we go to see the rushes and realize that it was not too bad. But we have to trust the director, so if we're showing off, tell him, not us!

DA Do you normally see your rushes? – because some actors prefer not to.

YM I like to go, not for narcissism, but to see how the character is progressing. I think, 'What's the peasant in South America going to think about it?' so it's important for me to see it.

DA Is your greatest fear before you do a take, or before you see the rushes?

YM The greatest fear is the first day; with Simone it was the same. The first day we are very afraid because there is a new family, a new story, and there is a new director. You talk with directors before you make the movie and they are very charming. They invite you to dinner and everything, they talk about your films: 'Oh, just fantastic, believe me!' etc. etc. Then on the first day it's, 'Come here! Shut up, everybody!' I understand why they do this, because you cannot be a director if you are not a dictator – it's impossible. I mean, you *could* be very nice and very polite, but they would kill you right away! So directors say, 'Once more!' I say nothing. 'What's wrong?' 'What's wrong?

It seemed fine to me!' You stay very calm, you do one, two, three, four takes . . . You become mad, but you are obedient.

DA You had a bad time with Godard and Gorin, didn't you, when you were doing *Tout Va Bien*?

YM *Oui*, but I still think Godard really was one of the best directors, maybe now not so much . . . I was nervous sometimes, and I do not want all movies to be made like that, but he made it very, very well, and it became a classic. Even in the movies which are not so well done, there are always sequences which are wonderful.

DA But he made you suffer?

YM Yes, but he suffered too, because he likes actors and at the same time he hates actors. In fact, he hates everybody. But he was a very charming man, it's true, and he was very nice with you: he was very frank, very quick. He wrote letters to me: 'What you are going to shoot is not what you are going to say. You're going to say the words, but what is important is what is behind the words, what is behind the situation.' Very wonderful, interesting letters. Then, we arrived on the set and the first day no one worked, he didn't talk to us at all. We shot and we didn't know what we shot, we acted and he said 'good', or 'not good', and then we finished: for two weeks it was like that. One night I said to him, 'Listen, tomorrow when I come to work I will wear dark glasses and I won't film and I won't do anything, because we don't know what we are doing and this is unacceptable.' He was afraid, of course, that maybe I would punch him on the nose, but I didn't want to, not at all – that is weakness. In fact, he came up to me with determination and very courageously, stood under my nose and said, 'I am the director and I'll shoot the film how I like.' But I said in truth what I thought, and we became very good friends.

DA Would you work with him again?

YM I would like to very much, but at the same time I know that when he says, 'Very good!' he also pinches you, really pinches you – you know what I mean? He's a very peculiar man, but I like him very much, and I must tell you he's also very shy.

DA Let's come on to . . .

YM Let's have a beer!

DA Well, let's have a beer in a moment. You've got to sing also . . .

YM No, I don't think so.

DA Let's come to the two films based on Pagnol, *Jean de Florette* and *Manon des sources*. I believe it was Simone Signoret who encouraged you to accept the part?

YM Well, Simone was fantastic about introducing the right people to each other. She knew very well that this man would work very well with this man or this woman, because she had the quality to be a human being with everyone: everybody knows this, but I like to repeat it. It's true, I didn't want to make the movies. I didn't want to look twenty years older. I said, 'Let Time do that, for Christ's sake!' Then my friend Claude Berri, the director, asked me to take a test with Coluche taking the part that Daniel Auteuil plays in the movies . . .

DA Really? Coluche in Daniel Auteuil's part?

YM Yes, yes, but as you know he talks with a Parisian accent, though he was wonderful in the test. So to help Claude Berri I said, 'OK, I'll do the test, but remember that you're a good friend and I don't want to make the movie, please, and I have to go on tour, so I don't want to play an old man now! Not so old, OK?' So I put on the moustache and the black hat and the accent, and when I saw the tests and I saw the face I said, 'My God, forget this *coquetterie*! Do it!' So that's it – I did it!

DA Did you base your performance on anybody in your childhood?

YM Yes, I thought of my family. When I put on the moustache and hat and the *velours* I felt at home, I felt very, very, very well, and I tell you that I want to continue to wear a moustache! To stay young in your mind, that is very important, but the face doesn't matter.

DA Can I ask you which actresses you've worked most closely with in your career?

YM Well, I was very lucky. First of all, of course, Simone Signoret, and then Catherine Deneuve, Ingrid Bergman, Marilyn Monroe, Shirley MacLaine, and Romy Schneider, etc. etc. . . . The actress's life is cruel, very cruel, you know? Her career is shorter than ours. In life, we cannot say to women, 'Well, you look older now, too old!' because it isn't true, but one director will say, 'I thought of you for the part, but you're too old!' Her life on the screen is very short. It's terrible, don't you think? This is life, but it's very cruel.

DA At one time there were rumours that you were going to stand for the Presidency of France, were there not? In one opinion poll, 30 per cent of the French population wanted you to be President.

YM Well, they asked me to go on television and I said, 'You ask for my opinion? OK, I give my opinion!' and I talked like I talk here. It was 1983, and I said that things aren't going very well. The people in the government are very honest, nice people, but you cannot find the solution to the problem of the economy just because you read Marx, or Mao Tse-tung, or Hegel, or Nietzsche. The problem of the economy was terrible, but they continued to talk and they accused the conservatives again. Of course, the conservatives are sometimes responsible, but too many big excuses! The government had the power, the full power, and still things weren't going very well.

DA And it just struck a chord with the French nation?

YM The majority of the people think the same thing. We didn't expect a miracle – I mean, nobody can work miracles, especially today – but try to do something! If you make a mistake, if you aren't capable of doing it, say so! Prove to me you are capable of doing something by yourself, and don't just say that things didn't work because the rich people are keeping their money! Rich people are very shrewd. They know very well that to save their money they have to give a little bit, but they won't give just like that, just because you are yelling!

DA But even though you didn't seek to be a Presidential candidate, weren't you tempted even very briefly by the fact that so many people, on the evidence of your speeches and opinions and your reputation, thought you could do the job? There are precedents!

YM No, because when you are President you need a party, and if you have a party – middle, left, right, it doesn't matter – it's like your family, and you must defend your own family instead of defending the truth. It's a trap! I know what I'm talking about, because I did it for years.

DA You're probably too honest.

YM No, I'm not too honest, I'm like everyone here. I've got my defects, I'm not Superman, I'm weak sometimes like anyone, but it's true I try to give a sense to my life. Don't cheat, because everyone lies to us so much, so many times, and when you have the chance to say the truth – what *you* consider the truth – say it and defend it! All the time I repeat the phrase of your writer Graham Greene, who said, 'I try to understand the truth, even if it compromises my ideology.' This is very tough, because it disturbs the people who think automatically, who believe just like that, and I was that way once, so I know what I'm talking about. To try to think for yourself is very hard, because you are alone instead of with thousands or millions of people, and people say that you're a traitor because you've got money, because you've become old, because anything . . . They don't say, 'Listen, maybe he's right!' Instead they say, 'No, no, no! He's not right! The family comes first!' *Voilà*!

DA I still think you could have done the job! I don't know how you feel now about the singing business . . .

YM I have never talked so much in my life, and now I'll try to sing a song without a piano, but the voice is tired now . . . [*He sings 'Autumn Leaves' in French. Applause*]

DA Not only without a piano, but without a microphone. Thank you very much indeed, Yves Montand.

11 Michael Cimino

Michael Cimino was born in 1943, the son of a music publisher, and he grew up in New York City and Old Westbury, Long Island. He attended Michigan State University between 1956 and 1959, and then entered Yale, from which he graduated in 1963 with an MFA in painting. He returned to New York, where he studied acting and ballet, and also attended the Directors' Unit of the Actors' Studio. He went to work for a company producing industrial and documentary films, and in the late 1960s became a highly successful director of television commercials before moving to Hollywood in 1971, where he began his film career as a screen-writer. He co-wrote the screenplays of *Silent Running* (1972, Douglas Trumbull) and *Magnum Force* (1973, Ted Post), and he was later to work, without credit, on the screenplay of *The Rose* (1979, Mark Rydell). His meeting with Clint Eastwood during the production of *Magnum Force* led to his debut as a director, *Thunderbolt and Lightfoot* (1974), which, like his next two films, he also co-wrote. The phenomenal success of his second movie, *The Deer Hunter* (1978), transformed him overnight into the most lionized film-maker in the United States. The film won five Oscars, including Best Picture and Best Director, and Michael Cimino was also named Best Director by the Directors' Guild. Two years later, universal adulation gave way to universal opprobrium when *Heaven's Gate* became the occasion of the most spectacular and widely-publicized débâcle in the history of the Hollywood cinema. The film opened in New York to poisonous reviews and was immediately withdrawn, to be released later in a heavily truncated version which was also panned and which was a disastrous box-office failure. The scandal culminated in the bankruptcy and liquidation of United Artists. The complete version of *Heaven's Gate* later opened to great critical acclaim in Britain and France, but it is fair to say that Cimino's reputation in the United States has never recovered from the anathemas pronounced in 1980. He worked briefly on *Footloose* (1984), which was finally directed by Herbert Ross, and then signed a long-term contract with

Dino de Laurentiis which has since produced three films: *Year of the Dragon* (1985), *The Sicilian* (1987) and *Dangerous Hours* (1990).

The following lecture took place on 11 August 1983. Michael Cimino was interviewed by Nigel Andrews, the film critic of the *Financial Times*.

Michael Cimino

Nigel Andrews There's a moment in *Heaven's Gate* where Kris Kristofferson turns to Isabelle Huppert and says, 'Do you want me to say "I told you so"? I told you so!' Well, it's not often a critic has the luxury of doing that himself, but the small band of people who loved *Heaven's Gate* way back when the then-notorious two-and-a-half hour version opened in Cannes are about the happiest people in town tonight, now that the complete version is about to open for an eight-performance run at the National Film Theatre. I think it's an occasion for a great deal of dancing in streets – on roller-skates, of course! [*Applause*] Michael, one of the most consistent and remarkable things about your films is the way that you use those big set-piece, non-dialogue sequences like the long dance sequence in *The Deer Hunter* or the Harvard Waltz and the roller-skating sequence in *Heaven's Gate*. Do you deliberately set out to make a film with this kind of set piece? Is it part of your vision of how you like to see America?

Michael Cimino I can't imagine a greater pleasure in film-making than working with music and dancers. It's possibly the most joyful work that you can do in film. There is something about the presence of music on the set. There's just a great sensual pleasure in doing it. Dancers, of course, are always in every country the hardest-working of performers, and always the lowest-paid as well. Whether it's deliberate from the outset it's hard to say. I don't think that I've ever begun with the idea of doing big set pieces. Somehow they find their way into the picture.

NA One of the things *Heaven's Gate* has been attacked for (I think quite unfairly) is that it's a Western which doesn't succeed as a Western. Some people have argued that it's not an authentic view of the West, and the roller-skating is a good example of the things that have been criticized as being anachronistic. Yet according to you, you researched all the details of period and setting and costume very thoroughly.

MC That is one of the most incomprehensible comments made during the initial run of the movie, and it took us very much by surprise because there is little in the film not based on photographic images of that period, which, as you know, coincided with the real explosion of still photography in America. People photographed absolutely everything: whole towns posed for photographs! I don't think there's a single structure, or a single piece of wardrobe, or anything visual in the picture that is not in some way based on a photograph of the period, right down to the shape of the logs in the log cabins. People's perception of the West is really based on old movies and on a lot of television, where they've become accustomed to back-lots and empty streets and little activity, so when suddenly they're presented with a street full of commerce and movement and noise, it seems wrong. They can't relate to the reality before them; they can only relate to the reality of movies that they've seen. There were people I know who questioned the legitimacy of telephone poles. People made astonishing statements like, 'How could you do that? Electricity wasn't invented yet!' They became dislocated because they had never seen those images before, they couldn't accept the fact that streets were crowded with traffic, but all they had to do was look at photos of the period. The roller-skating was thought to be absolutely ridiculous, yet we found photos of a town where there was not only one roller-skating rink but two, and there were also tennis courts. Can you imagine if we had shown tennis as well? [*Laughter*] We would have been run out of town completely.

NA Some critics have detected the influence of John Ford in *Heaven's Gate*. Were you aware of that?

MC Certainly everyone working in the cinema – at least, everyone in America – works in the shadow of Ford, and if you like Ford it's impossible not to be in some way influenced by what he's done. I think you can't praise Ford enough, and no one has given us better images of the West than Ford and Hawks have. Yet as authentic as Ford would be with images of army life and so on, he exercised the prerogative of every director, which is to exaggerate what he felt it necessary to make a point. The history of the West was certainly not written in Monument

Valley, and there were many Indian tribes which never set foot there, but you believe and accept it. He loved music, and in *My Darling Clementine*, when he couldn't figure out any other way to play the damned tune, he had Henry Fonda whistle the title song! Ford loved hearing music, and I think that's evident in his films. As I was saying, there's a great joy that a filmmaker takes in using music and using it well. I think it's irresistible.

NA Another thing that's very consistent in your movies – even in *Thunderbolt and Lightfoot*, where one of the main towns in the film is called Warsaw – is the interest in East European, Russian, German immigrants rather than, as one might have supposed, Italian immigrants, because you yourself are a third-generation Italian–American. Why have you been drawn towards this particular group of American immigrants?

MC I suppose because I have a certain familiarity with it. I was raised in an area where there were a lot of Russians and Poles, and I remember when I was very young that the Mass was conducted in Polish. Later on I was the best man at a wedding very similar to the one we see in *The Deer Hunter*. For some reason it feels closer to me than anything to do with Italy or the Italian experience in America, which actually seems very far away from me, at least spiritually.

NA Can you tell us a little about your background? How did you get into the film industry?

MC I kind of stumbled into it. I was actually intent on being an architect, and I had no contact at all with anything to do with the theatre or film. For some reason it just took me over. I began by studying acting and ballet in New York and while I was doing that I began to write, mostly out of necessity. Somehow there it was.

NA Did you write with movies immediately in mind?

MC I started writing screenplays principally because I didn't have the money to buy books or to option properties. At that time you only had a chance to direct if you owned a screenplay which some star wanted to do, and that's precisely what happened with *Thunderbolt and Lightfoot*. Clint originally wanted to buy it and direct it himself, so it was a matter of holding out and saying, 'No, I won't sell it because I would like to direct it.' It's a very difficult thing to hold out at an early stage like that. Especially with Eastwood.

NA Before we move on to *Thunderbolt and Lightfoot*, what about the two films you co-scripted: *Magnum Force* and *Silent Running*? I understand that you didn't actually collaborate in person with the other scriptwriter in either case, but that you both did separate versions which became the final script.

MC Well, John Milius was in the process of writing the original screenplay for *Magnum Force*. Clint had meant to do *Thunderbolt and Lightfoot* first, but then John had a chance to direct his first picture, which was *Dillinger*, and he left off writing *Magnum* in the middle, so Clint asked me if I would finish the screenplay and rewrite it. That meant postponing *Thunderbolt* until *Magnum Force* was written.

NA Although you wrote and directed it, *Thunderbolt and Lightfoot* was very much a Clint Eastwood production: it was made for his company and he was in the starring role. How much control did he insist on having in the movie, for instance, in terms of ratios of footage featuring Clint Eastwood, and things like that?

MC Well, Clint was wonderful. We're still really good friends. He was exceptionally professional and very knowledgeable about the actual mechanics of making a film . . . and of course, he's now directed many pictures. I will tell you that there was absolutely no interference, and in fact I was very worried about that. He was known, and is still known, to be quite tough on directors and I worried about when he might make his move, so we thought we'd be very clever and we scheduled the first three days of shooting without Clint. We knew that he wouldn't get there until just before his day of work, which was the third day, and we made every effort to be a day and a half ahead of schedule before he arrived, because it was his company, of course, and I knew that if he showed up on the set and the crew stopped what they were doing and all went over and started chatting with him, the game was lost. So we worked very hard the first three days and sure enough, the third day Clint turned up. He got out of his car, and I just watched him out of the corner of my eye walking across this field. We were doing the scene with Jeff [Bridges] driving the truck, and I had one eye on Clint and one eye on the crew, just waiting to see what would happen. Well, we were working so hard and so fast that the crew kept right on going and nobody left, and I think Clint was a little surprised that nobody stopped work: they barely said hello. That was the first real triumph, and I'm very pleased with that. However, I did always go to him at night and ask him if he was happy with what was being shot, or if there was anything he was concerned about, and his answer was always, 'Look, I love the script, I didn't change a word in it and I want your vision of it. Whatever it is you want to see in the picture, that's what I want to see.' It's not the way that people usually think of Eastwood.

NA Have you generally got on well with your actors?

MC I've had rather good luck with actors. All the actors I've worked with I've liked very much, and fortunately I'm still friends with all of them. I would work with Jeff always. He's exactly as he appears on film; he's really absolutely wonderful to work with, and he's not afraid to try anything. And Bob, of course: there's no better instrument that a director could hope to have than Bob De Niro. Kristofferson is an extraordinary man. I ran into Jack Nicholson, and he said he thought Kristofferson did a remarkable job in *Heaven's Gate*, and that he didn't know anyone else who could have done it because it needed something more than an actor could bring to it. That's quite a compliment coming from Nicholson, who's a pretty critical guy. One of the things that hurt me about the reaction to the film was not what people said about me at all, but the fact that they ignored Kris's work, because he worked so terribly hard.

NA There's a marvellous little scene in *Thunderbolt and Lightfoot* where they discover the horde of loot hidden in a one-room schoolhouse, which has been preserved from the century before as a museum. That seems to be a kind of emblem of the America that you like to visualize, where everyone is together and there is only one class, one people, despite all the different immigrants. Is that fair, or am I having a delirium of interpretation?

MC The territory that *Thunderbolt and Lightfoot* moves through, and the territory in *Heaven's Gate* and parts of *The Deer Hunter*, is real Lewis and Clark[1] country, and a good many of the highways that we used are the old Lewis and Clark trails. There is a sense of it vanishing, and you feel it most acutely when you see little one-room schoolhouses which are just disintegrating. There are a lot of them in Montana – I think we looked at damn near all of them for the movie – and everywhere you go there are these crumbling ghostly buildings, so I saw it as emblematic of a world that was disappearing rather quickly.

NA As I understand it, you wrote something like a dozen screenplays after *Thunderbolt and Lightfoot*, and some of these projects have been announced, like *The Fountainhead*, *The Dogs of War* and an original screenplay of your own called *Pearl*. Is there anything you would like to say about why they didn't materialize, or is it something you would rather put out of your mind?

MC For some reason it seems that if I have a meeting with *anyone*, it gets into the press! It's difficult to have even the most casual conversation about a project now. Most directors are constantly talking about new projects and developing scripts which they discard after working on them for a time, and no one ever hears about it, but it seems that if I just mention an idea, or if I work a bit on a project which doesn't go, it makes some kind of news. I think it's very boring, but there it is. *Pearl* was meant to be the story of Janis Joplin, and it was going to be set against the background of the anti-war movement in New York City and throughout the country during the 1960s. Bette Midler became attracted to the project, and I was offered it while I was on the River Kwai in Thailand, in the middle of doing the Russian Roulette sequences for *The Deer Hunter*. It was simply not possible for me to do it, so the picture was made completely differently by someone else.[2] It's not the screenplay I had written, and it didn't come out the way I envisioned it. It was meant to be something very different.

NA Did you have any casting in mind?

MC We wanted the two men in *Coming Home*: Bruce Dern was meant to play the manager, and Jon Voight was meant to be the marine who went AWOL. The girl was the big problem. It's the same problem that you'd face if you tried to do a picture about Mick Jagger. How can you find someone who can create that much energy and electricity, and who can sing that way and do what he does on stage, and not have it be him? It was going to be very difficult, and as it turned out, when Bette Midler did it she didn't really use any of Joplin's music. She had special arrangements, which probably for her was the right thing to do, but it wasn't the sort of music that Joplin made.

NA How about *The Fountainhead*? What attracted you to the novel?

MC I suppose because it was about a man dealing with critics! [*Laughter*] The thing that moved me towards it originally was my own interest in architecture, which was what I intended to do before I got side-tracked by this movie business. I'd always wanted very much to do something about Frank Lloyd Wright, but the rights were always very complicated. Robert Redford and I both tried independently to get the rights, and they were not possible to get, so somehow – I've forgotten how, exactly – we got around to *The Fountainhead*. Of course, rumour has it that Ayn Rand based much of the novel on Wright in the first place. It seemed a good story, about somebody strong. There's a famous scene where Howard Roark, having been literally destroyed by critics – one in particular – is approached by one of them at a building site after he's lost his practice and has really been out on the street. This critic introduces himself and says, 'I've been responsible for destroying you. All these commissions could have been yours, but I prevented you from getting them, and now this stuff is being done by inferior architects. What do you think of me?' And Roark looks at him and says, 'But I *don't* think of you!' and walks away. That's the kind of character! . . . although on closer study of the book I realized that it's really more a story about the girl than it is about Roark. Roark is unchanging from the beginning to the end, and it was a great shock to me when I saw that it's Dominique who's really central and the more complex character. I suppose it's not surprising, since it was written by a woman.

NA What did you think of the King Vidor version?

MC Oh, it's just not what I would have done with it, I think.

NA And the actors?

MC As I said, the intention was to use Redford, but again, the girl would have been very difficult to find, because one of the marvellous things in the Vidor movie was Patricia Neal, and she's a hard act to follow at that age.

NA Moving on towards *The Deer Hunter*, you yourself were called up and were attached to the Green Berets, but you didn't go to Vietnam, is that correct?

MC Well, it's a little backwards! I was in Texas training as a medic with a Green Beret unit, and then after I was released from that training I was called up for duty in Vietnam, because medics could be called up as individuals then. However, I didn't go.

NA You have said, I believe, that you used the Russian Roulette sequences purely, or mainly, for dramatic reasons. What do you say to people who argue that they are a libel against the

Vietnamese, and that they give a totally distorted view of what the war was about?

MC It seems that in *The Deer Hunter* people accused me of being right-wing, and in *Heaven's Gate* they accused me of being left-wing! I get accused of being so many things. I think it's important to remember that we are making movies, we are not writing history: we're not attempting to lecture people. That's why I was so put off by the title of this programme: 'The *Guardian* Lecture'! I couldn't imagine myself lecturing at all. It should be 'the *Guardian* Chat', maybe. The last thing one hopes for with a film is to be pretentious, or to instruct anyone. That seems a rather dreadful notion. What *was* true of *The Deer Hunter* is that we did an enormous amount of research. We did have hundreds of tapes, we did talk to hundreds of veterans, paraplegics, people who saw a lot of action. Joann Carelli, who produced *The Deer Hunter*, and *Heaven's Gate* as well, spent literally months and months in New York looking through millions of feet of news film at NBC, ABC and CBS. It was a horrendous process because this stuff is uncatalogued; there was very little order to it. Here was this priceless material in boxes and on the floor, and any producer at the network could just go in and snip out a chunk, and the film might be lost for ever. Joann looked at a great deal of stuff, and then we put together an eight-hour inauguration programme for all of the crew, the actors and everybody who worked on the picture. Everybody looked at it and anybody on the crew who had questions could ask them, and if the art director, or the costume people, or whoever wanted clips or blow-ups from it for their work, they could have them. It was a project library for us which we carried around. Many of the reporters who filed those stories were at work in Bangkok when we got there. They had not returned to the States because they were covering Cambodia, so when we brought that material with us we set up a screening for them at a hotel in Bangkok, and a lot of guys in UPI were able to look at film that they themselves had shot, but had never got a chance to see. In addition to film research we did other kinds of research, and there were *some* – not a lot of – accounts of Russian Roulette being played in South-East Asia. In fact, the man who plays Pierre in *The Deer Hunter* claims that a friend of his was lost in just such a game. He's not an actor – indeed, there are many non-actors in both *The Deer Hunter* and *Heaven's Gate* – but he was with the French at Dien Bien Phu, and he was involved in a lot of interesting activities with gold and guns. We also met a man who claimed to have seen Russian Roulette played with women. So while there are many more people who say that it never existed, there are those people who make a case for it quite adamantly and claim to have witnessed it. I think its immaterial, and when I'm asked about why I used it I've always said it was a dramatic device. When you think about it, how else can you convey the tension of combat? You can do what Andy Warhol did many years ago and make a film called *Sleep* and just show people sleeping, but how do you dramatize it in a story where you're going to spend more than twenty minutes on it? How can you create the tension of waiting for something to happen? When you talk to a lot of Vet's they speak about the endless waiting, and there's a kind of eruption of action – very brief, very horrific – and then the waiting again. It seemed an ideal way of dramatizing, if not the reality of combat in Asia, then the *emotional* reality, and I think the proof of that is the reaction of veterans, which has really been in a way the most rewarding. Almost all the veterans I know, or who have written to me about it, say that they feel as though they're back in 'Nam, especially when they hear the sound of the choppers, and not just any chopper sound, but that particular sound which we laboured over for three days to get precisely right. That's what's important about it, and if one is to say anything about the Russian Roulette *which pertains to the film*, I think it's that. It made the emotional tension of people in war real. I think it's begging the question to ask whether it happened or not. It doesn't matter if it happened, and even if it *did* happen it wouldn't matter, in my opinion.

NA We're going to see a short clip from *The Deer Hunter* now. I should just point out that there are a few frames missing from this print when the deer is shot. Perhaps they're missing accidentally, but it seems more likely that they were tastefully cut, because one does in fact see the deer fall. It's always a shock to see film mutilated, but I guess there are some films that people feel compelled to meddle with.
[*At this point a noisy and abusive demonstration by Animal Rights activists erupts in the auditorium. The protesters demand to know if the deer is really killed and accuse Michael Cimino of cruelty to animals during the filming of Heaven's Gate.*]

NA We'll carry on this interview with the order of questions I have chosen and not the order of questions that you have chosen. [*Continued shouting and abuse*] If the question has not been answered to your satisfaction before the end of the evening, then you may protest. Until then, why not leave the interview the way it's going? [*Applause*]

MC If you'd been quiet long enough I could have answered your question, but you keep talking after you ask it. The answer to it is no, the deer was not killed, and that's what's so interesting about the fact that someone saw fit to cut this. No one ever protests about violence in horror films and pictures like *The Texas Chainsaw Massacre*. No one protests about what happens to *people*, let alone what happens to children, in films like that. I think what's happened in the case of *The Deer Hunter* and *Heaven's Gate* is that you come to know the people so well and to have such an affection for them and to believe in them so much as real people, that you believe all the other things in the picture on the same level, so if you see a hunting sequence you take it as something literal. Of course we did not kill the deer! Those deer came from a game preserve! Had we killed those deer we ourselves would have been killed!
[*Continued shouting and abuse*]

NA Let him answer.

MC Please, I did you the courtesy of listening to your question; why don't you listen to my answer? All the game in *The Deer Hunter* came from the game preserve in New Jersey, of all places, and they were transported to the state of Washington. Those sequences were accomplished with tranquillizers, in the same way that game wardens work all over the world when they tag animals for conservation purposes, and absolutely no harm comes to those animals. Indeed, they were also very expensive. Obviously somebody thought that the shot of the deer on the ground was too real, but nevertheless I can assure you without any equivocation that no harm whatever came to those animals. With respect to *Heaven's Gate*, no horses were killed; as a matter of fact, there was quite a remarkable safety record on the picture. There were one or two injuries: a stuntwoman banged her knee in a battle sequence, and there was a wagon sequence where somebody injured a shoulder, but apart from minor scrapes and bruises really not much happened, and many, many safety precautions were taken. The veterinarian who worked on the film has issued a statement about how well the animals were cared for.

Demonstrator How about the horses that were blown up?

MC There were no horses blown up.

Demonstrator Excuse me, I saw the pictures in the *Daily Mirror*! [*Derisive laughter*]

NA Before the time to be devoted to this talk runs out completely, can I know if there are any people here who have actually seen Michael Cimino killing an animal so that we can have something verifiable to argue about? I'm going to move on from the high-priority topic of violence to animals to the relatively low-priority topic of violence to humans. [*Further shouting and abuse*] There's a great deal of violence in *Heaven's Gate*, which is about an era of critical confrontation between two classes: the wealthy landowners and stockgrowers in Wyoming in the 1890s embark on a land war against the immigrants. As you said, *The Deer Hunter* has been accused of having a right-wing message, but *Heaven's Gate* seems to be pro-socialist and anti-capitalist. Do you think that these political descriptions are worth discussing, or do you think that your films have a unity that is actually apolitical, or which transcends politics?

MC I think it is probably better discussed by people who don't make films. I find it fascinating that people can make so many interpretations of a film, or draw out so many layers of meaning. I don't think I set out particularly to make a political statement. As a matter of fact, I think that any picture that deals with war automatically becomes an anti-war statement if it's a good picture. I don't think there's any way you could make a good picture about war which would be anything *but* that. As for drawing political conclusions, I leave that to the people who write about film. I don't really feel adequate discussing those questions.

NA You say that you don't set out to make a political statement, but some critics have suggested that, for example, the closing scene of *The Deer Hunter* is a kind of commentary on the American experience of Vietnam. Doesn't the 'God Bless America' scene have political implications?

MC I would rephrase what you said just a little bit. I don't know if I said I wasn't conscious of the implications. What I tried to say (and perhaps didn't do it well enough) is that I didn't intend some kind of political *statement*. The singing of 'God Bless America' at the end was an expression of some feeling that those people had which could not be expressed in any other way. It had to be expressed in song. There was no other way for them to talk about their grief, or to express to each other what they felt. As it happens, we were in a restaurant in Pittsburgh before that sequence was made – so nobody there had any way of knowing what we were going to do – and a group of people just broke into that song. It was this unabashed expression of feeling about the country. I don't think you have to be very political to love your country. I think that's a rather simple emotion, it doesn't need to be too complicated. The primary thing was to find a way for those characters to express things that could not be verbalized, and what could be better than a song that they all knew? Most people don't remember lyrics, but those lyrics stay with you because you learn them in school; a national anthem is the kind of thing that everybody knows. It seemed a natural thing to do. An anthem to America.

NA Both *The Deer Hunter* and *Heaven's Gate* were photographed, quite amazingly, by Vilmos Zsigmond, and yet both have a very different style. How closely do you discuss with Zsigmond the kind of strategy you want for the overall look of a film?

MC We discuss it quite a lot, and we usually reconnoitre prior to shooting. We do fairly extensive make-up tests, and we always try to shoot some film at night in the areas where we hope to do night work, or in an existing interior that we're not building. In the case of *The Deer Hunter* it was very necessary and important to do that because, as some of you may know, although *The Deer Hunter* was shot with the look of the Fall to legitimate the inclusion of the hunting season, it was actually shot during one of the hottest summers in some twenty or thirty years in America. It was so hot that Meryl and Bob had to change clothes and have their hair dried between takes in some of the scenes. Because it was supposed to be Fall, every camera set-up had to be prepared and protected, in that the grass had to be brown and the trees had to be stripped of leaves, so there was no possibility of changing your mind once you arrived on location. It all had to be pre-planned, because if we had moved the camera five degrees, you would have seen wonderful flowers and leaves and green grass! It needed to be planned very precisely, and that extended to our decision to film it very sharply with lots of back-lighting and so forth. In fact, you begin to determine the look of a movie before you've shot a foot of film by virtue of the choices you make in the selection of locations. The minute you choose mountains; the minute you choose a valley, or a river, or a lake; the minute you choose a town which has a north–south axis on Main Street, as opposed to an east–west axis; the minute you do that, then automatically you start giving yourself back-light as opposed to cross-light at a certain time of day, and you're making choices before the cameraman is ever on the show. Then you add to that decisions about the colours of the costumes and so forth, so that the determination of the look of the film begins very early on. In the case of *Heaven's Gate*, we decided that since most of the interiors would be heated by wood-burning stoves, they would be smoky and hazy (which, of course, is another thing that a lot of people have complained about), and that the exteriors, in contrast to that, would be relatively sharp, and the battle dusty and confusing. I think that combat is often confusing. It's difficult to see, and when you have hundreds of wagons and people and shots being fired, that's what you'd get, that's what it would look like. We just reinforced it a little bit.

NA There are often very long scenes in your films with virtually no dialogue at all, and yet the narrative is pushed forward. Do you think that that may be one reason why critics who favour the filmed-play ethos react against your movies?

MC I think that there's now an expectation, particularly because of television, that you should know everything about a character the minute he makes his entrance, and in fact Americans tend to be that way. When you meet an American on a plane he will tell you the story of his life in an hour, and you'll know everything you do and don't want to know about him and every member of his family, including his salary and his insurance policy. I don't know why this is, but it seems to be so, and that's very much how we do television. You get everything about a character very quickly, so you don't have to guess about what his reaction will be over the course of a film, or a television show, and that, of course, helps them to make successful comedy. The audiences are just slightly ahead of the reaction and they know there's going to be a laugh, so then they laugh. I'm trying to do something a little different. My attitude is to do without dialogue as much as possible, and it always pains me to have to do a long exposition scene, but invariably there they are, and you have to do them somehow and get by them. If you can dramatize it without words and with just behaviour, I think it's more powerful, and as far as the cutting goes it's a cleaner way of working – a way of working where you can't make excuses. It's much harder to cover things up, and so you have to be quite sure of what you're doing.

NA One of the reasons that people were so hostile to *Heaven's Gate* in America (and this is something which even people who don't like the film in Britain can't quite understand) was that it's a Western. To what do you attribute the fact that the Western is so unpopular?

MC That's a difficult question to answer simply. It's got to do with the fact that so many Westerns were made over a long period of time, and a lot of them made carelessly or badly, and as a result people lost interest in them. After you get a lot of bad work, any genre suffers. But I don't think it has as much to do with the public as it has to do with the media's presentation of *Heaven's Gate* to the public. When they showed it in Los Angeles on KTV, and most recently in Canada, the ratings were extraordinarily high, so people do want to see it. But none of us wants to appear ignorant, and when the press of the world has told everyone that this is the worst movie ever made, it's pretty hard to want to be seen coming out of the theatre. [*Laughter*] I think that the curiosity was there to see the picture, but there was a kind of injunction *not* to see it. This extraordinary thing that's happening at the NFT, with the press treating it almost as if it's an opening two years after the fact, is really rather remarkable (and also rather courageous, I might add), and it's broken down that injunction a bit. I think people are now saying, 'Well, let me go and see for myself!' and the fact that they come out and say, 'Gee, it's not as bad as we thought!' is an amazing turnaround for anyone to make, because it isn't a simple film. It's a complex film and there are a lot of lines to follow, a lot of things that are developing in it.

NA After the adverse press reaction in New York when the film was first shown, it was withdrawn and you cut it down from three hours forty minutes to two hours twenty-five minutes. You are quoted as saying that 'the missing step of public previews clouded my perception of the film.' What is your perception of the film now, and what is your attitude to the two alternative versions?

MC I can't really answer that yet; I think I'm still sorting it out. I can only tell you that we intended to do something not unlike what Kubrick did with *2001*. As you know, when he opened *2001* it also received a bad reaction from the critics and it wasn't immediately successful. He was still tinkering with the film, still exploring possibilities of changing sequences and adding and subtracting material, and we thought we might do the same thing, since the original opening was only meant to be in one theatre in New York and one in Los Angeles, and we hadn't even made any 35mm prints. Since we had had no screenings of the film, we thought that we'd use the opening in New York as a kind of series of previews and that we'd do what Kubrick did, which was to edit things, take things out, experiment with it. When you've worked for several years on something that's so long and so complex, and you have so much footage, and you've spent so much time editing and dubbing, you need some way of refreshing your vision and your reaction to what you've done. It just didn't turn out that way; it didn't become the process that we'd hoped it would become. I'm still sorting out my reaction to it.

NA Do you feel you were stampeded into making a decision by the press reaction before you really wanted to or felt ready?

MC It's still difficult to say. It was such a hot, charged atmosphere, there seemed to be so much strong feeling that I think it will take me a while before I can come back and really look at it objectively. It's very hard for me to view any of it objectively at this point.

NA Was it difficult to make the cut version?

MC It was difficult continuing to work because the media were all over us constantly, to the point where we literally had television crews camped outside my cutting room at MGM waiting for me to leave so that they could do an interview on the run. People would leave notes on my car and somehow climb over the fence and get on to the lot. Every day there was some incident or another. So I would often sleep in the cutting room, or I would make sure I was there at six o'clock every morning, and then I wouldn't leave until after midnight. Usually they were pretty tired by then and would go away. All we were trying to do was a job of work, and that didn't make it any easier.

NA How do you think the Hollywood establishment has reacted to it all?

MC I think that the people who make movies and run the studios, and most of the people I know, understand what happened. Those people don't take it nearly as seriously as the press takes it, otherwise we wouldn't be involved in any other projects. We have been offered projects by UA and by MGM which we've actually turned down. They see it as an over-reaction, and as something to do with things other than the merits of the film itself.

NA I want to ask you a question about Michael Cimino, the notorious monomaniac, whom we've heard so much about. I have a quotation here by your producer on *Heaven's Gate* from an interview with *Rolling Stone*, where she says, 'We should have said, "No, Michael, no – you *cannot* build the town larger than you said! No, Michael, no – you *cannot* have a thousand extras when you said a hundred!" Everyone was afraid to say no to Michael.' Why is everyone afraid of you?

MC God, I don't know! I'm not very big! I don't know what it is. I think one works as hard as one can, and one tries to get the best possible work from oneself and from other people. Maybe it's because I ask people for a lot. The odd thing is, when you ask people for a lot you usually get it, and they give you everything they can. This may sound terribly melodramatic, but I think that everybody in some way wants to experience some transcendent moment in their work. It's like some great moment in football where everything is clicking, and the quarterback gets off a great pass and the receiver is there at the right moment, and everybody is just doing the right thing, and everybody is out of themselves just a little bit. Money and all other considerations aside, I think that everybody wants that kind of moment, and maybe the problem is that I go after that unashamedly. Many people are . . . perhaps 'afraid' is not the right word, but *reluctant* to go for it!!! If I had to do it all again, perhaps I would listen to Joann a bit more about some things, but you do get somewhat over-enthusiastic if you feel what you're doing is good, and when you're getting something very special you want to get as much out of it as you can. And there the possibility is! You have this momentary control because another film that you've done has been successful, you have this glorious set, these wonderful actors, one of the greatest cameramen in the world and this fantastic light, and you have the paint-brush in your hand. It's a question of whether you want to use it or not. Sometimes, yes, you *do* exceed the parameters that you've been given, and the only defence I can make is to say that it's in the interest of getting something special. For example, there is a shot in *The Deer Hunter* after Bob comes back from Vietnam. He goes out hunting and he's walking along the ridge of mountains, and there's the most amazing light and the most extraordinary reflection of sky in a small lake in front of him, with the mist coming up off the mountains. All that happened in two minutes. It's my custom to go to the location before anybody else in the morning (I'm usually the first one there), and I was standing up on the hill when I saw this incredible sight, and I just started screaming to get the cameras. The operator ran with the camera and the tripod and the zoom lens on, and Bob came running from his trailer, putting on his clothes, and I just said, 'You get there and put the camera here!' and 'Bob! Stop running, start acting!' The camera was only half on the tripod. We made the shot, and then the mist disappeared; that shot would have been gone for ever. It's like falling in love, you know. You've got to take advantage of it!

Notes

1 The US explorers Meriwether Lewis (1774–1809) and William Clark (1770–1838). They were the leaders of the first overland expedition from the east coast of the United States to the Pacific and back (1804–06).

2 *The Rose* (1979, Mark Rydell). A version of *The Dogs of War* appeared in 1980, directed by John Irvin.